VOLUME TWO

ONI PRESS

AN ONI PRESS PUBLICATION

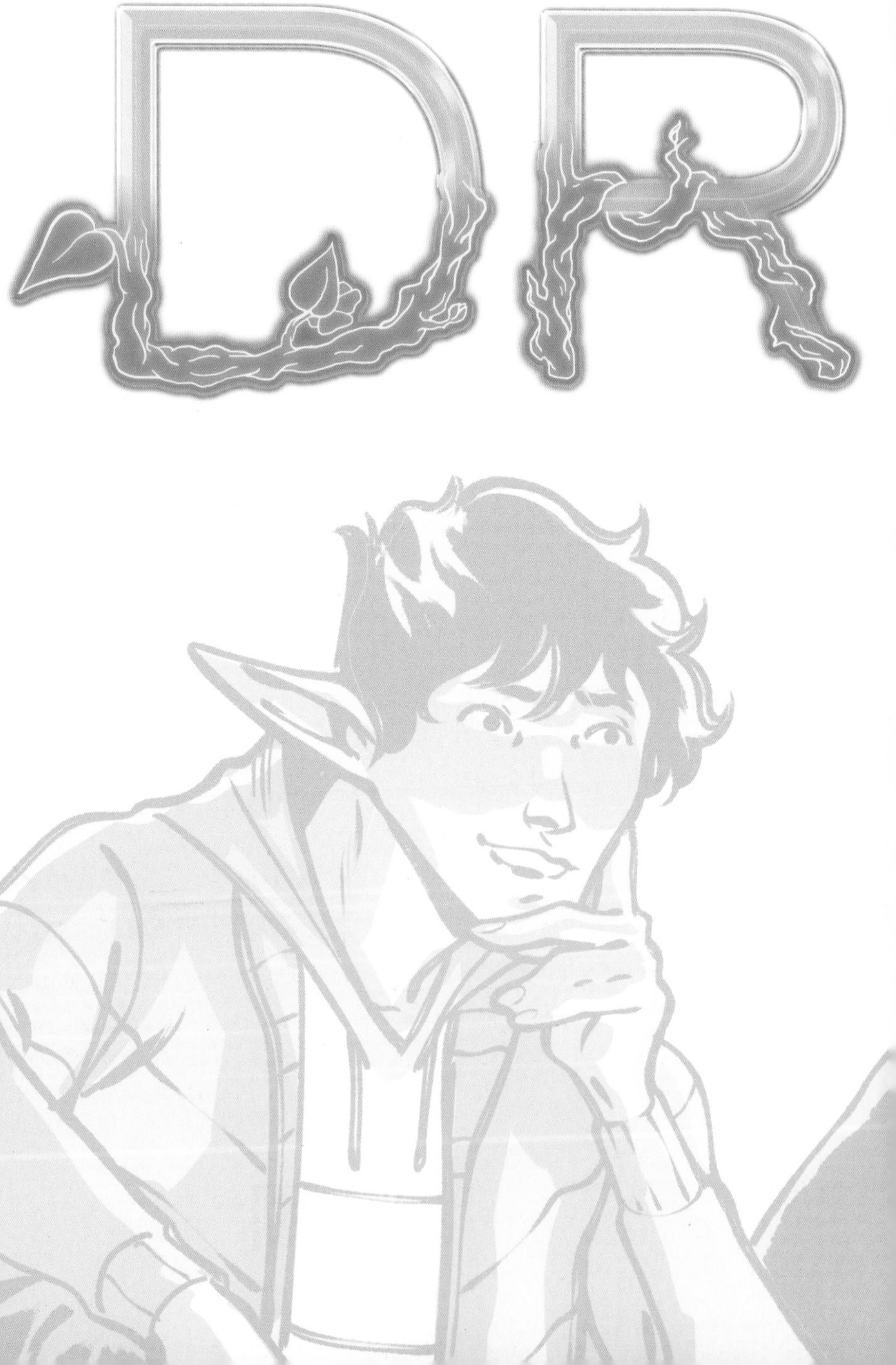
DR

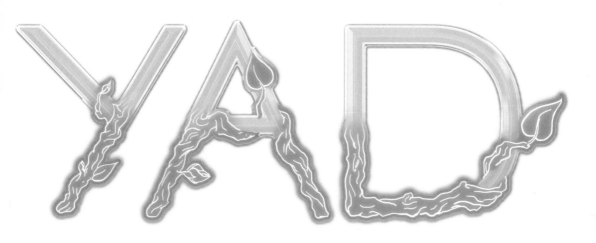

YAD

VOLUME TWO

CREATED BY KURTIS WIEBE
AND JUSTIN BARCELO

Written by **Kurtis Wiebe**
Illustrated by **Justin Barcelo**
With Inking Assistance by
Jeremy Lawson [Chapter 9]

Colored by **Francesco Segala**
Lettered by **Jim Campbell**

Cover by **Tomas Oleksak**

Edited by **Jasmine Amiri**
Designed by **Kate Z. Stone**

PUBLISHED BY ONI PRESS, INC.

James Lucas Jones, president & publisher **Sarah Gaydos**, editor in chief **Charlie Chu**, e.v.p. of creative & business development **Brad Rooks**, director of operations **Amber O'Neill**, special projects manager **Margot Wood**, director of marketing & sales **Katie Sainz**, marketing manager **Tara Lehmann**, publicist **Holly Aitchison**, consumer marketing manager **Troy Look**, director of design & production **Kate Z. Stone**, senior graphic designer **Hilary Thompson**, graphic designer **Sarah Rockwell**, graphic designer **Angie Knowles**, digital prepress lead **Vincent Kukua**, digital prepress technician **Shawna Gore**, senior editor **Amanda Meadows**, senior editor **Robert Meyers**, senior editor, licensing **Jasmine Amiri**, senior editor **Grace Scheipeter**, editor **Zack Soto**, editor **Chris Cerasi**, editorial coordinator **Steve Ellis**, vice president of games **Ben Eisner**, game developer **Michelle Nguyen**, executive assistant **Jung Lee**, logistics coordinator **Joe Nozemack**, publisher emeritus

onipress.com
facebook.com/onipress
twitter.com/onipress
instagram.com/onipress

lionforge.com
facebook.com/lionforge
twitter.com/lionforge
instagram.com/lionforge

@KurtisWiebe
@ohnoJustinO
@FrancescoSegala
@CampbellLetters

First Edition: September 2021
ISBN 978-1-62010-935-9
eISBN 978-1-62010-948-9

DRYAD Volume 2, September 2021. Published by Oni-Lion Forge Publishing Group, LLC, 1319 SE Martin Luther King Jr. Blvd., Suite 240, Portland, OR 97214. Dryad is ™ & © 2021 Kurtis Wiebe and Justin Osterling. All rights reserved. Oni Press logo and icon ™ & © 2021 Oni-Lion Forge Publishing Group, LLC. All rights reserved. Oni Press logo and icon artwork created by Keith A. Wood. The events, institutions, and characters presented in this book are fictional. Any resemblance to actual persons, living or dead, is purely coincidental. No portion of this publication may be reproduced, by any means, without the express written permission of the copyright holders.

Printed in Canada.

Library of Congress Control Number: 2020937769

1 3 5 7 9 10 8 6 4 2

CHAPTER SIX

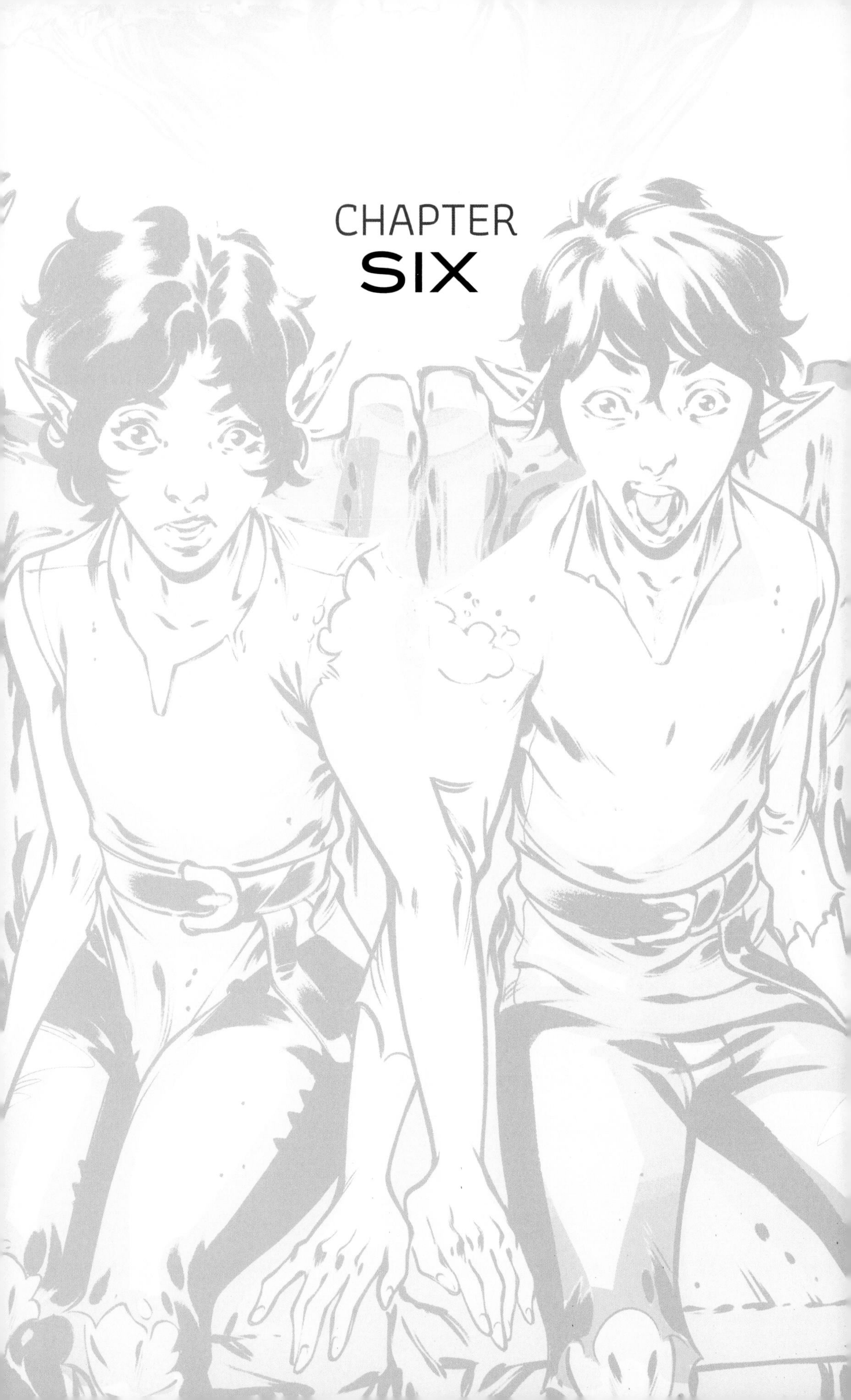

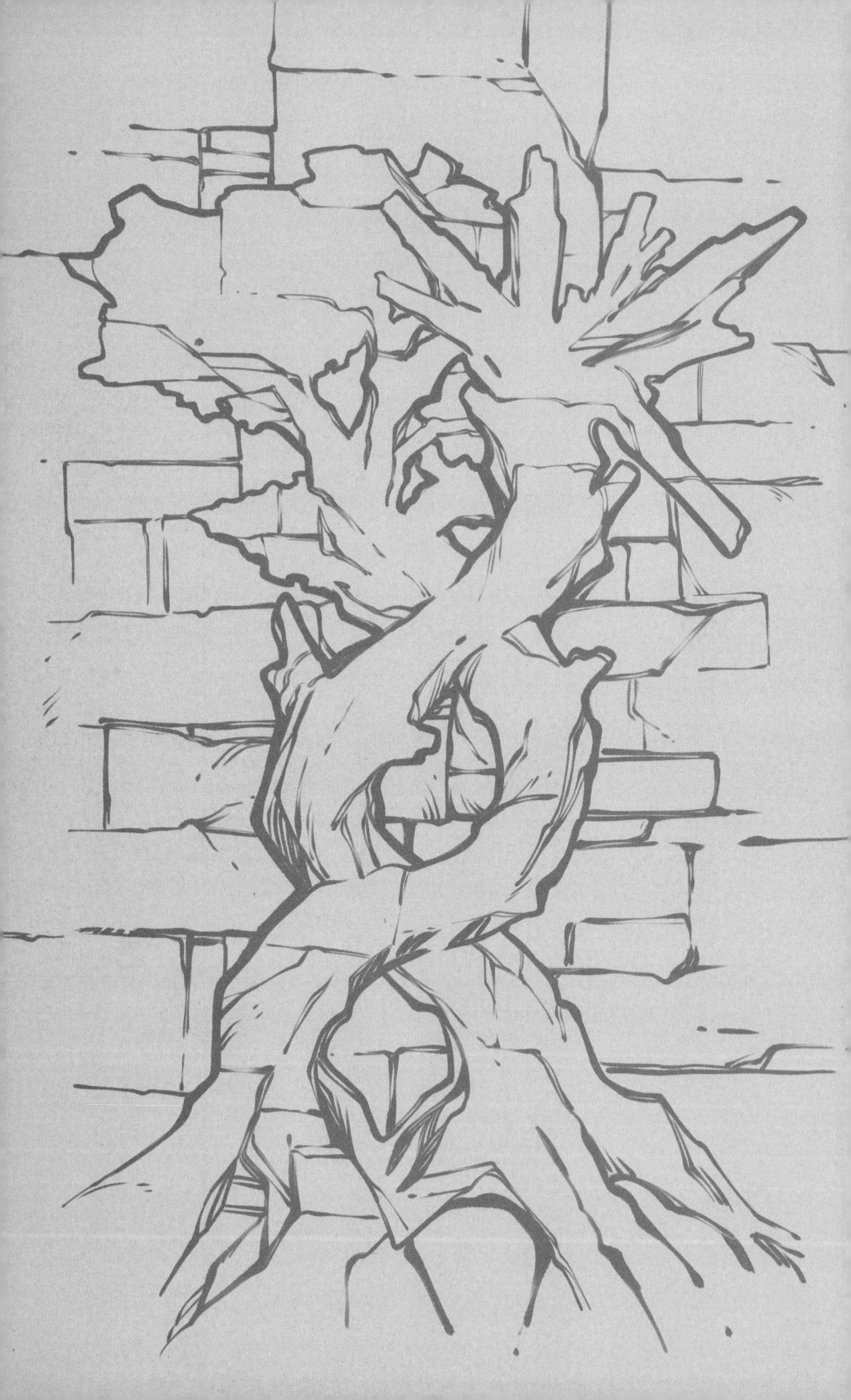

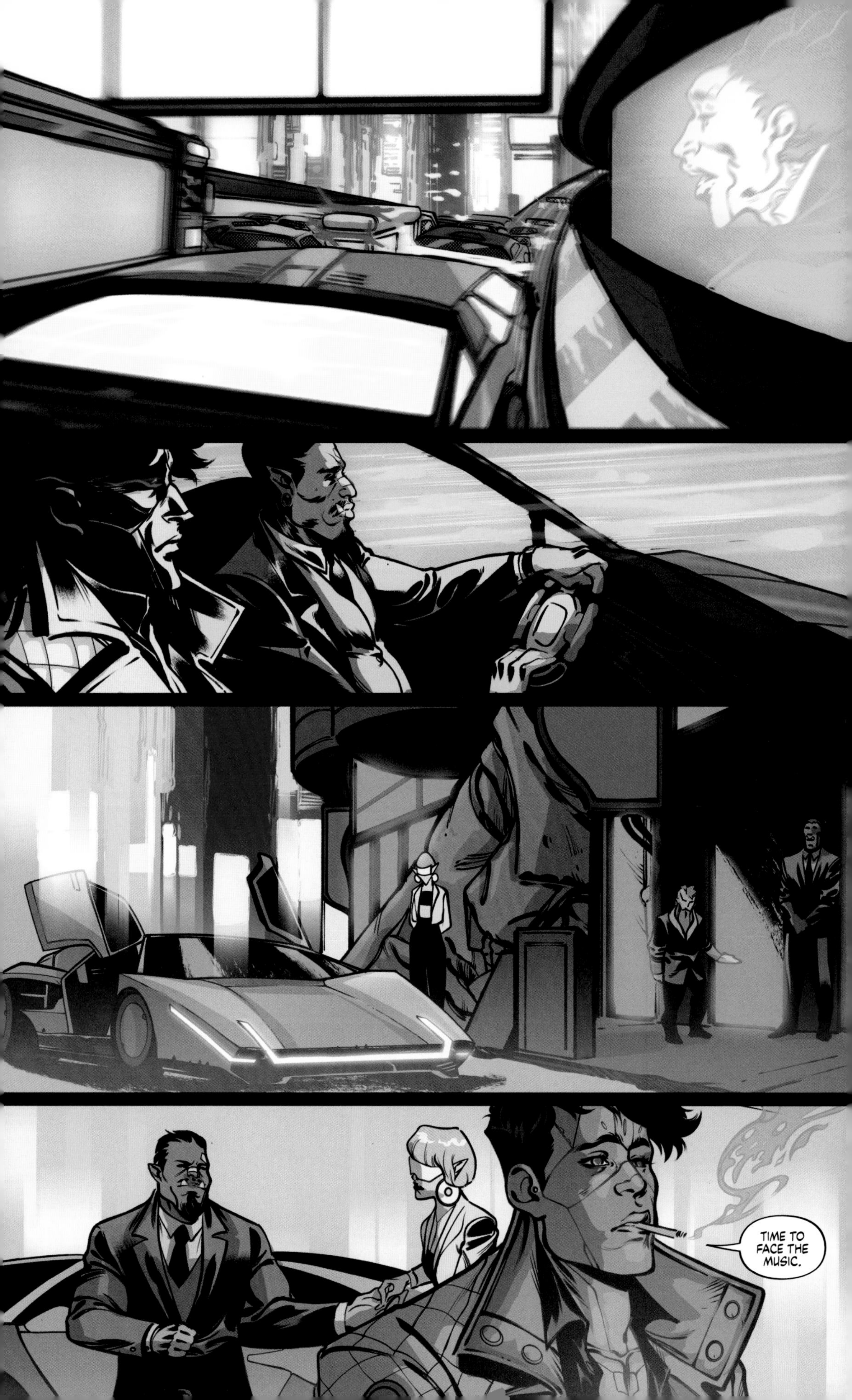
TIME TO FACE THE MUSIC.

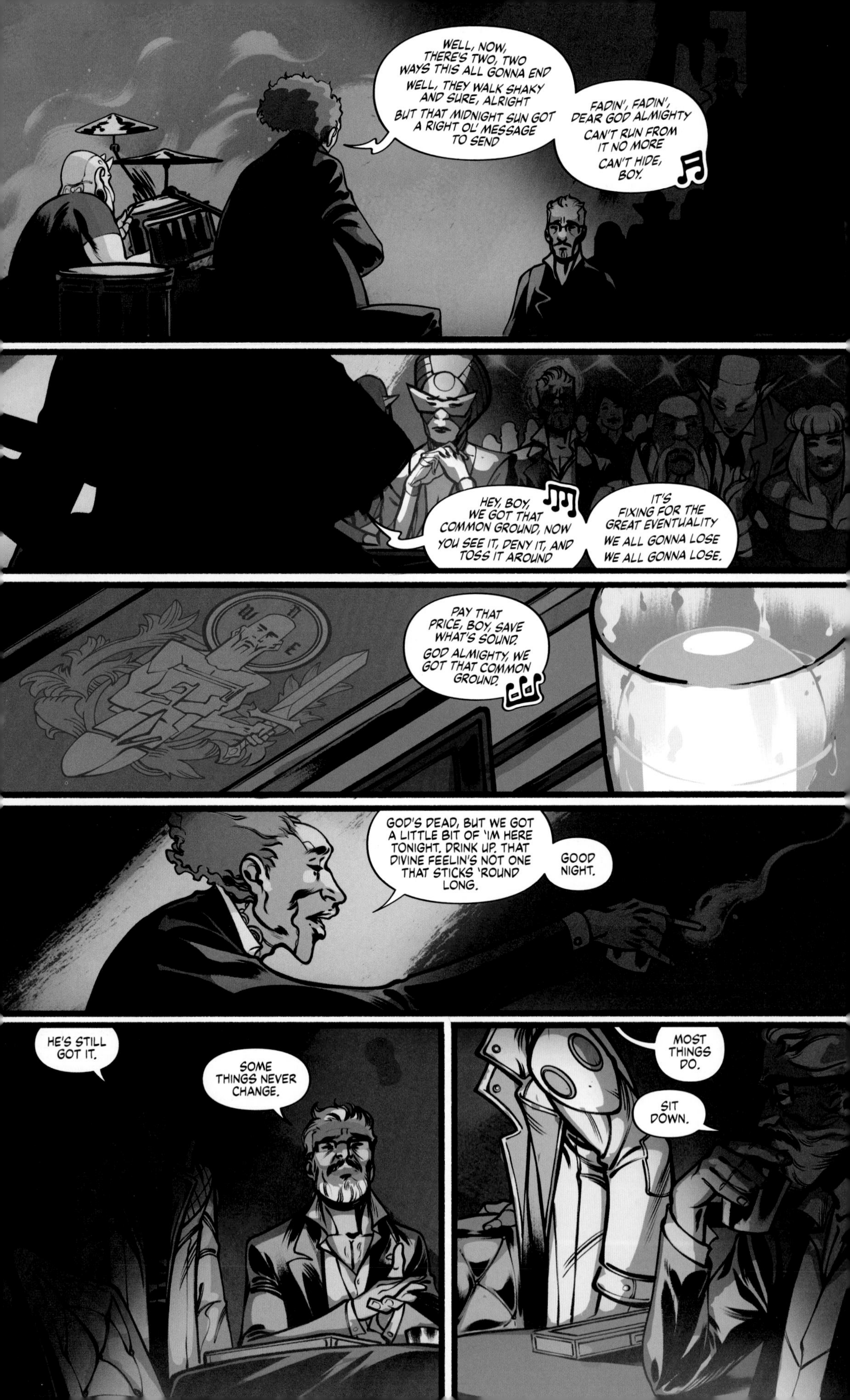
WELL, NOW, THERE'S TWO, TWO WAYS THIS ALL GONNA END
WELL, THEY WALK SHAKY AND SURE, ALRIGHT
BUT THAT MIDNIGHT SUN GOT A RIGHT OL' MESSAGE TO SEND
FADIN', FADIN', DEAR GOD ALMIGHTY
CAN'T RUN FROM IT NO MORE
CAN'T HIDE, BOY.
HEY, BOY, WE GOT THAT COMMON GROUND, NOW
YOU SEE IT, DENY IT, AND TOSS IT AROUND
IT'S FIXING FOR THE GREAT EVENTUALITY
WE ALL GONNA LOSE
WE ALL GONNA LOSE.
PAY THAT PRICE, BOY, SAVE WHAT'S SOUND.
GOD ALMIGHTY, WE GOT THAT COMMON GROUND.
GOD'S DEAD, BUT WE GOT A LITTLE BIT OF 'IM HERE TONIGHT. DRINK UP. THAT DIVINE FEELIN'S NOT ONE THAT STICKS 'ROUND LONG.
GOOD NIGHT.
HE'S STILL GOT IT.
SOME THINGS NEVER CHANGE.
MOST THINGS DO.
SIT DOWN.

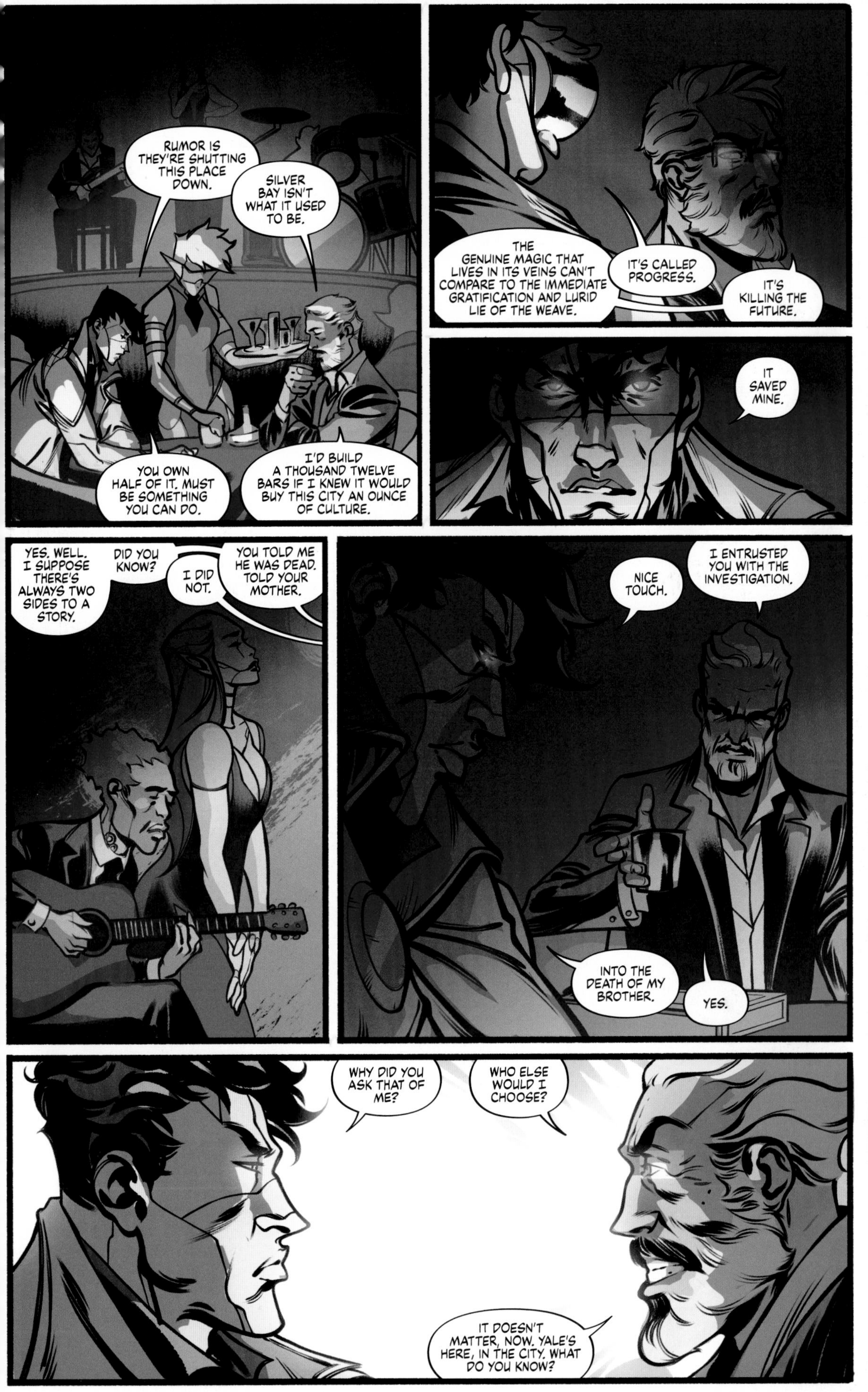
RUMOR IS THEY'RE SHUTTING THIS PLACE DOWN.
SILVER BAY ISN'T WHAT IT USED TO BE.
YOU OWN HALF OF IT. MUST BE SOMETHING YOU CAN DO.
I'D BUILD A THOUSAND TWELVE BARS IF I KNEW IT WOULD BUY THIS CITY AN OUNCE OF CULTURE.
THE GENUINE MAGIC THAT LIVES IN ITS VEINS CAN'T COMPARE TO THE IMMEDIATE GRATIFICATION AND LURID LIE OF THE WEAVE.
IT'S CALLED PROGRESS.
IT'S KILLING THE FUTURE.
IT SAVED MINE.
YES. WELL. I SUPPOSE THERE'S ALWAYS TWO SIDES TO A STORY.
DID YOU KNOW?
I DID NOT.
YOU TOLD ME HE WAS DEAD. TOLD YOUR MOTHER.
NICE TOUCH.
I ENTRUSTED YOU WITH THE INVESTIGATION.
INTO THE DEATH OF MY BROTHER.
YES.
WHY DID YOU ASK THAT OF ME?
WHO ELSE WOULD I CHOOSE?
IT DOESN'T MATTER, NOW. YALE'S HERE, IN THE CITY. WHAT DO YOU KNOW?

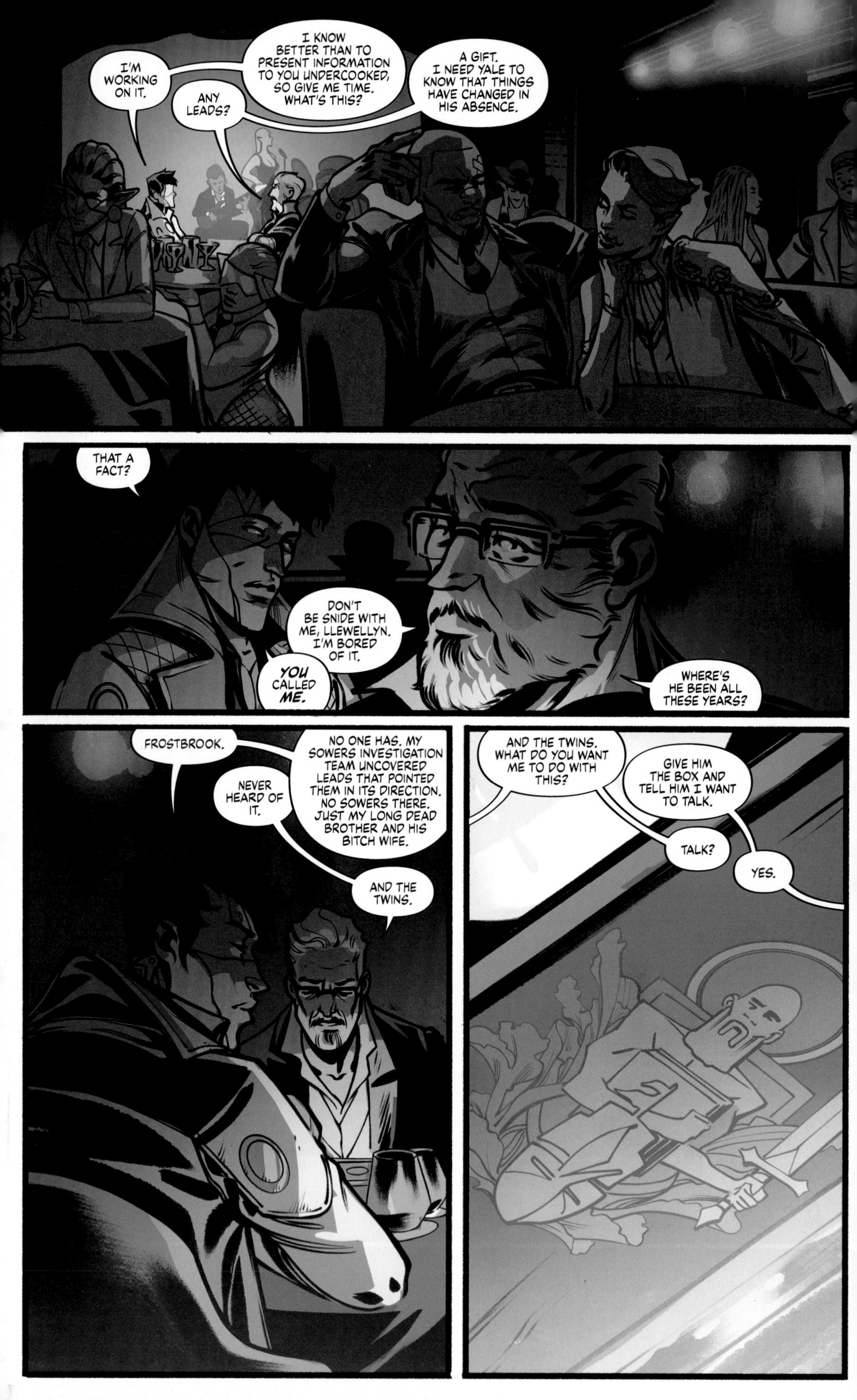
ANY LEADS?
I'M WORKING ON IT.
I KNOW BETTER THAN TO PRESENT INFORMATION TO YOU UNDERCOOKED, SO GIVE ME TIME. WHAT'S THIS?
A GIFT. I NEED YALE TO KNOW THAT THINGS HAVE CHANGED IN HIS ABSENCE.
THAT A FACT?
DON'T BE SNIDE WITH ME, LLEWELLYN. I'M BORED OF IT.
YOU CALLED ME.
WHERE'S HE BEEN ALL THESE YEARS?
FROSTBROOK.
NEVER HEARD OF IT.
NO ONE HAS. MY SOWERS INVESTIGATION TEAM UNCOVERED LEADS THAT POINTED THEM IN ITS DIRECTION. NO SOWERS THERE. JUST MY LONG DEAD BROTHER AND HIS BITCH WIFE.
AND THE TWINS.
AND THE TWINS. WHAT DO YOU WANT ME TO DO WITH THIS?
GIVE HIM THE BOX AND TELL HIM I WANT TO TALK.
TALK?
YES.

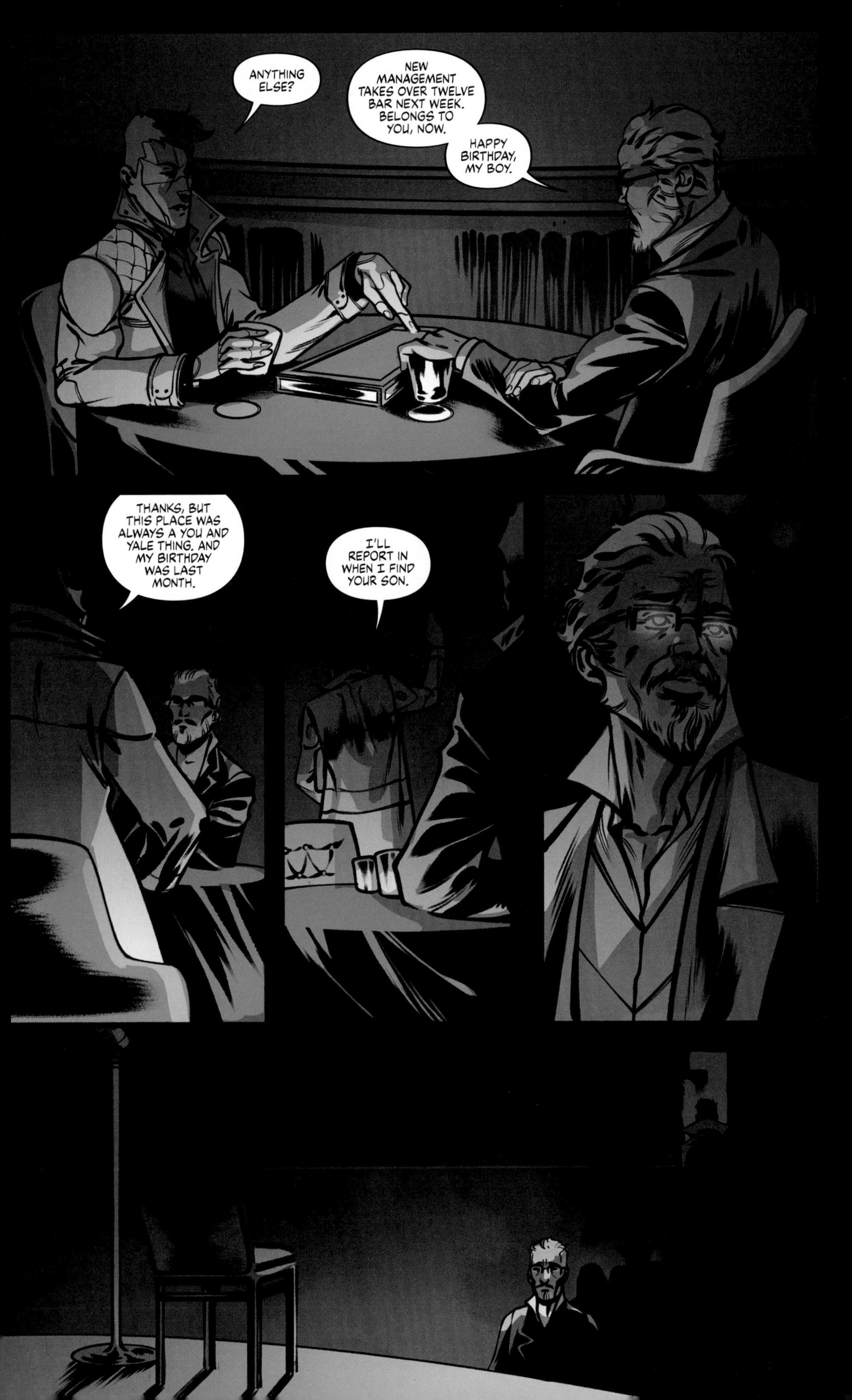
ANYTHING ELSE?
NEW MANAGEMENT TAKES OVER TWELVE BAR NEXT WEEK. BELONGS TO YOU, NOW.
HAPPY BIRTHDAY, MY BOY.
THANKS, BUT THIS PLACE WAS ALWAYS A YOU AND YALE THING. AND MY BIRTHDAY WAS LAST MONTH.
I'LL REPORT IN WHEN I FIND YOUR SON.

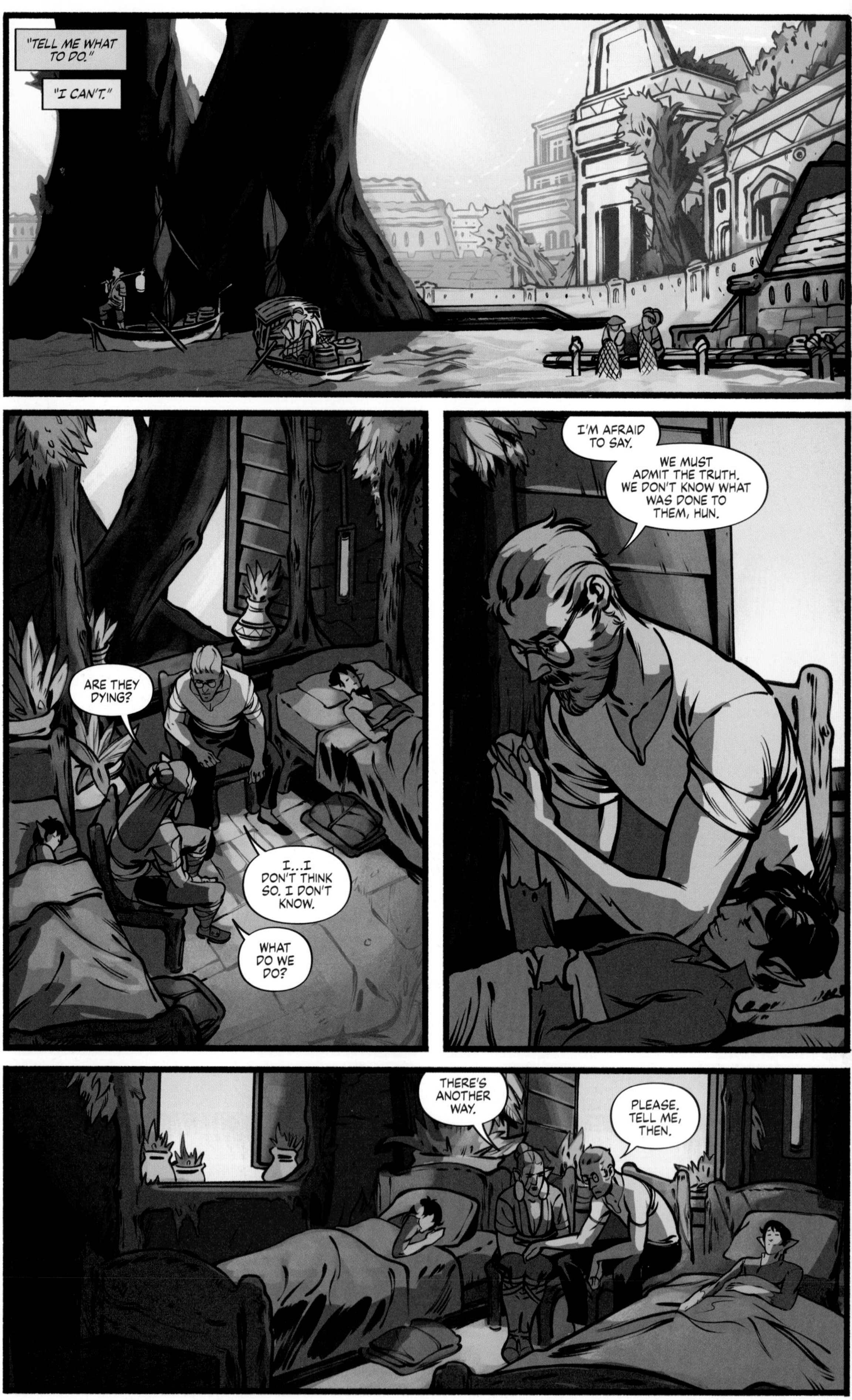
"TELL ME WHAT TO DO."
"I CAN'T."
ARE THEY DYING?
I...I DON'T THINK SO. I DON'T KNOW.
WHAT DO WE DO?
I'M AFRAID TO SAY.
WE MUST ADMIT THE TRUTH. WE DON'T KNOW WHAT WAS DONE TO THEM, HUN.
THERE'S ANOTHER WAY.
PLEASE. TELL ME, THEN.

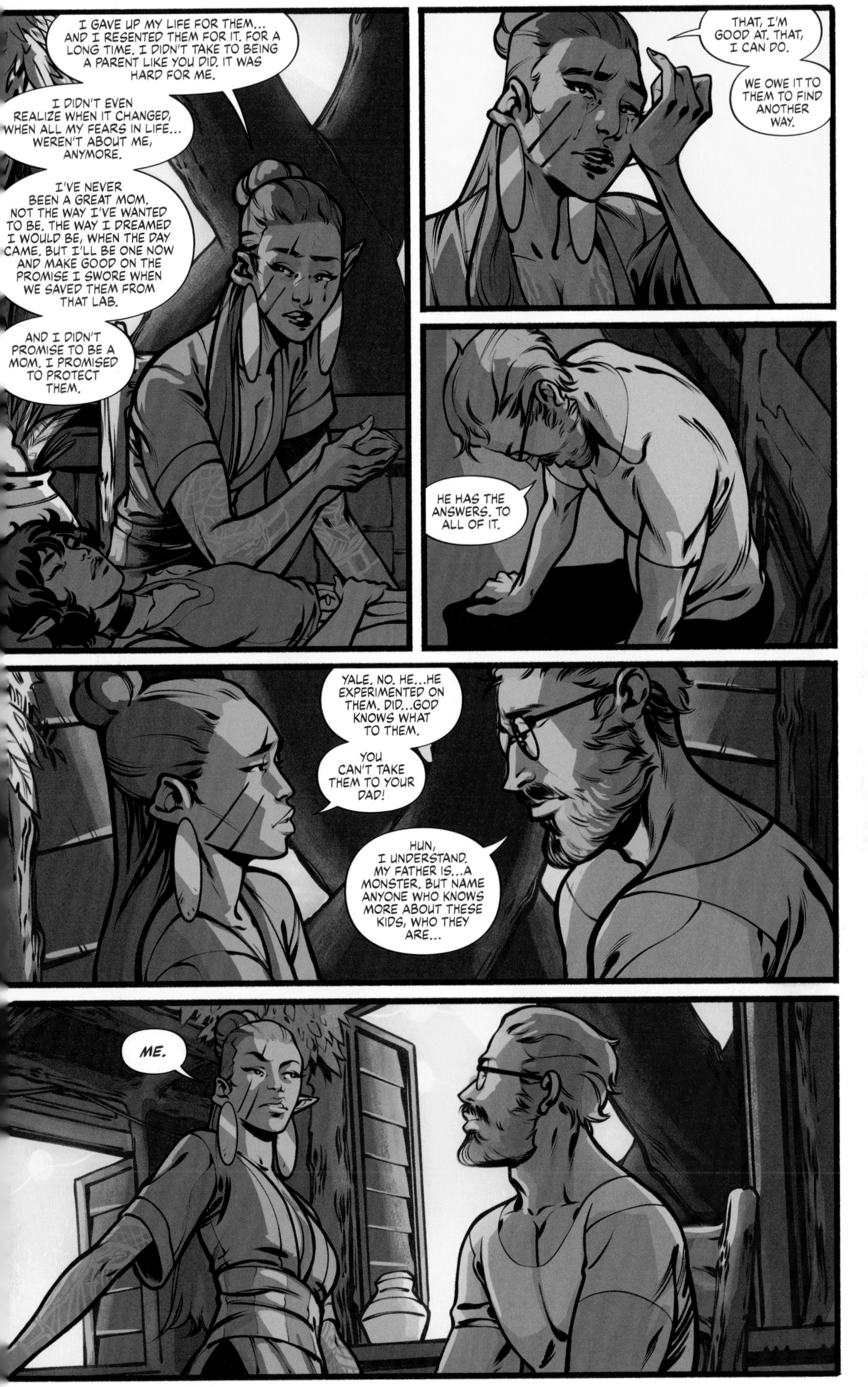
I GAVE UP MY LIFE FOR THEM... AND I RESENTED THEM FOR IT. FOR A LONG TIME. I DIDN'T TAKE TO BEING A PARENT LIKE YOU DID. IT WAS HARD FOR ME.
I DIDN'T EVEN REALIZE WHEN IT CHANGED, WHEN ALL MY FEARS IN LIFE... WEREN'T ABOUT ME, ANYMORE.
I'VE NEVER BEEN A GREAT MOM. NOT THE WAY I'VE WANTED TO BE. THE WAY I DREAMED I WOULD BE, WHEN THE DAY CAME. BUT I'LL BE ONE NOW AND MAKE GOOD ON THE PROMISE I SWORE WHEN WE SAVED THEM FROM THAT LAB.
AND I DIDN'T PROMISE TO BE A MOM. I PROMISED TO PROTECT THEM.
THAT, I'M GOOD AT. THAT, I CAN DO.
WE OWE IT TO THEM TO FIND ANOTHER WAY.
HE HAS THE ANSWERS. TO ALL OF IT.
YALE. NO. HE...HE EXPERIMENTED ON THEM. DID...GOD KNOWS WHAT TO THEM.
YOU CAN'T TAKE THEM TO YOUR DAD!
HUN, I UNDERSTAND. MY FATHER IS...A MONSTER. BUT NAME ANYONE WHO KNOWS MORE ABOUT THESE KIDS, WHO THEY ARE...
ME.

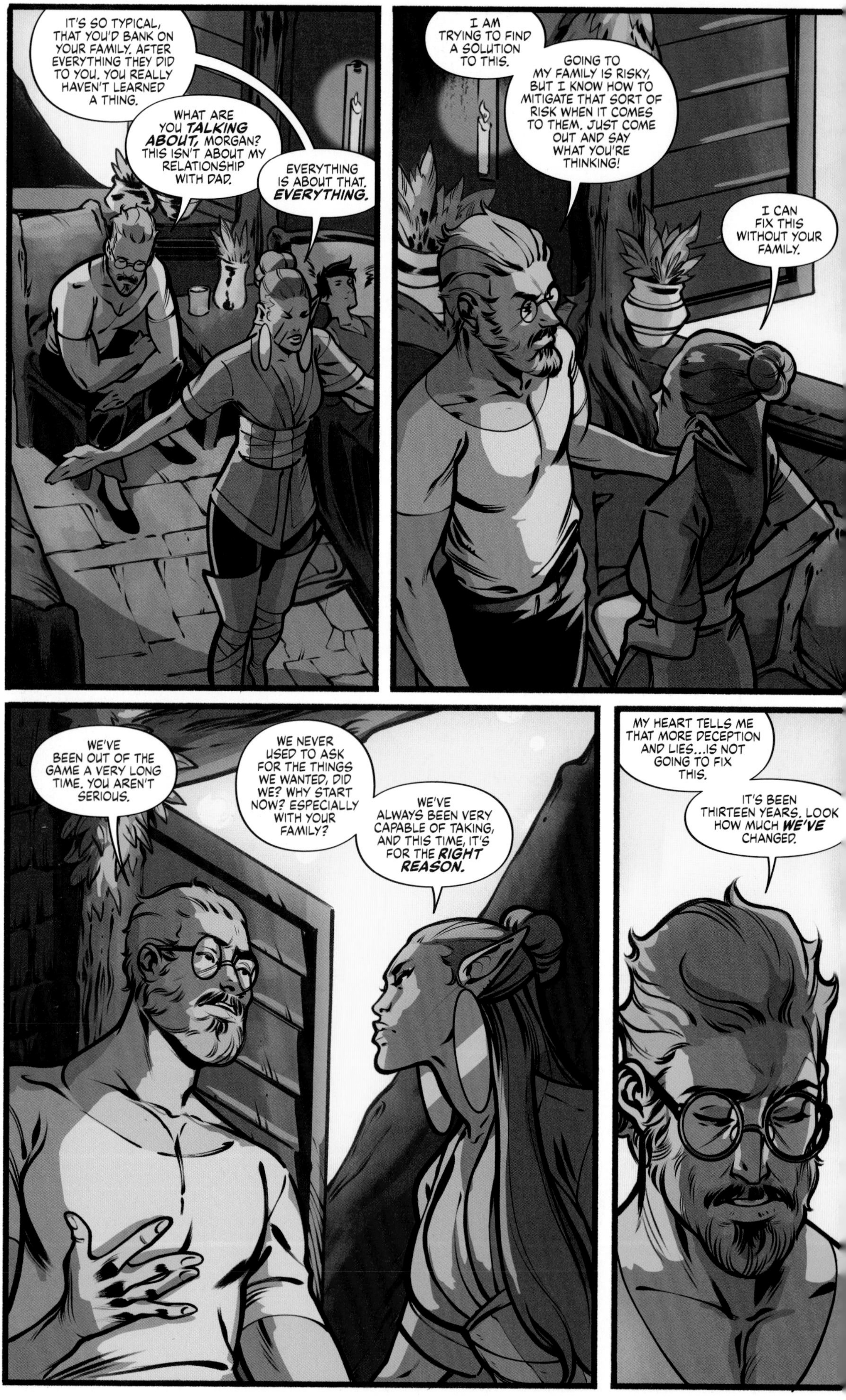
IT'S SO TYPICAL, THAT YOU'D BANK ON YOUR FAMILY. AFTER EVERYTHING THEY DID TO YOU. YOU REALLY HAVEN'T LEARNED A THING.
WHAT ARE YOU TALKING ABOUT, MORGAN? THIS ISN'T ABOUT MY RELATIONSHIP WITH DAD.
EVERYTHING IS ABOUT THAT. EVERYTHING.
I AM TRYING TO FIND A SOLUTION TO THIS.
GOING TO MY FAMILY IS RISKY, BUT I KNOW HOW TO MITIGATE THAT SORT OF RISK WHEN IT COMES TO THEM. JUST COME OUT AND SAY WHAT YOU'RE THINKING!
I CAN FIX THIS WITHOUT YOUR FAMILY.
WE'VE BEEN OUT OF THE GAME A VERY LONG TIME. YOU AREN'T SERIOUS.
WE NEVER USED TO ASK FOR THE THINGS WE WANTED, DID WE? WHY START NOW? ESPECIALLY WITH YOUR FAMILY?
WE'VE ALWAYS BEEN VERY CAPABLE OF TAKING, AND THIS TIME, IT'S FOR THE RIGHT REASON.
MY HEART TELLS ME THAT MORE DECEPTION AND LIES...IS NOT GOING TO FIX THIS.
IT'S BEEN THIRTEEN YEARS. LOOK HOW MUCH WE'VE CHANGED.

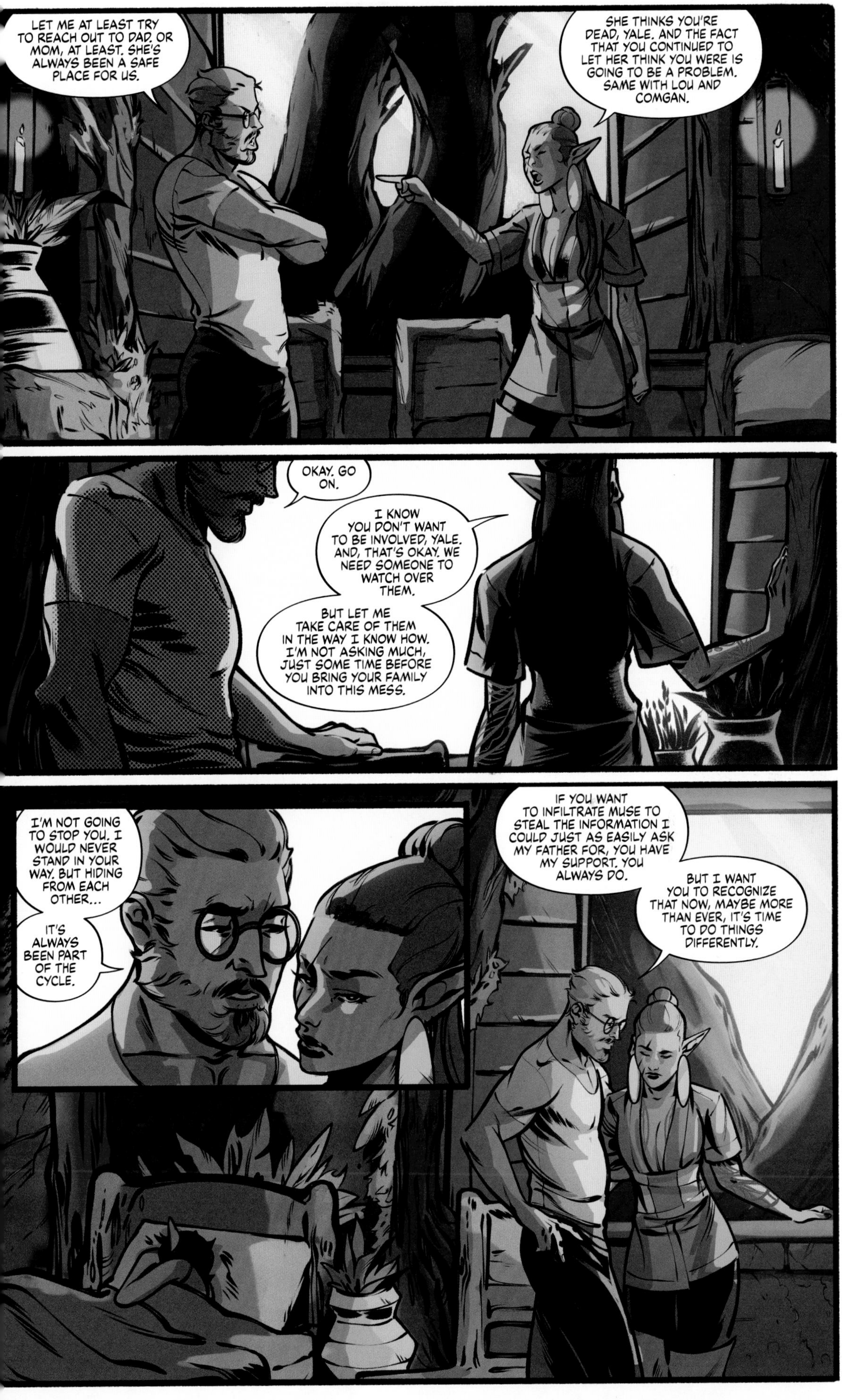
LET ME AT LEAST TRY TO REACH OUT TO DAD. OR MOM, AT LEAST. SHE'S ALWAYS BEEN A SAFE PLACE FOR US.
SHE THINKS YOU'RE DEAD, YALE. AND THE FACT THAT YOU CONTINUED TO LET HER THINK YOU WERE IS GOING TO BE A PROBLEM. SAME WITH LOU AND COMGAN.
OKAY. GO ON.
I KNOW YOU DON'T WANT TO BE INVOLVED, YALE. AND, THAT'S OKAY. WE NEED SOMEONE TO WATCH OVER THEM.
BUT LET ME TAKE CARE OF THEM IN THE WAY I KNOW HOW. I'M NOT ASKING MUCH, JUST SOME TIME BEFORE YOU BRING YOUR FAMILY INTO THIS MESS.
I'M NOT GOING TO STOP YOU. I WOULD NEVER STAND IN YOUR WAY. BUT HIDING FROM EACH OTHER...
IT'S ALWAYS BEEN PART OF THE CYCLE.
IF YOU WANT TO INFILTRATE MUSE TO STEAL THE INFORMATION I COULD JUST AS EASILY ASK MY FATHER FOR, YOU HAVE MY SUPPORT. YOU ALWAYS DO.
BUT I WANT YOU TO RECOGNIZE THAT NOW, MAYBE MORE THAN EVER, IT'S TIME TO DO THINGS DIFFERENTLY.

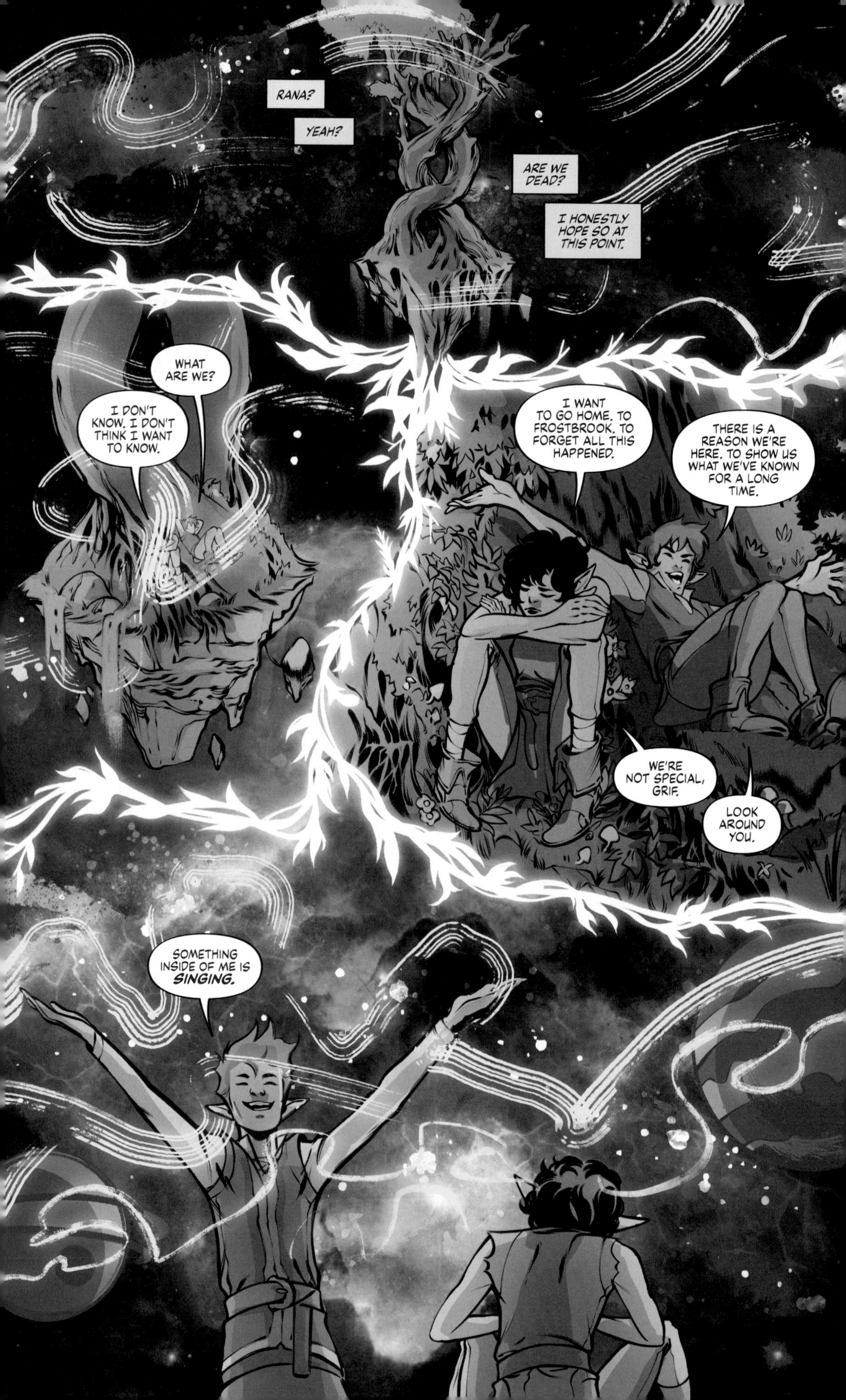
RANA?
YEAH?
ARE WE DEAD?
I HONESTLY HOPE SO AT THIS POINT.
WHAT ARE WE?
I DON'T KNOW. I DON'T THINK I WANT TO KNOW.
I WANT TO GO HOME. TO FROSTBROOK. TO FORGET ALL THIS HAPPENED.
THERE IS A REASON WE'RE HERE. TO SHOW US WHAT WE'VE KNOWN FOR A LONG TIME.
WE'RE NOT SPECIAL, GRIF.
LOOK AROUND YOU.
SOMETHING INSIDE OF ME IS **SINGING.**

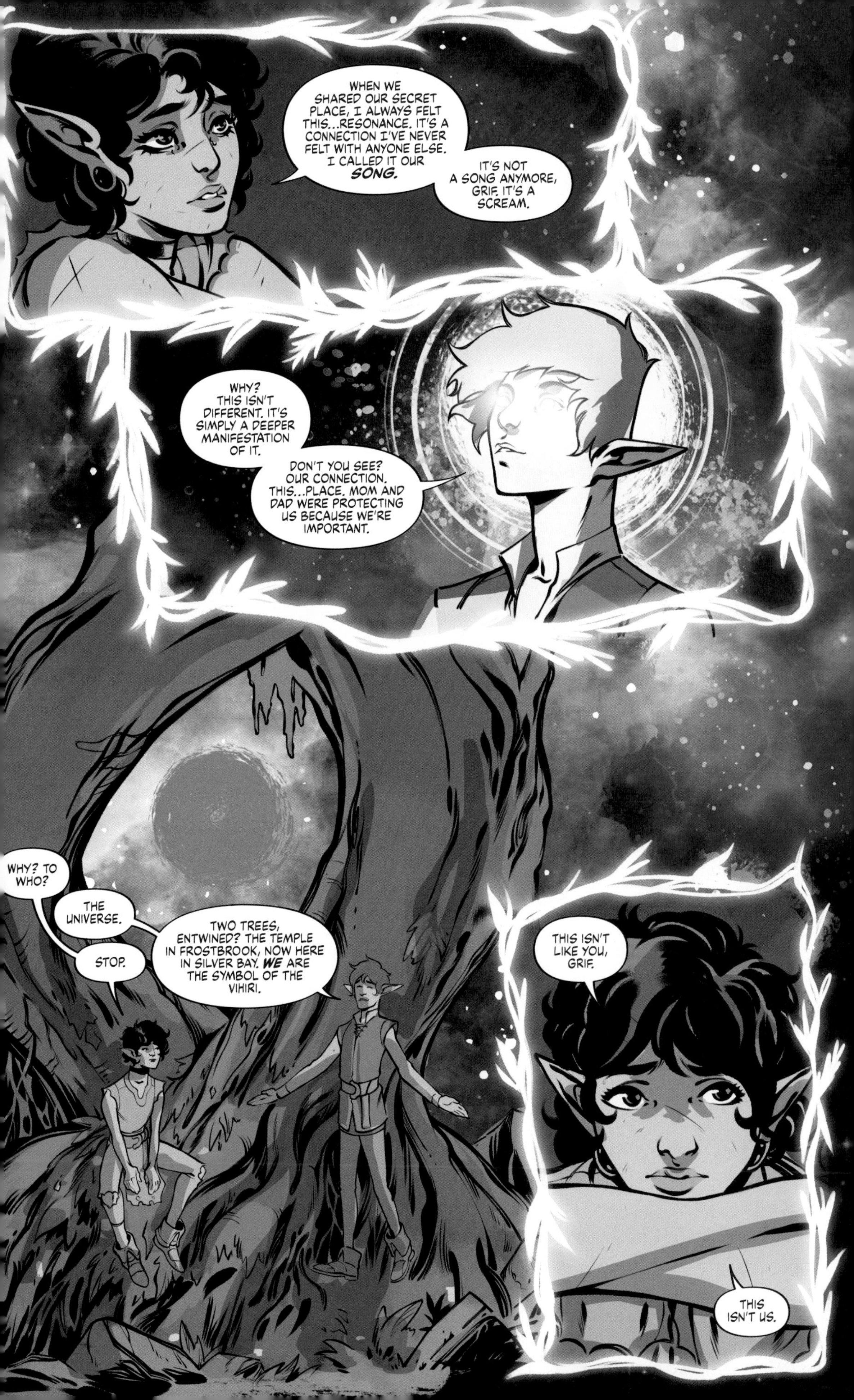
WHEN WE SHARED OUR SECRET PLACE, I ALWAYS FELT THIS...RESONANCE. IT'S A CONNECTION I'VE NEVER FELT WITH ANYONE ELSE. I CALLED IT OUR *SONG.*
IT'S NOT A SONG ANYMORE, GRIF. IT'S A SCREAM.
WHY? THIS ISN'T DIFFERENT. IT'S SIMPLY A DEEPER MANIFESTATION OF IT.
DON'T YOU SEE? OUR CONNECTION. THIS...PLACE. MOM AND DAD WERE PROTECTING US BECAUSE WE'RE IMPORTANT.
WHY? TO WHO?
THE UNIVERSE.
STOP.
TWO TREES, ENTWINED? THE TEMPLE IN FROSTBROOK, NOW HERE IN SILVER BAY. *WE* ARE THE SYMBOL OF THE VIHIRI.
THIS ISN'T LIKE YOU, GRIF.
THIS ISN'T US.

STRANGEST THING, PARKER. AN INFINITE HORIZON AS A PRISON.

NO WAY I'M GETTING OUT OF THIS.

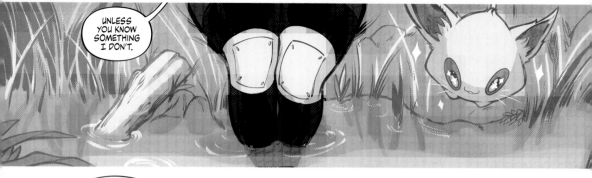

UNLESS YOU KNOW SOMETHING I DON'T.

DON'T SWEAT IT, PAL. YOU WERE ALWAYS CUTE BUT SO, SO DUMB.

THIS ONE... IT'S ON ME. CAN'T BELIEVE I WALKED RIGHT INTO THIS SHIT.

CONDITION: RED

EMERGENCY

WELL, BOY. IF YOU MANAGE TO FIND A CONNECTION TO THE WEAVE, LET ME KNOW. LOOKS LIKE I'VE GOT THINGS TO DEAL WITH IN THE REAL WORLD.

eep

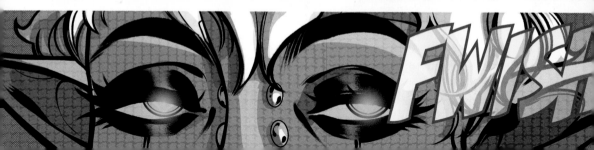

FW

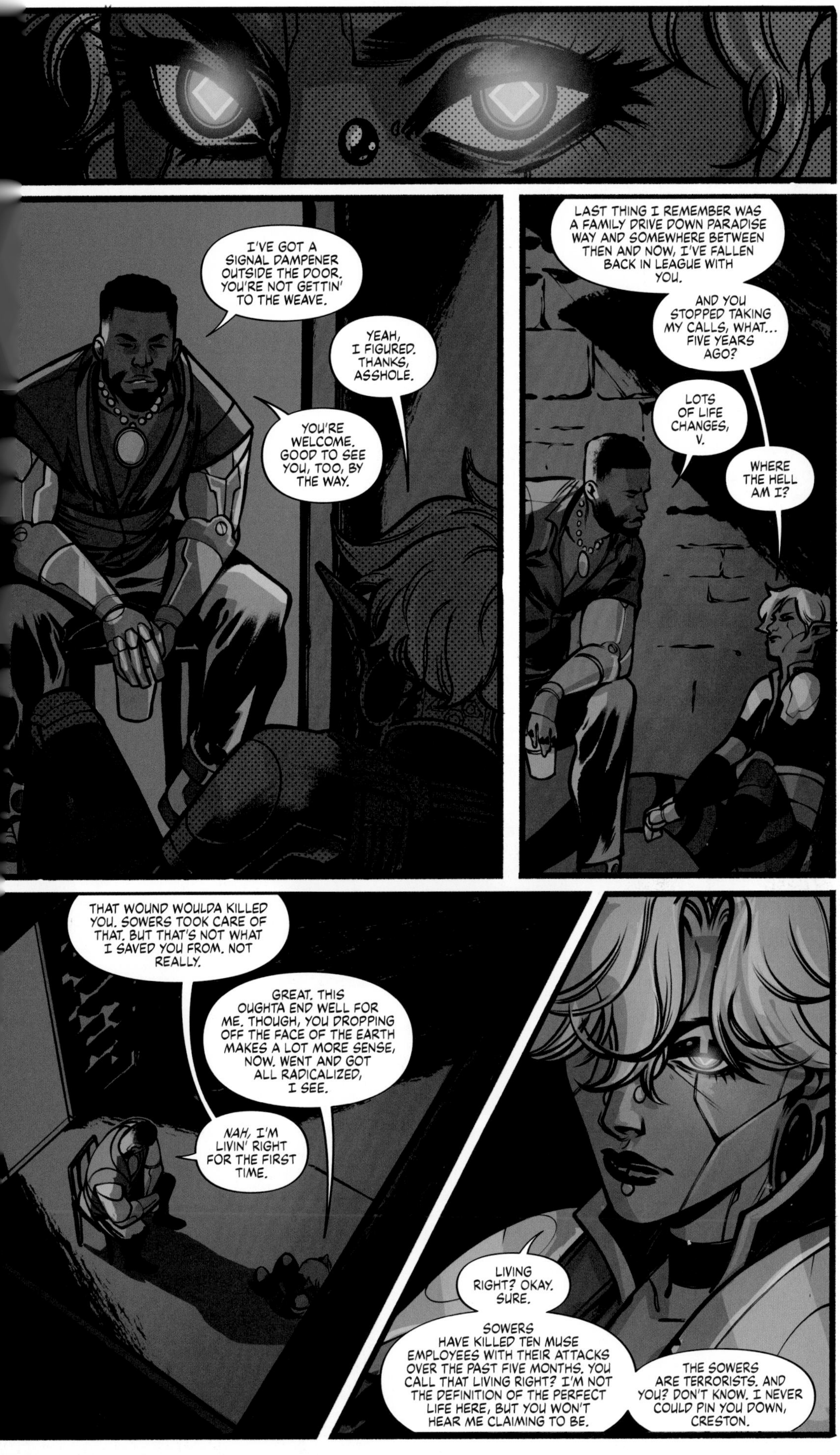
I'VE GOT A SIGNAL DAMPENER OUTSIDE THE DOOR. YOU'RE NOT GETTIN' TO THE WEAVE.
YEAH, I FIGURED. THANKS, ASSHOLE.
YOU'RE WELCOME. GOOD TO SEE YOU, TOO, BY THE WAY.
LAST THING I REMEMBER WAS A FAMILY DRIVE DOWN PARADISE WAY AND SOMEWHERE BETWEEN THEN AND NOW, I'VE FALLEN BACK IN LEAGUE WITH YOU.
AND YOU STOPPED TAKING MY CALLS, WHAT... FIVE YEARS AGO?
LOTS OF LIFE CHANGES, V.
WHERE THE HELL AM I?
THAT WOUND WOULDA KILLED YOU. SOWERS TOOK CARE OF THAT. BUT THAT'S NOT WHAT I SAVED YOU FROM. NOT REALLY.
GREAT. THIS OUGHTA END WELL FOR ME. THOUGH, YOU DROPPING OFF THE FACE OF THE EARTH MAKES A LOT MORE SENSE, NOW. WENT AND GOT ALL RADICALIZED, I SEE.
NAH, I'M LIVIN' RIGHT FOR THE FIRST TIME.
LIVING RIGHT? OKAY. SURE.
SOWERS HAVE KILLED TEN MUSE EMPLOYEES WITH THEIR ATTACKS OVER THE PAST FIVE MONTHS. YOU CALL THAT LIVING RIGHT? I'M NOT THE DEFINITION OF THE PERFECT LIFE HERE, BUT YOU WON'T HEAR ME CLAIMING TO BE.
THE SOWERS ARE TERRORISTS. AND YOU? DON'T KNOW. I NEVER COULD PIN YOU DOWN, CRESTON.

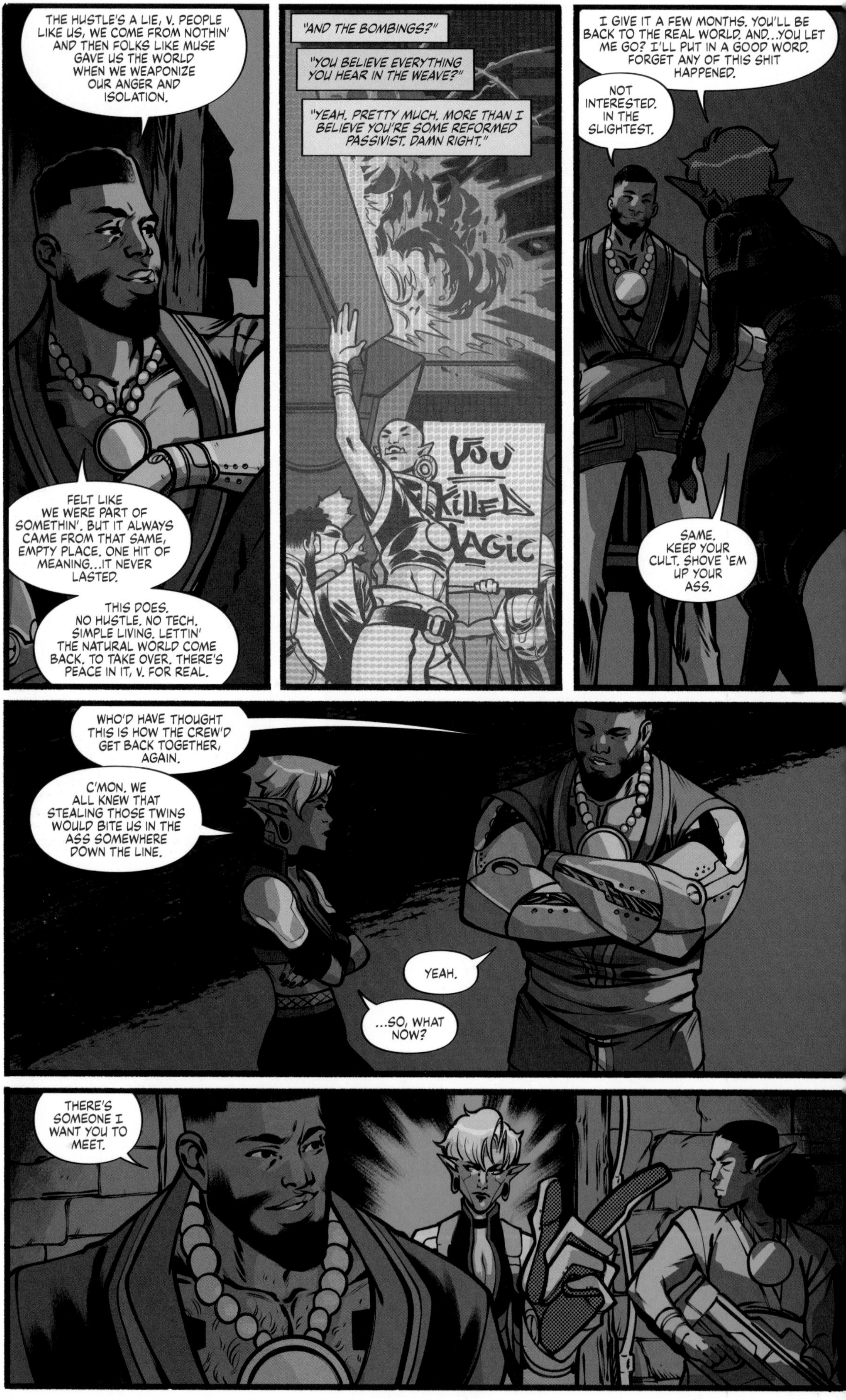
THE HUSTLE'S A LIE, V. PEOPLE LIKE US, WE COME FROM NOTHIN' AND THEN FOLKS LIKE MUSE GAVE US THE WORLD WHEN WE WEAPONIZE OUR ANGER AND ISOLATION.
FELT LIKE WE WERE PART OF SOMETHIN'. BUT IT ALWAYS CAME FROM THAT SAME, EMPTY PLACE. ONE HIT OF MEANING...IT NEVER LASTED.
THIS DOES. NO HUSTLE. NO TECH. SIMPLE LIVING. LETTIN' THE NATURAL WORLD COME BACK. TO TAKE OVER. THERE'S PEACE IN IT, V. FOR REAL.
"AND THE BOMBINGS?"
"YOU BELIEVE EVERYTHING YOU HEAR IN THE WEAVE?"
"YEAH. PRETTY MUCH. MORE THAN I BELIEVE YOU'RE SOME REFORMED PASSIVIST. DAMN RIGHT."
YOU KILLED MAGIC
I GIVE IT A FEW MONTHS. YOU'LL BE BACK TO THE REAL WORLD. AND...YOU LET ME GO? I'LL PUT IN A GOOD WORD. FORGET ANY OF THIS SHIT HAPPENED.
NOT INTERESTED. IN THE SLIGHTEST.
SAME. KEEP YOUR CULT. SHOVE 'EM UP YOUR ASS.
WHO'D HAVE THOUGHT THIS IS HOW THE CREW'D GET BACK TOGETHER, AGAIN.
C'MON. WE ALL KNEW THAT STEALING THOSE TWINS WOULD BITE US IN THE ASS SOMEWHERE DOWN THE LINE.
YEAH.
...SO, WHAT NOW?
THERE'S SOMEONE I WANT YOU TO MEET.

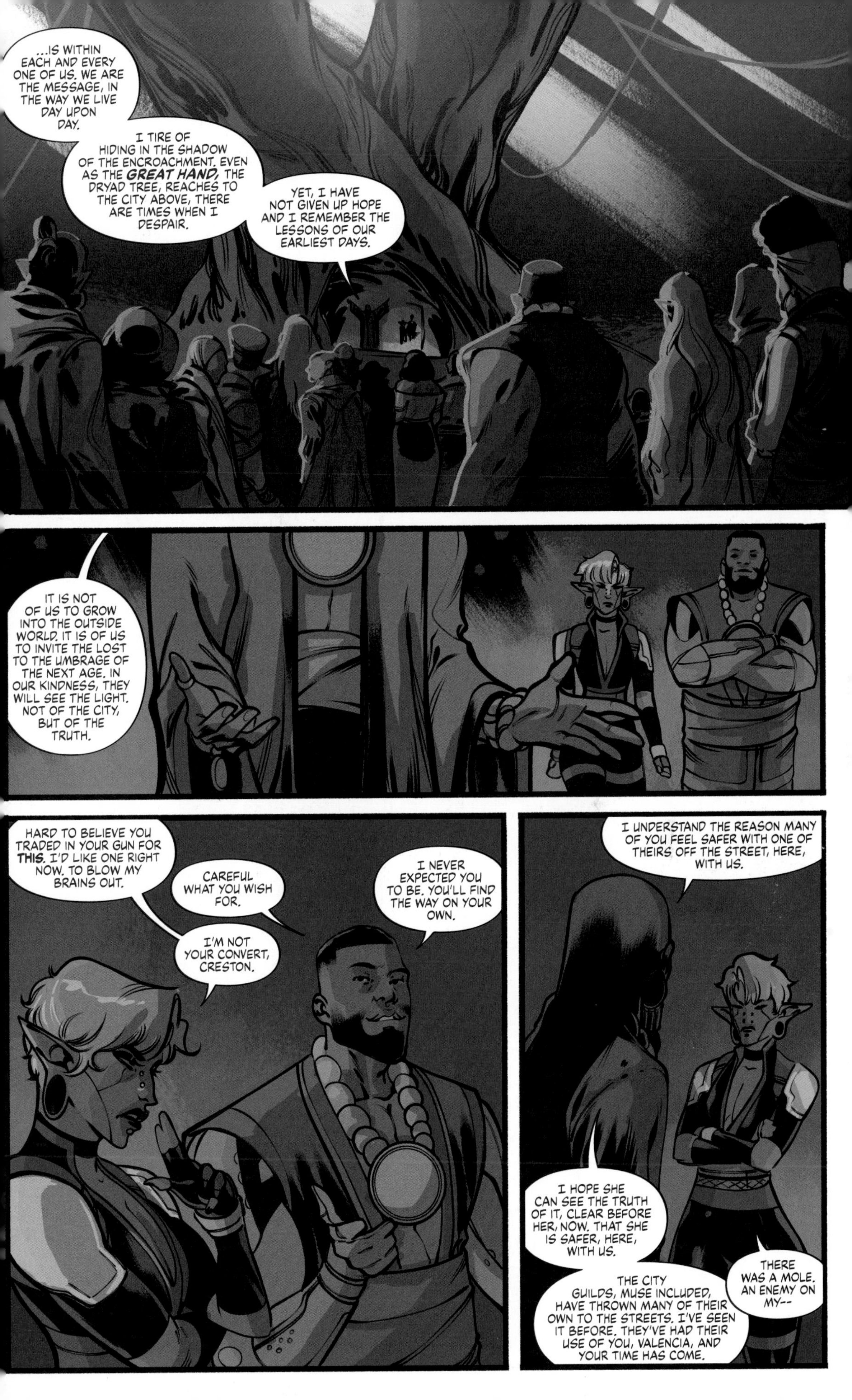
...IS WITHIN EACH AND EVERY ONE OF US. WE ARE THE MESSAGE, IN THE WAY WE LIVE DAY UPON DAY.
I TIRE OF HIDING IN THE SHADOW OF THE ENCROACHMENT. EVEN AS THE **GREAT HAND,** THE DRYAD TREE, REACHES TO THE CITY ABOVE, THERE ARE TIMES WHEN I DESPAIR.
YET, I HAVE NOT GIVEN UP HOPE AND I REMEMBER THE LESSONS OF OUR EARLIEST DAYS.
IT IS NOT OF US TO GROW INTO THE OUTSIDE WORLD. IT IS OF US TO INVITE THE LOST TO THE UMBRAGE OF THE NEXT AGE. IN OUR KINDNESS, THEY WILL SEE THE LIGHT. NOT OF THE CITY, BUT OF THE TRUTH.
HARD TO BELIEVE YOU TRADED IN YOUR GUN FOR **THIS**. I'D LIKE ONE RIGHT NOW. TO BLOW MY BRAINS OUT.
CAREFUL WHAT YOU WISH FOR.
I'M NOT YOUR CONVERT, CRESTON.
I NEVER EXPECTED YOU TO BE. YOU'LL FIND THE WAY ON YOUR OWN.
I UNDERSTAND THE REASON MANY OF YOU FEEL SAFER WITH ONE OF THEIRS OFF THE STREET, HERE, WITH US.
I HOPE SHE CAN SEE THE TRUTH OF IT, CLEAR BEFORE HER, NOW. THAT SHE IS SAFER, HERE, WITH US.
THERE WAS A MOLE. AN ENEMY ON MY--
THE CITY GUILDS, MUSE INCLUDED, HAVE THROWN MANY OF THEIR OWN TO THE STREETS. I'VE SEEN IT BEFORE. THEY'VE HAD THEIR USE OF YOU, VALENCIA, AND YOUR TIME HAS COME.

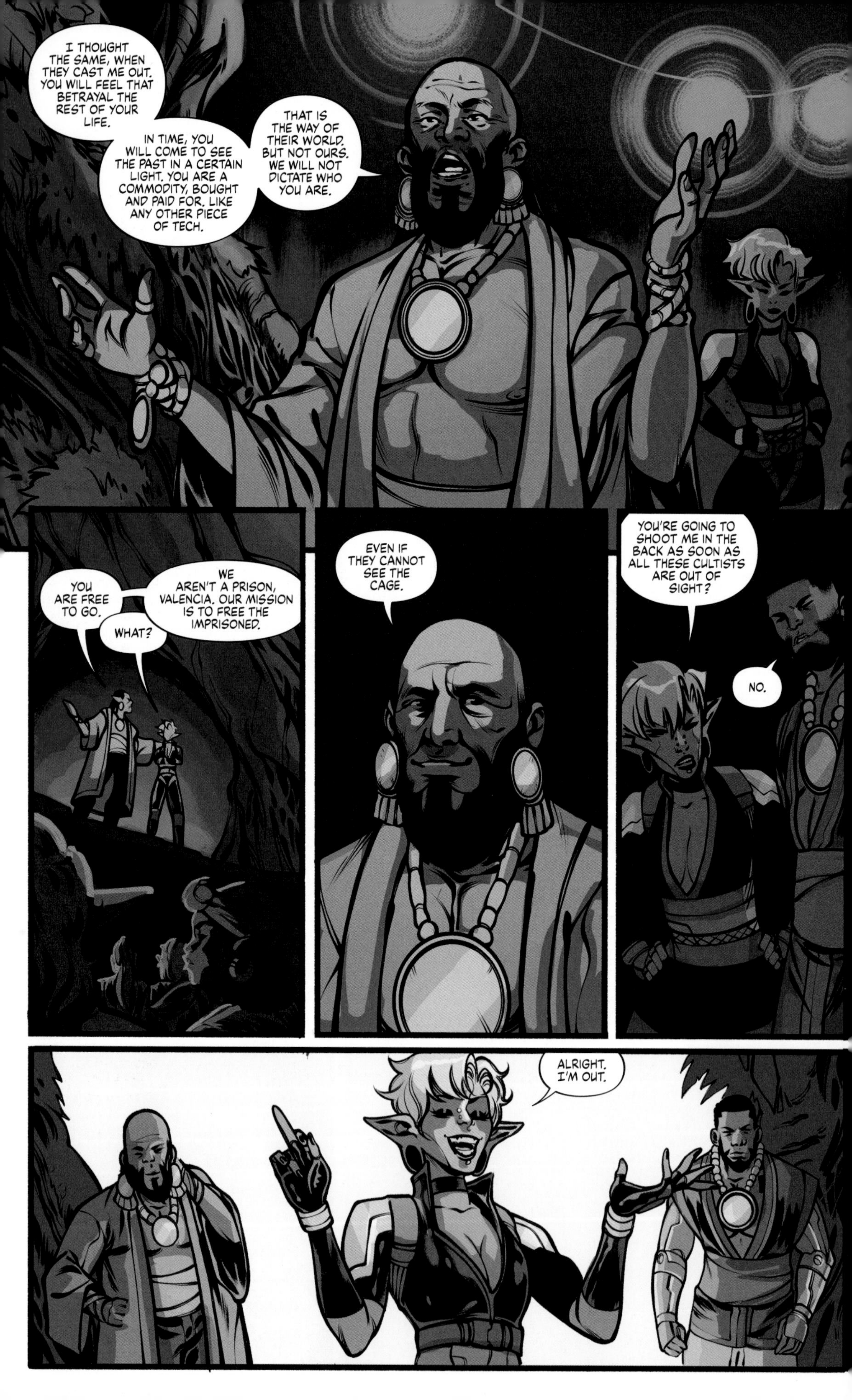
I THOUGHT THE SAME, WHEN THEY CAST ME OUT. YOU WILL FEEL THAT BETRAYAL THE REST OF YOUR LIFE.
IN TIME, YOU WILL COME TO SEE THE PAST IN A CERTAIN LIGHT. YOU ARE A COMMODITY, BOUGHT AND PAID FOR. LIKE ANY OTHER PIECE OF TECH.
THAT IS THE WAY OF THEIR WORLD. BUT NOT OURS. WE WILL NOT DICTATE WHO YOU ARE.
YOU ARE FREE TO GO.
WHAT?
WE AREN'T A PRISON, VALENCIA. OUR MISSION IS TO FREE THE IMPRISONED.
EVEN IF THEY CANNOT SEE THE CAGE.
YOU'RE GOING TO SHOOT ME IN THE BACK AS SOON AS ALL THESE CULTISTS ARE OUT OF SIGHT?
NO.
ALRIGHT. I'M OUT.

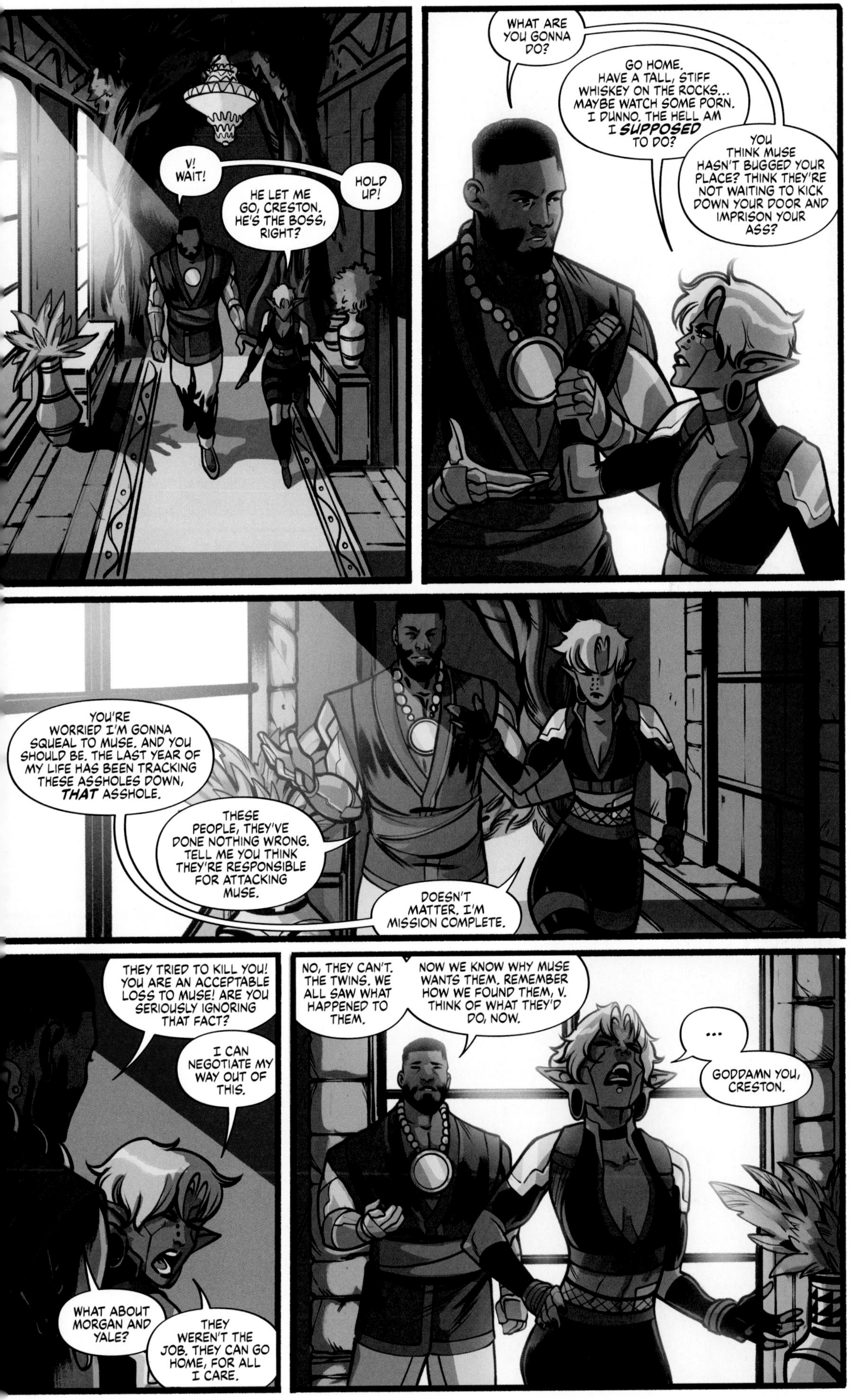
V! WAIT!
HOLD UP!
HE LET ME GO, CRESTON. HE'S THE BOSS, RIGHT?
WHAT ARE YOU GONNA DO?
GO HOME. HAVE A TALL, STIFF WHISKEY ON THE ROCKS... MAYBE WATCH SOME PORN. I DUNNO. THE HELL AM I SUPPOSED TO DO?
YOU THINK MUSE HASN'T BUGGED YOUR PLACE? THINK THEY'RE NOT WAITING TO KICK DOWN YOUR DOOR AND IMPRISON YOUR ASS?
YOU'RE WORRIED I'M GONNA SQUEAL TO MUSE. AND YOU SHOULD BE. THE LAST YEAR OF MY LIFE HAS BEEN TRACKING THESE ASSHOLES DOWN, THAT ASSHOLE.
THESE PEOPLE, THEY'VE DONE NOTHING WRONG. TELL ME YOU THINK THEY'RE RESPONSIBLE FOR ATTACKING MUSE.
DOESN'T MATTER. I'M MISSION COMPLETE.
THEY TRIED TO KILL YOU! YOU ARE AN ACCEPTABLE LOSS TO MUSE! ARE YOU SERIOUSLY IGNORING THAT FACT?
I CAN NEGOTIATE MY WAY OUT OF THIS.
WHAT ABOUT MORGAN AND YALE?
THEY WEREN'T THE JOB. THEY CAN GO HOME, FOR ALL I CARE.
NO, THEY CAN'T. THE TWINS. WE ALL SAW WHAT HAPPENED TO THEM.
NOW WE KNOW WHY MUSE WANTS THEM. REMEMBER HOW WE FOUND THEM, V. THINK OF WHAT THEY'D DO, NOW.
...
GODDAMN YOU, CRESTON.

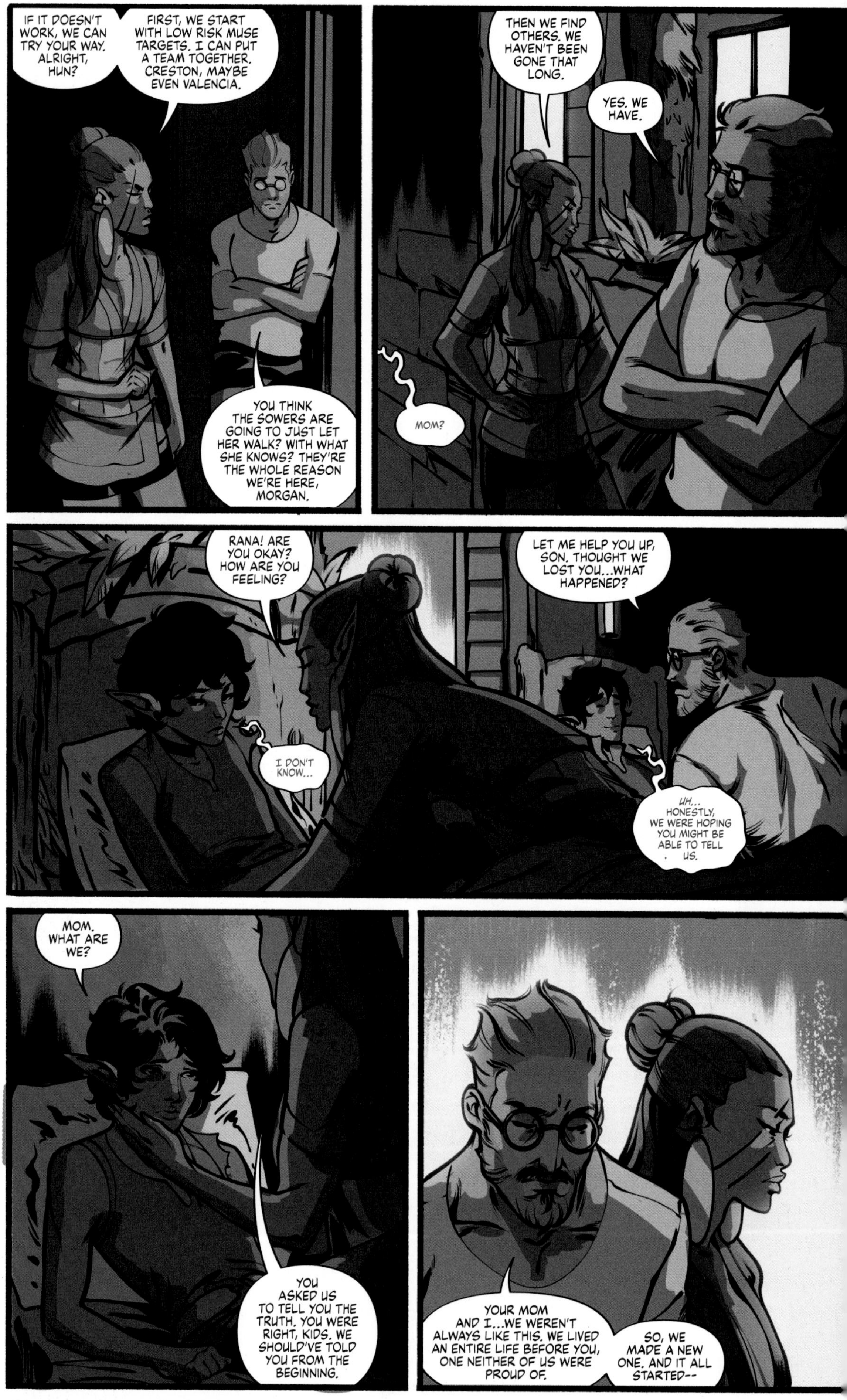
IF IT DOESN'T WORK, WE CAN TRY YOUR WAY. ALRIGHT, HUN?
FIRST, WE START WITH LOW RISK MUSE TARGETS. I CAN PUT A TEAM TOGETHER. CRESTON, MAYBE EVEN VALENCIA.
YOU THINK THE SOWERS ARE GOING TO JUST LET HER WALK? WITH WHAT SHE KNOWS? THEY'RE THE WHOLE REASON WE'RE HERE, MORGAN.
THEN WE FIND OTHERS. WE HAVEN'T BEEN GONE THAT LONG.
YES. WE HAVE.
MOM?
RANA! ARE YOU OKAY? HOW ARE YOU FEELING?
I DON'T KNOW...
LET ME HELP YOU UP, SON. THOUGHT WE LOST YOU...WHAT HAPPENED?
UH... HONESTLY, WE WERE HOPING YOU MIGHT BE ABLE TO TELL US.
MOM. WHAT ARE WE?
YOU ASKED US TO TELL YOU THE TRUTH. YOU WERE RIGHT, KIDS. WE SHOULD'VE TOLD YOU FROM THE BEGINNING.
YOUR MOM AND I...WE WEREN'T ALWAYS LIKE THIS. WE LIVED AN ENTIRE LIFE BEFORE YOU, ONE NEITHER OF US WERE PROUD OF.
SO, WE MADE A NEW ONE. AND IT ALL STARTED--

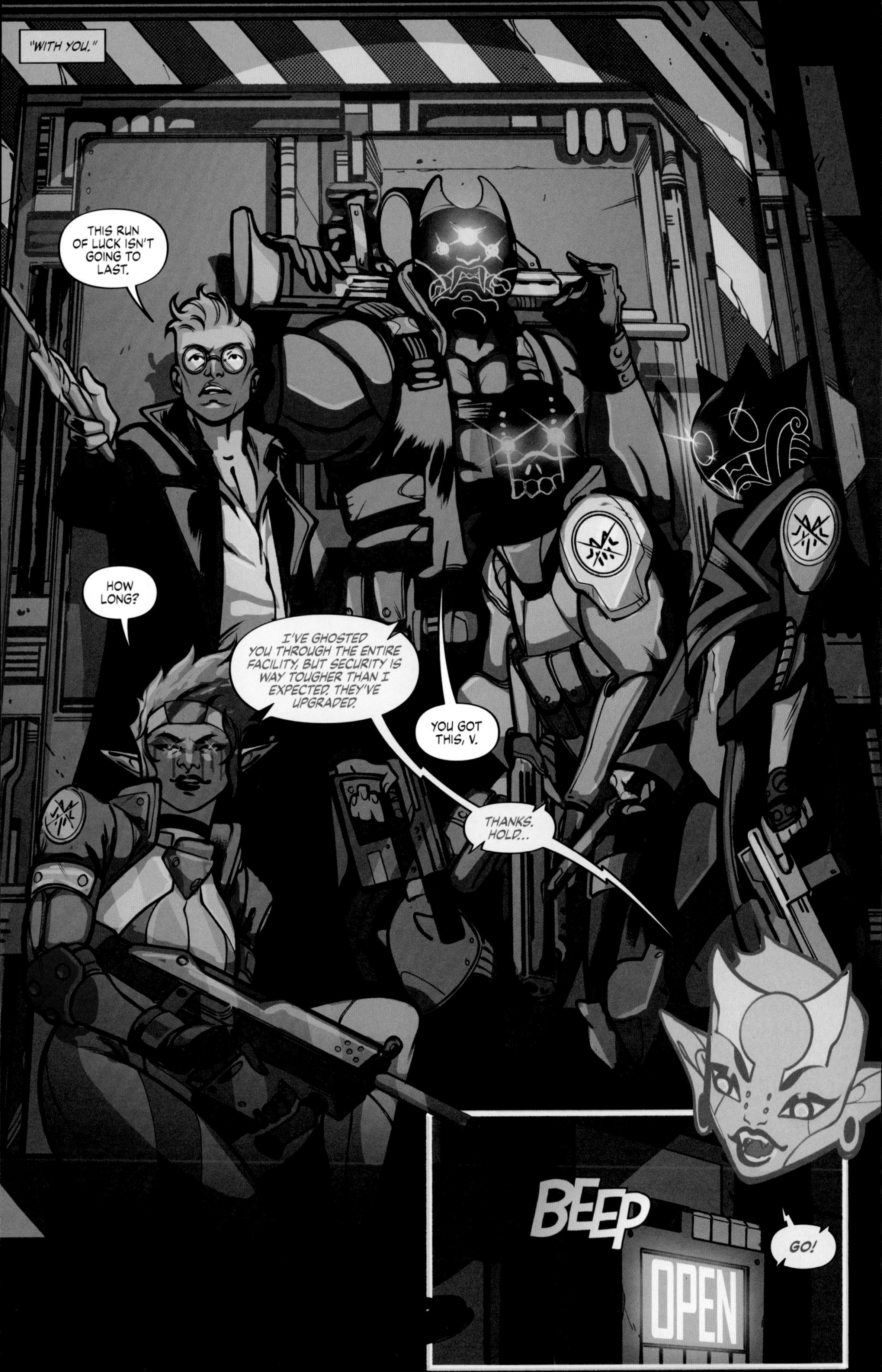
"WITH YOU."
THIS RUN OF LUCK ISN'T GOING TO LAST.
HOW LONG?
I'VE GHOSTED YOU THROUGH THE ENTIRE FACILITY, BUT SECURITY IS WAY TOUGHER THAN I EXPECTED. THEY'VE UPGRADED.
YOU GOT THIS, V.
THANKS. HOLD...
BEEP
OPEN
GO!

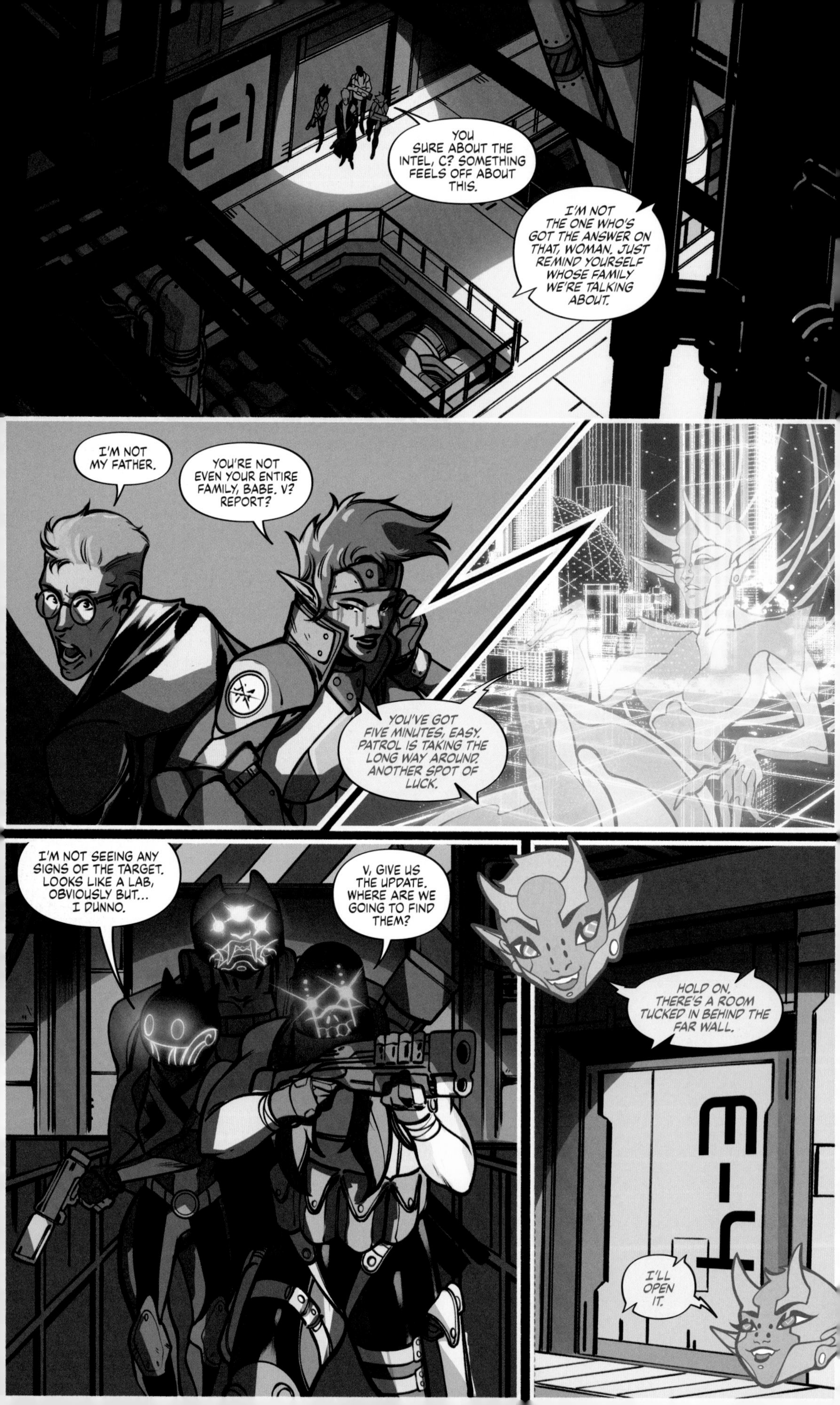
E-1
YOU SURE ABOUT THE INTEL, C? SOMETHING FEELS OFF ABOUT THIS.
I'M NOT THE ONE WHO'S GOT THE ANSWER ON THAT, WOMAN. JUST REMIND YOURSELF WHOSE FAMILY WE'RE TALKING ABOUT.
I'M NOT MY FATHER.
YOU'RE NOT EVEN YOUR ENTIRE FAMILY, BABE. V? REPORT?
YOU'VE GOT FIVE MINUTES, EASY. PATROL IS TAKING THE LONG WAY AROUND. ANOTHER SPOT OF LUCK.
I'M NOT SEEING ANY SIGNS OF THE TARGET. LOOKS LIKE A LAB, OBVIOUSLY BUT... I DUNNO.
V, GIVE US THE UPDATE. WHERE ARE WE GOING TO FIND THEM?
HOLD ON. THERE'S A ROOM TUCKED IN BEHIND THE FAR WALL.
I'LL OPEN IT.

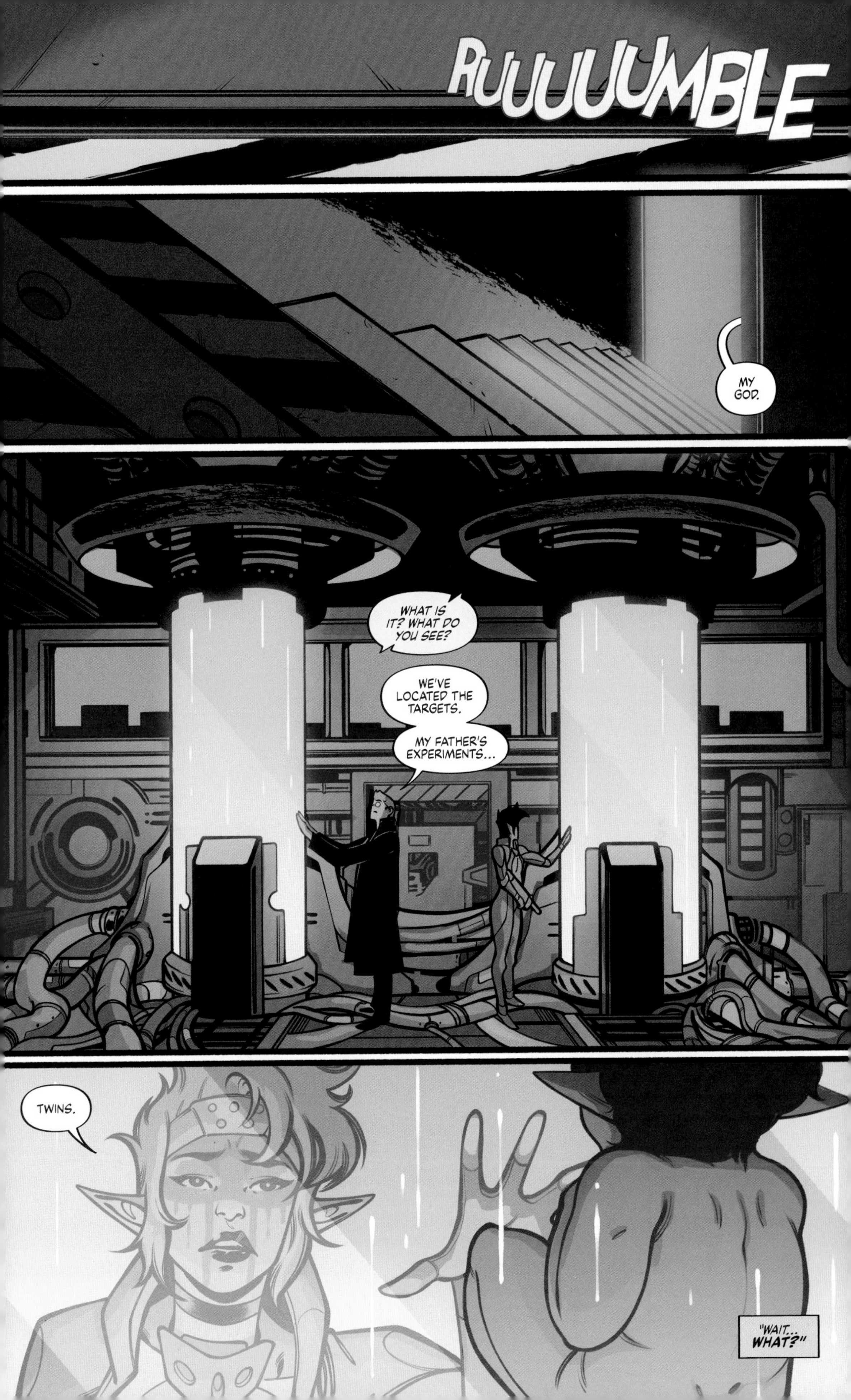
RUUUUUMBLE
MY GOD.
WHAT IS IT? WHAT DO YOU SEE?
WE'VE LOCATED THE TARGETS.
MY FATHER'S EXPERIMENTS...
TWINS.
"WAIT... WHAT?"

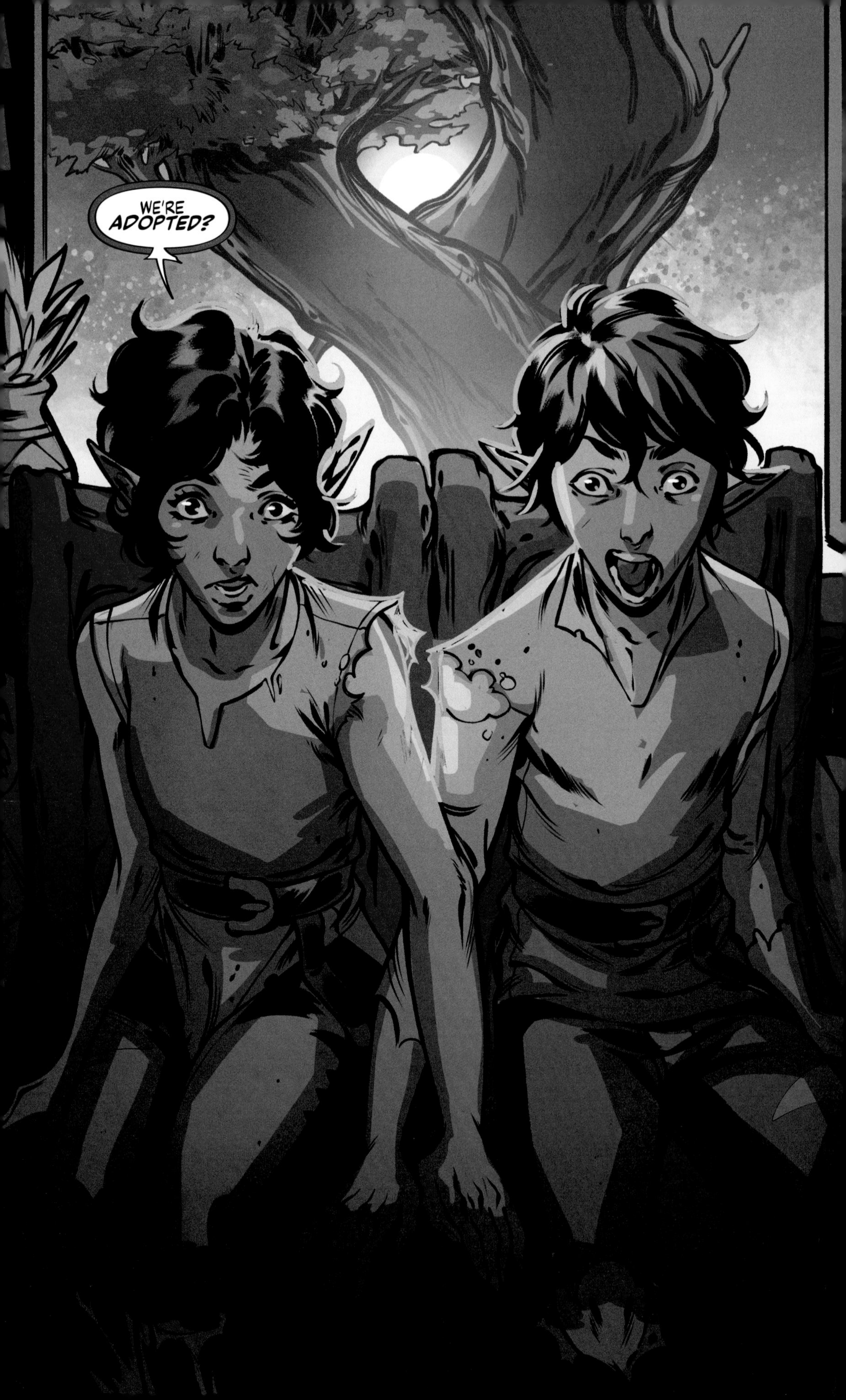
WE'RE ADOPTED?

CHAPTER
SEVEN

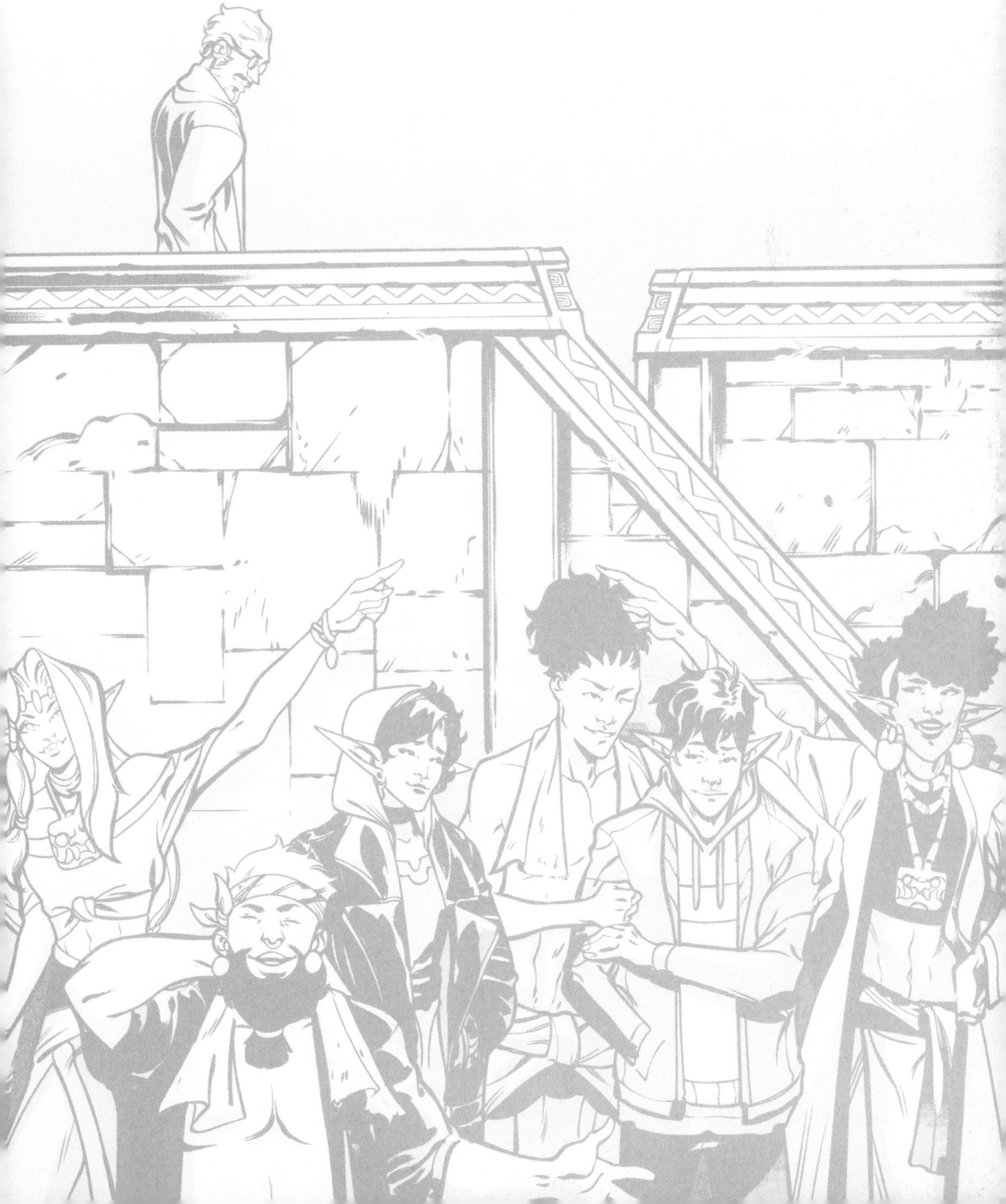

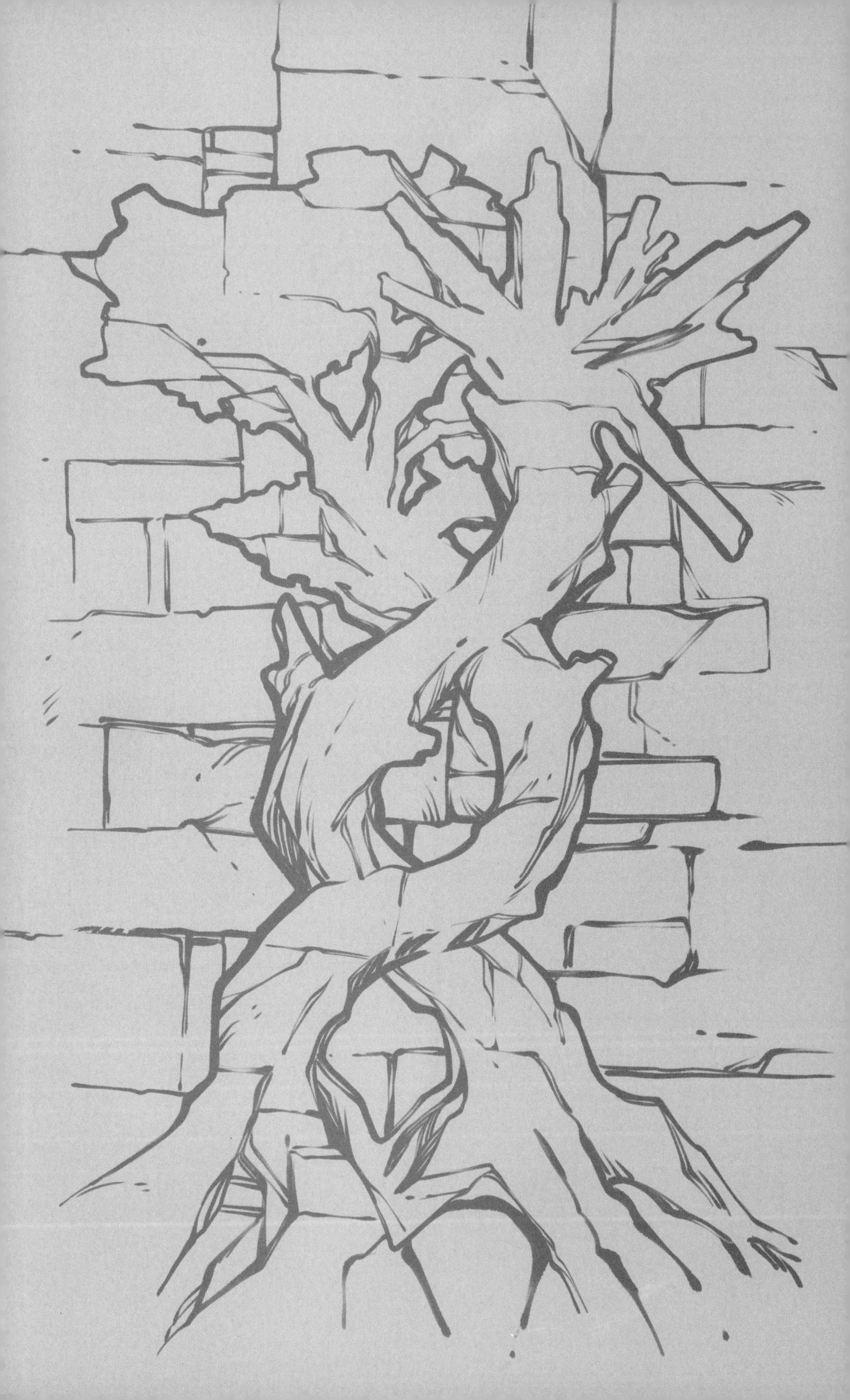

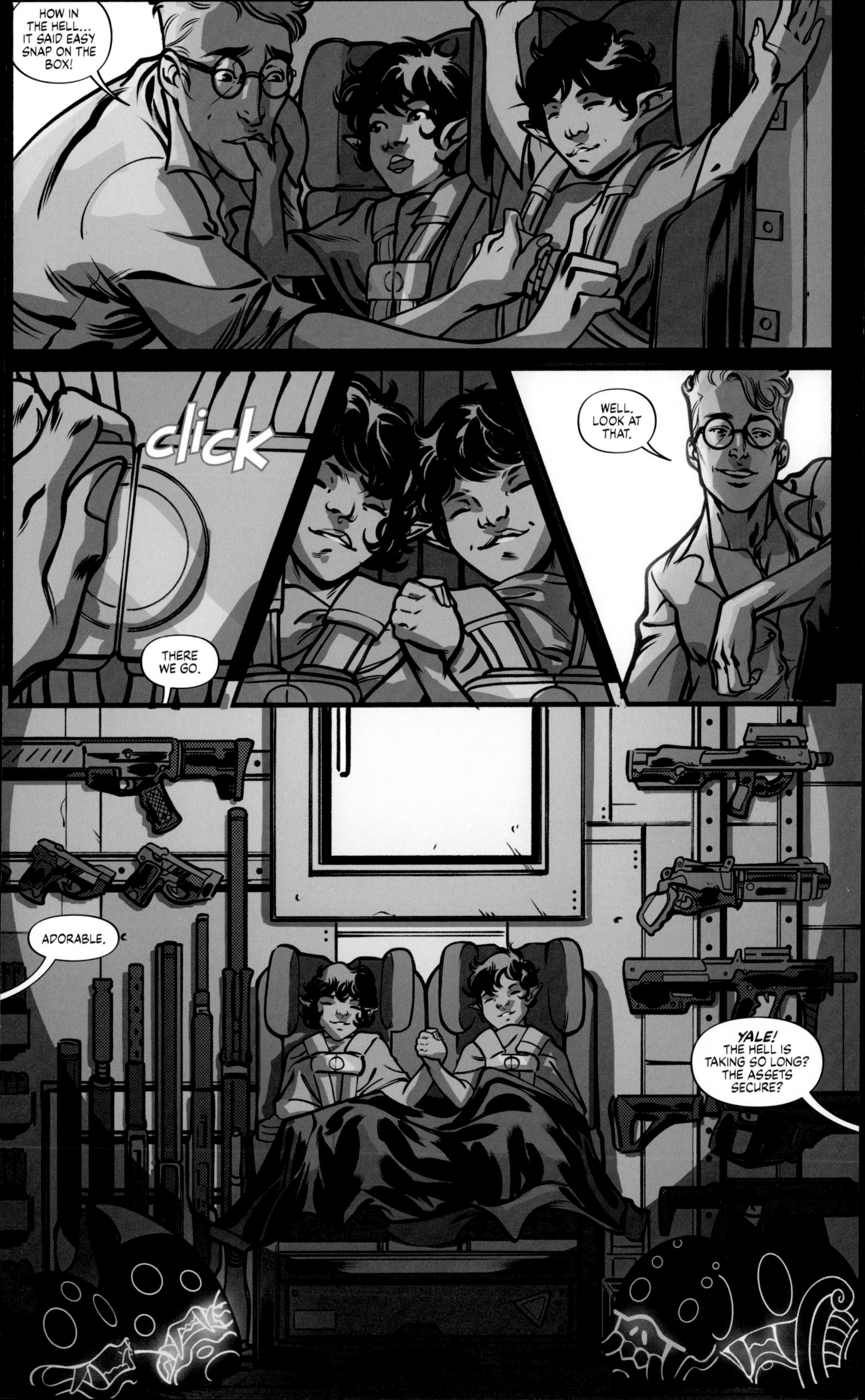
HOW IN THE HELL... IT SAID EASY SNAP ON THE BOX!
CLICK
THERE WE GO.
WELL. LOOK AT THAT.
ADORABLE.
YALE! THE HELL IS TAKING SO LONG? THE ASSETS SECURE?

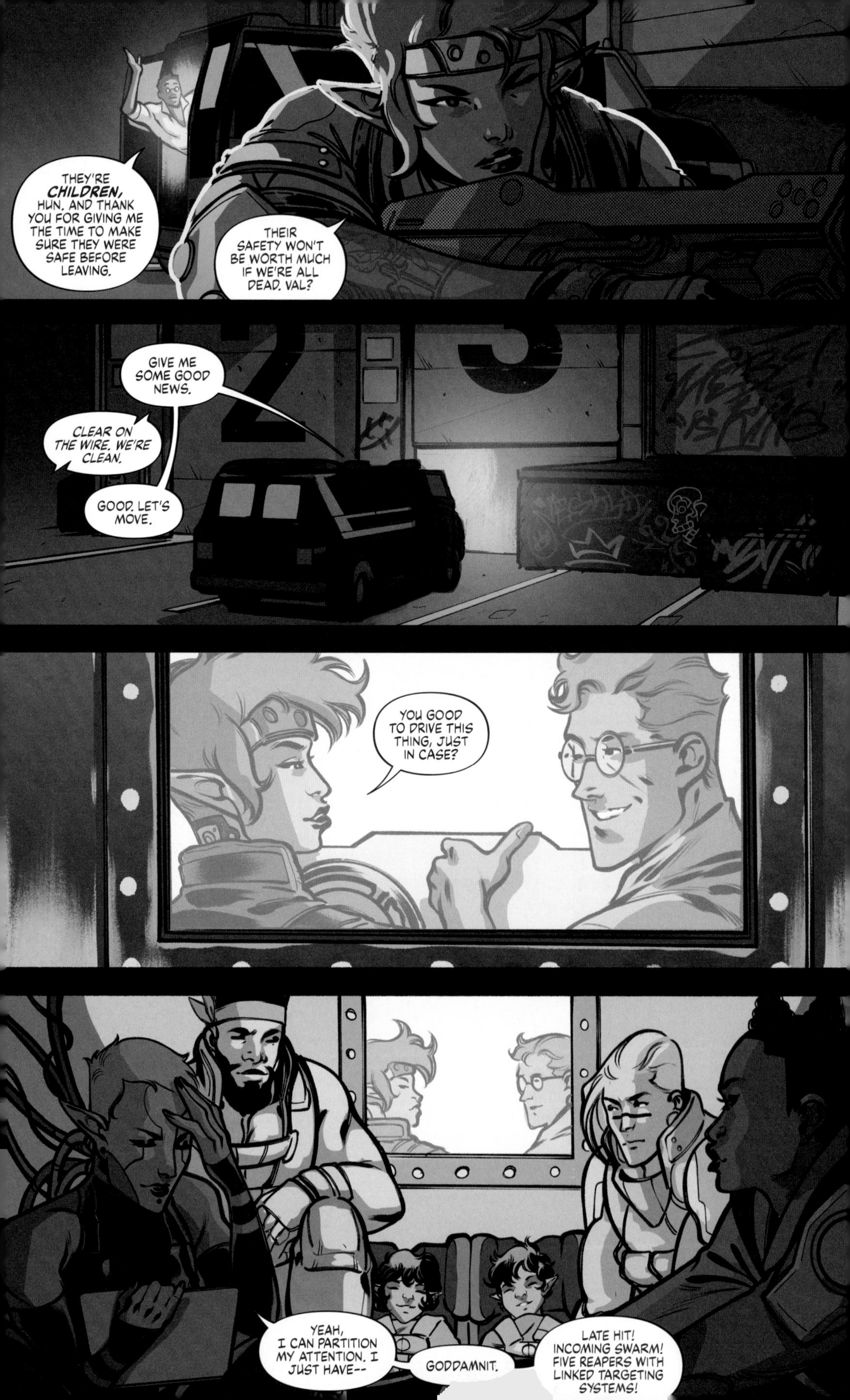
THEY'RE *CHILDREN,* HUN. AND THANK YOU FOR GIVING ME THE TIME TO MAKE SURE THEY WERE SAFE BEFORE LEAVING.
THEIR SAFETY WON'T BE WORTH MUCH IF WE'RE ALL DEAD. VAL?
GIVE ME SOME GOOD NEWS.
CLEAR ON THE WIRE. WE'RE CLEAN.
GOOD. LET'S MOVE.
YOU GOOD TO DRIVE THIS THING, JUST IN CASE?
YEAH, I CAN PARTITION MY ATTENTION. I JUST HAVE--
GODDAMNIT.
LATE HIT! INCOMING SWARM! FIVE REAPERS WITH LINKED TARGETING SYSTEMS!

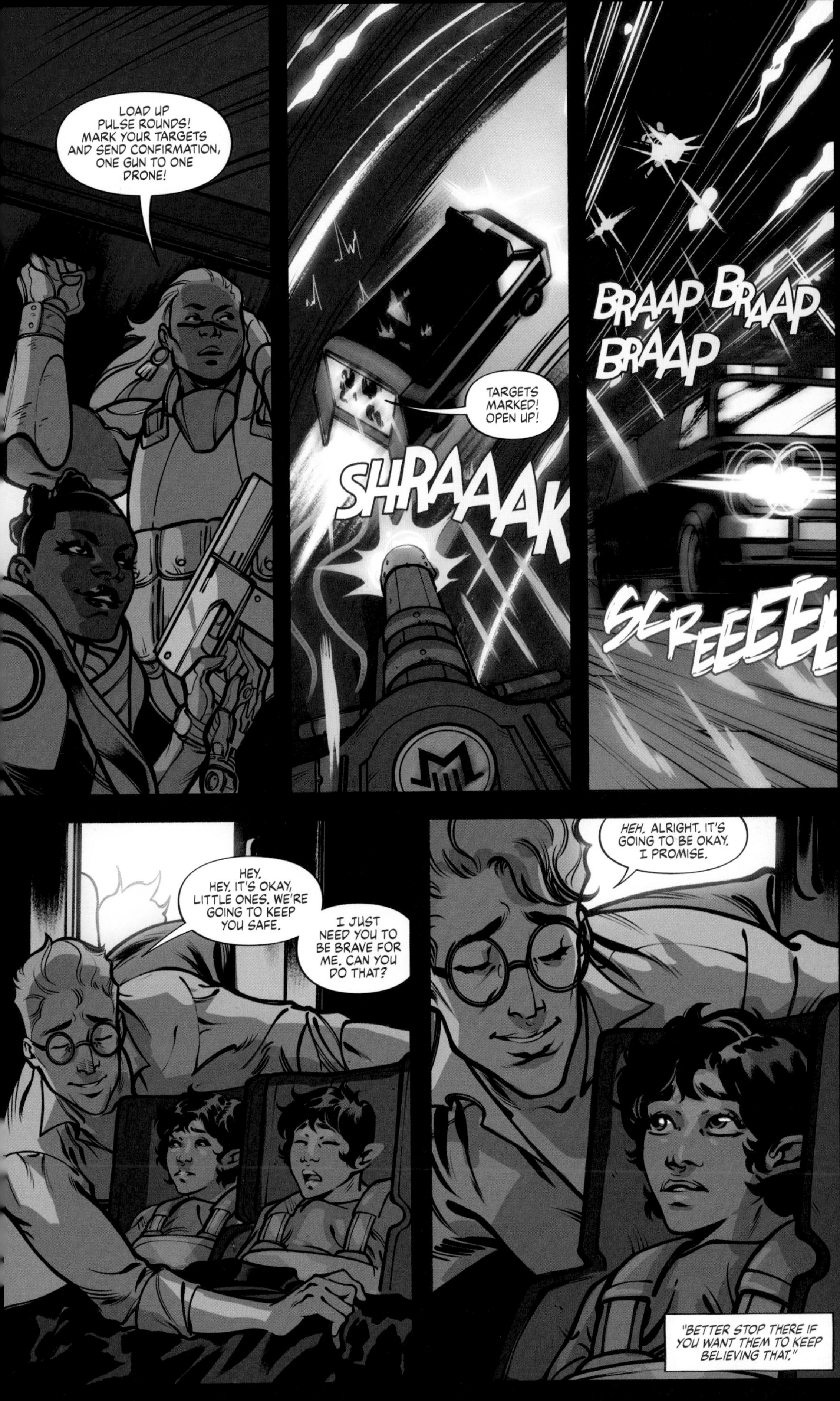
LOAD UP PULSE ROUNDS! MARK YOUR TARGETS AND SEND CONFIRMATION, ONE GUN TO ONE DRONE!
TARGETS MARKED! OPEN UP!
SHRAAAAK
BRAAP BRAAP BRAAP
SCREEEEEE
HEY. HEY. IT'S OKAY, LITTLE ONES. WE'RE GOING TO KEEP YOU SAFE.
I JUST NEED YOU TO BE BRAVE FOR ME. CAN YOU DO THAT?
HEH. ALRIGHT. IT'S GOING TO BE OKAY. I PROMISE.
"BETTER STOP THERE IF YOU WANT THEM TO KEEP BELIEVING THAT."

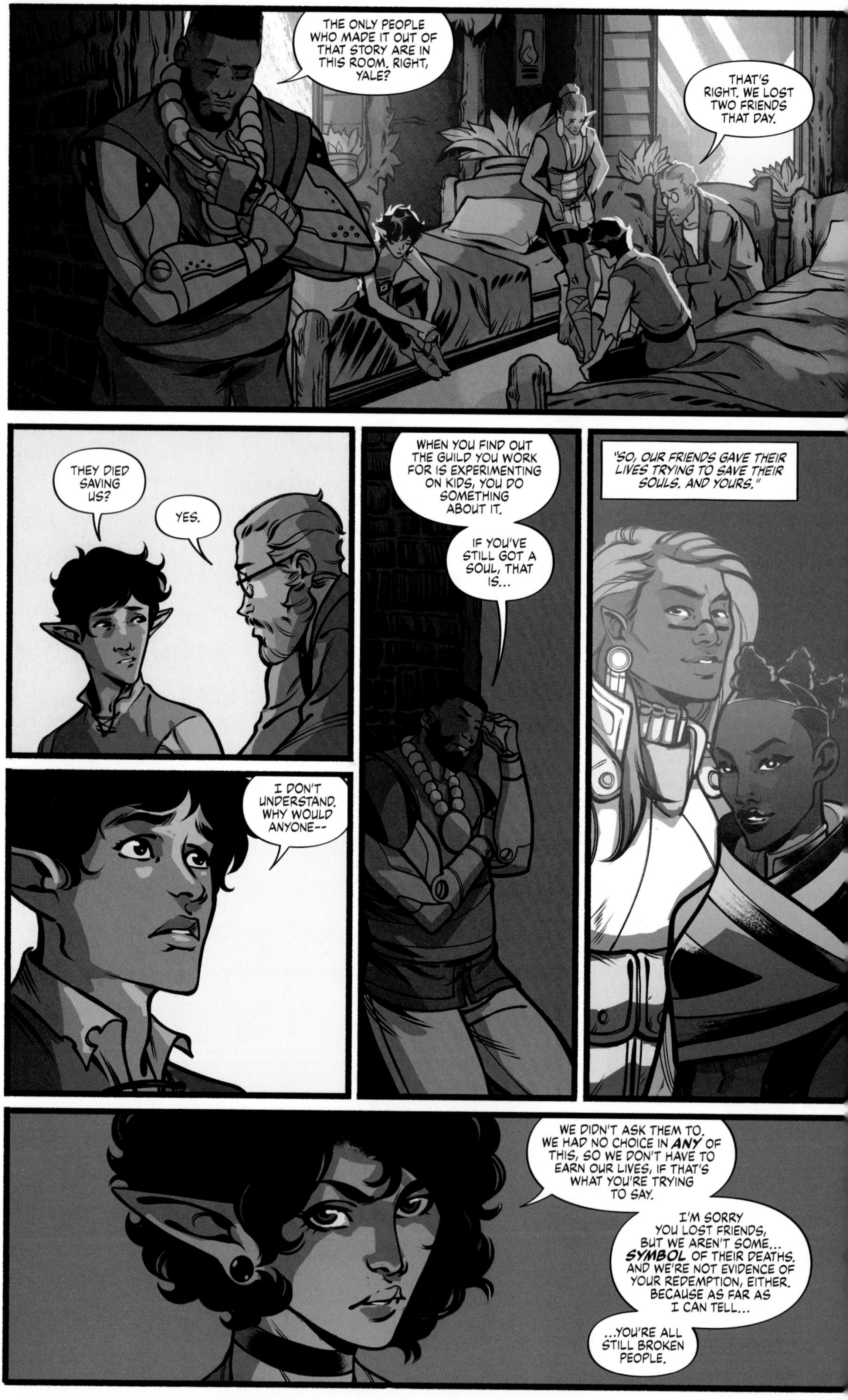
THE ONLY PEOPLE WHO MADE IT OUT OF THAT STORY ARE IN THIS ROOM. RIGHT, YALE?
THAT'S RIGHT. WE LOST TWO FRIENDS THAT DAY.
THEY DIED SAVING US?
YES.
I DON'T UNDERSTAND. WHY WOULD ANYONE--
WHEN YOU FIND OUT THE GUILD YOU WORK FOR IS EXPERIMENTING ON KIDS, YOU DO SOMETHING ABOUT IT.
IF YOU'VE STILL GOT A SOUL, THAT IS...
"SO, OUR FRIENDS GAVE THEIR LIVES TRYING TO SAVE THEIR SOULS. AND YOURS."
WE DIDN'T ASK THEM TO. WE HAD NO CHOICE IN *ANY* OF THIS, SO WE DON'T HAVE TO EARN OUR LIVES, IF THAT'S WHAT YOU'RE TRYING TO SAY.
I'M SORRY YOU LOST FRIENDS, BUT WE AREN'T SOME... **SYMBOL** OF THEIR DEATHS. AND WE'RE NOT EVIDENCE OF YOUR REDEMPTION, EITHER. BECAUSE AS FAR AS I CAN TELL...
...YOU'RE ALL STILL BROKEN PEOPLE.

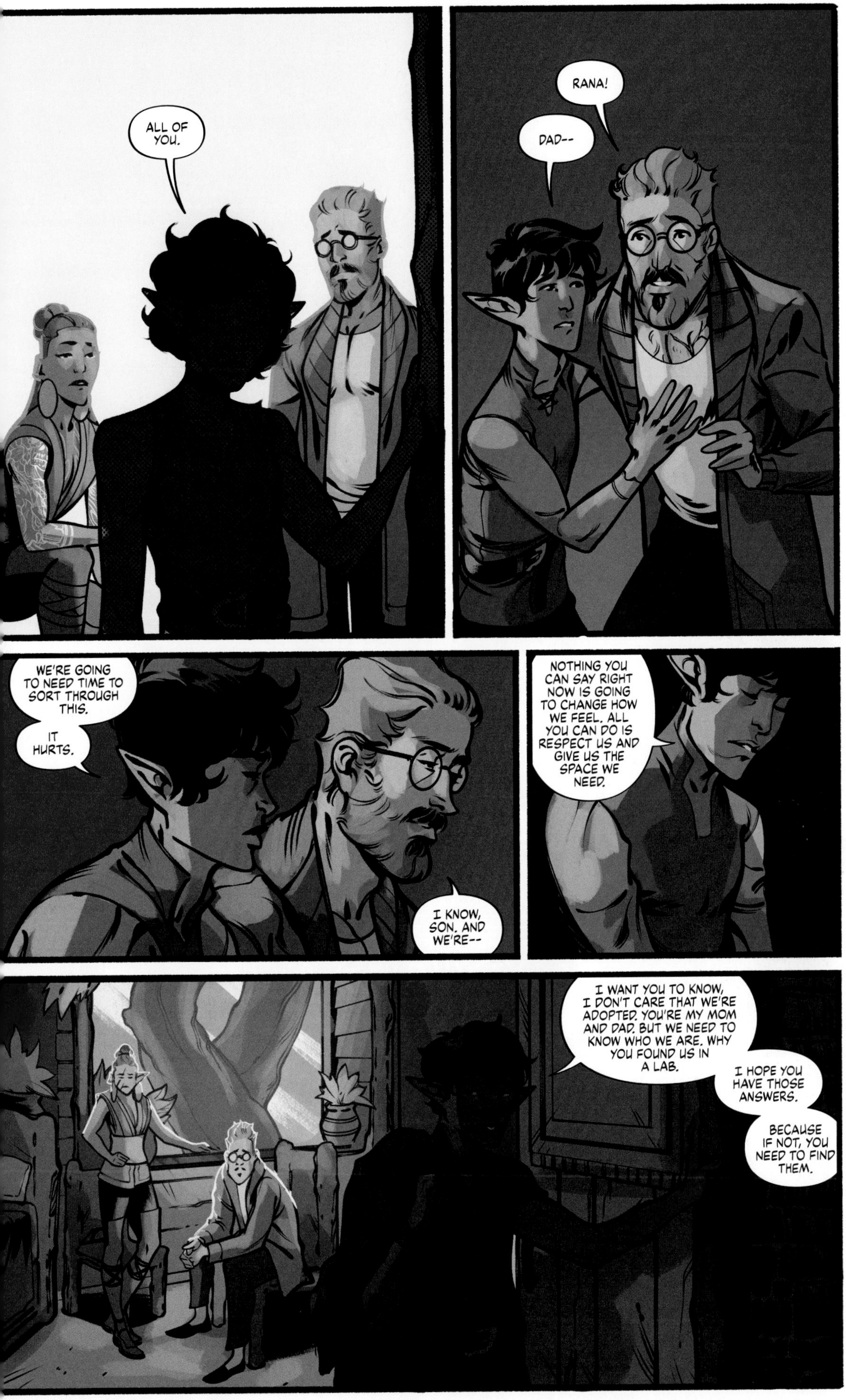
ALL OF YOU.
RANA!
DAD--
WE'RE GOING TO NEED TIME TO SORT THROUGH THIS.
IT HURTS.
I KNOW, SON. AND WE'RE--
NOTHING YOU CAN SAY RIGHT NOW IS GOING TO CHANGE HOW WE FEEL. ALL YOU CAN DO IS RESPECT US AND GIVE US THE SPACE WE NEED.
I WANT YOU TO KNOW, I DON'T CARE THAT WE'RE ADOPTED. YOU'RE MY MOM AND DAD. BUT WE NEED TO KNOW WHO WE ARE. WHY YOU FOUND US IN A LAB.
I HOPE YOU HAVE THOSE ANSWERS.
BECAUSE IF NOT, YOU NEED TO FIND THEM.

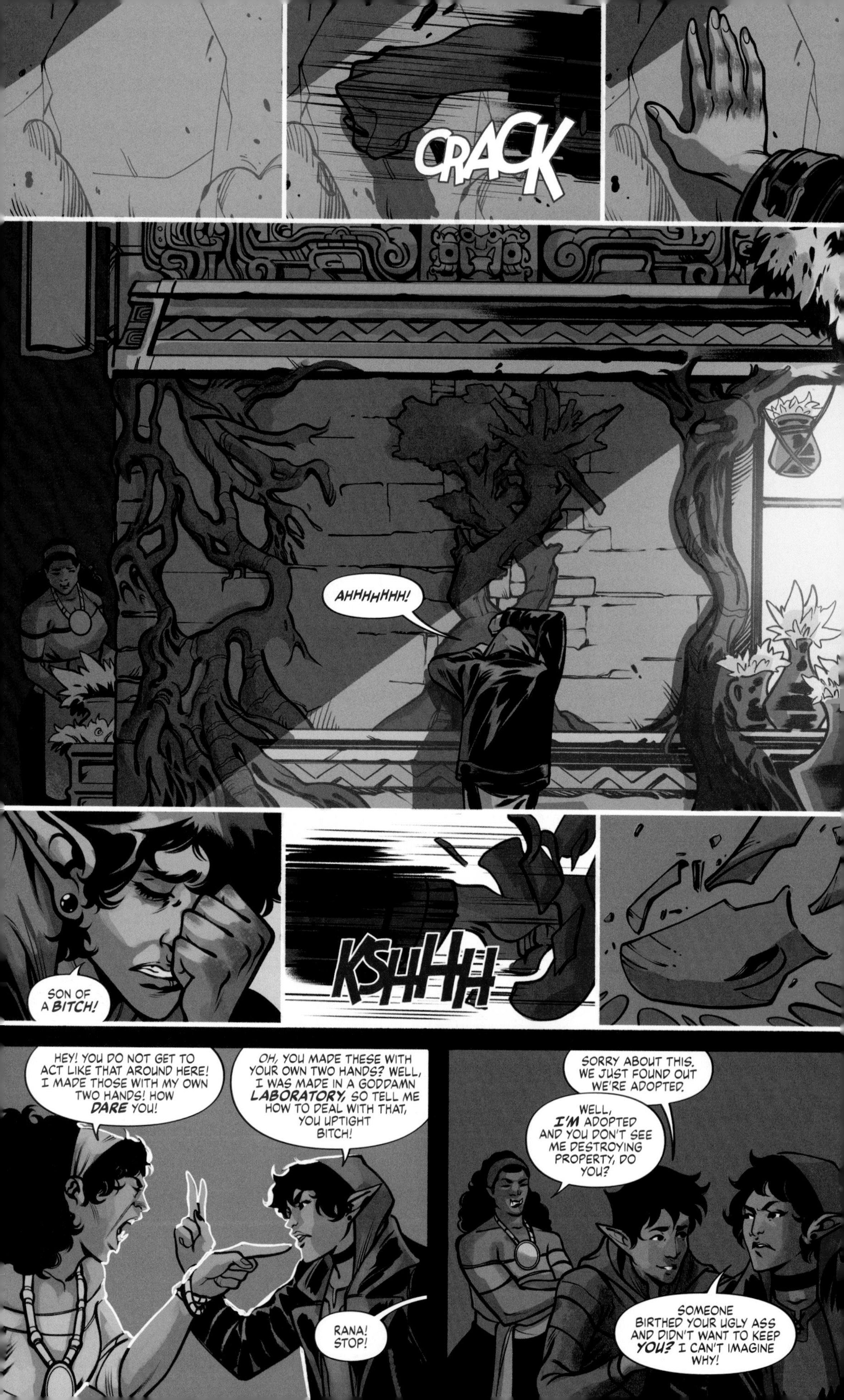
CRACK
AHHHHHHH!
SON OF A BITCH!
KSHHHH
HEY! YOU DO NOT GET TO ACT LIKE THAT AROUND HERE! I MADE THOSE WITH MY OWN TWO HANDS! HOW DARE YOU!
OH, YOU MADE THESE WITH YOUR OWN TWO HANDS? WELL, I WAS MADE IN A GODDAMN LABORATORY, SO TELL ME HOW TO DEAL WITH THAT, YOU UPTIGHT BITCH!
RANA! STOP!
SORRY ABOUT THIS. WE JUST FOUND OUT WE'RE ADOPTED.
WELL, I'M ADOPTED AND YOU DON'T SEE ME DESTROYING PROPERTY, DO YOU?
SOMEONE BIRTHED YOUR UGLY ASS AND DIDN'T WANT TO KEEP YOU? I CAN'T IMAGINE WHY!

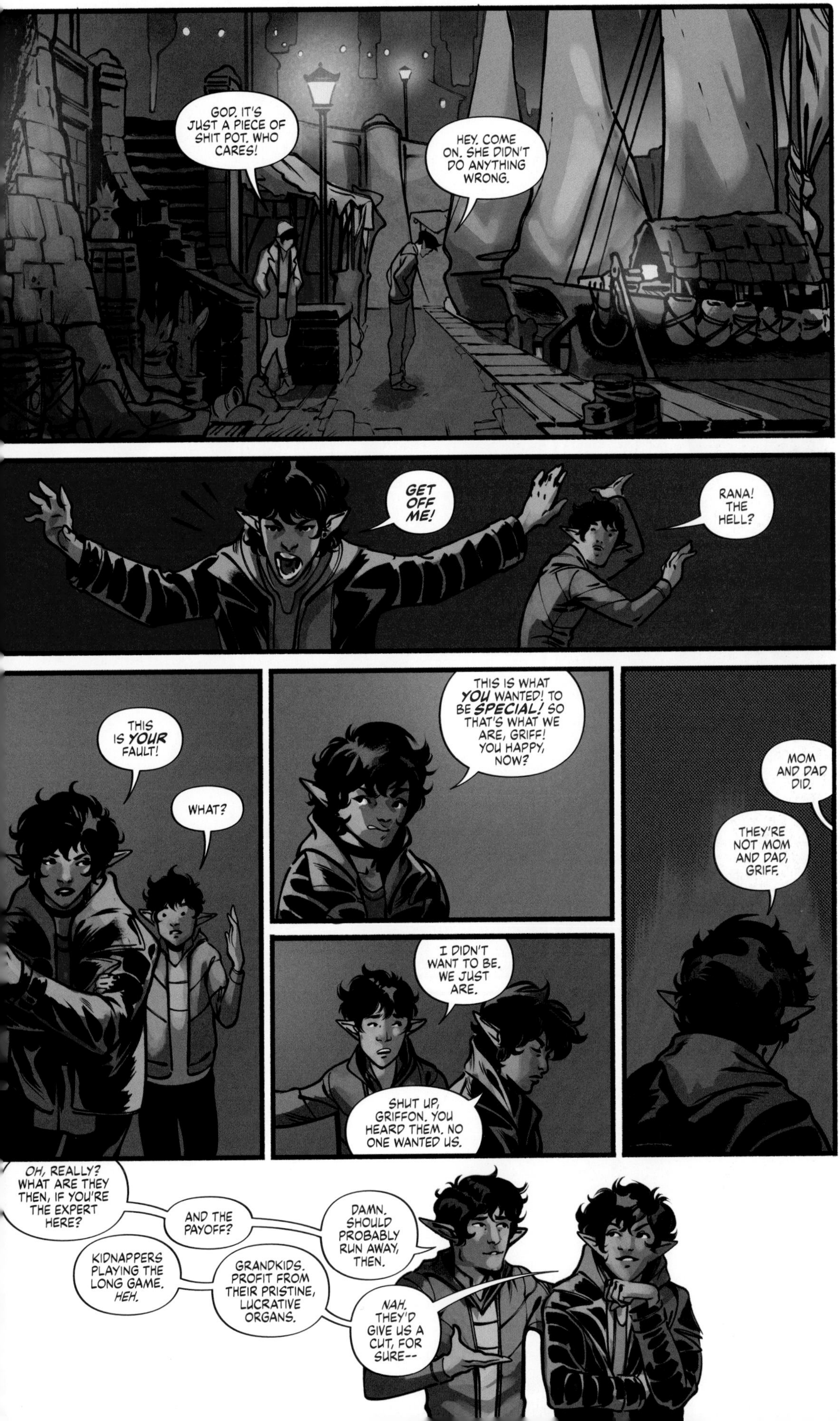

GOD. IT'S JUST A PIECE OF SHIT POT. WHO CARES!
HEY. COME ON. SHE DIDN'T DO ANYTHING WRONG.
GET OFF ME!
RANA! THE HELL?
THIS IS YOUR FAULT!
WHAT?
THIS IS WHAT YOU WANTED! TO BE SPECIAL! SO THAT'S WHAT WE ARE, GRIFF! YOU HAPPY, NOW?
I DIDN'T WANT TO BE. WE JUST ARE.
SHUT UP, GRIFFON. YOU HEARD THEM. NO ONE WANTED US.
MOM AND DAD DID.
THEY'RE NOT MOM AND DAD, GRIFF.
OH, REALLY? WHAT ARE THEY THEN, IF YOU'RE THE EXPERT HERE?
KIDNAPPERS PLAYING THE LONG GAME. HEH.
AND THE PAYOFF?
GRANDKIDS. PROFIT FROM THEIR PRISTINE, LUCRATIVE ORGANS.
DAMN. SHOULD PROBABLY RUN AWAY, THEN.
NAH. THEY'D GIVE US A CUT, FOR SURE--

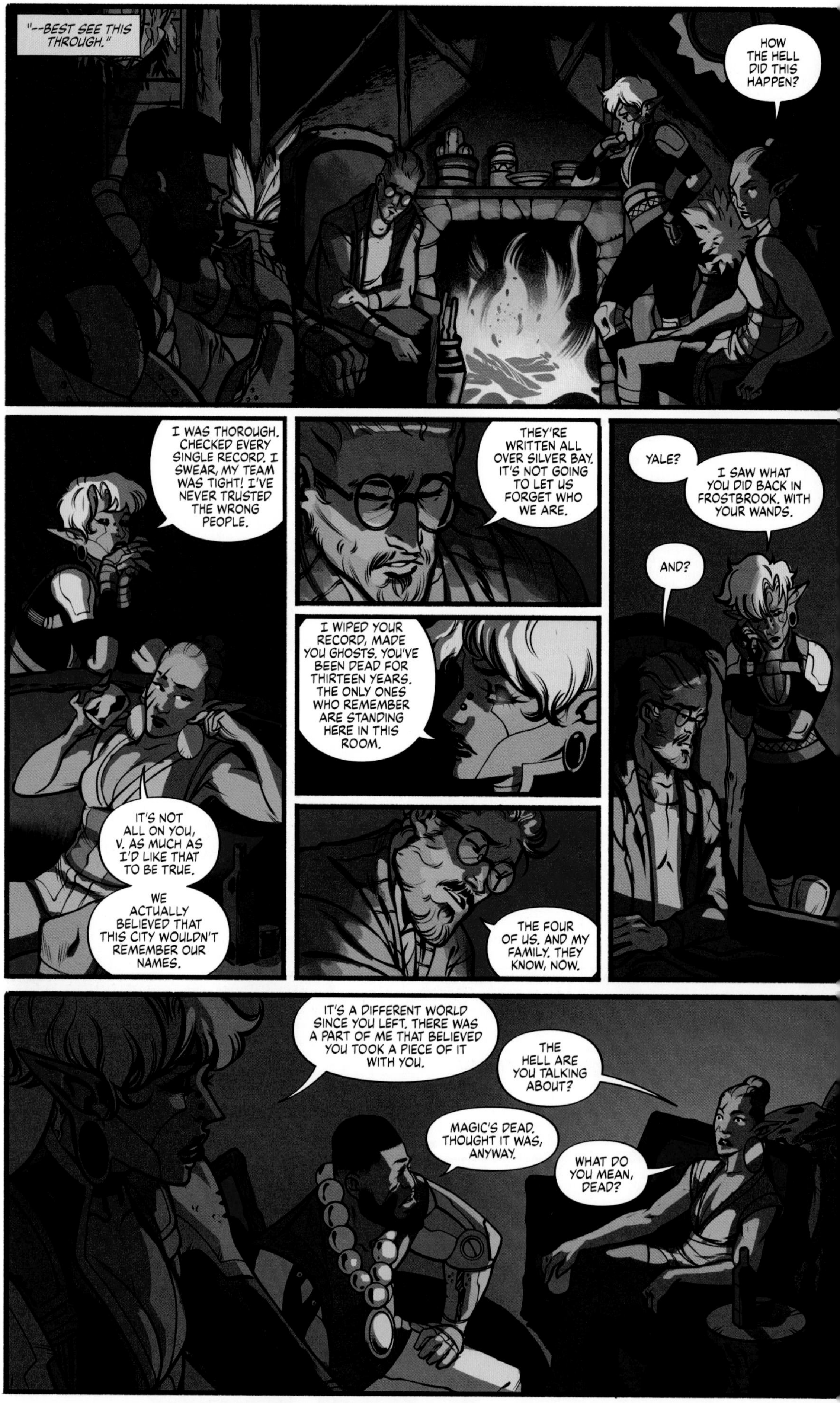
"--BEST SEE THIS THROUGH."
HOW THE HELL DID THIS HAPPEN?
I WAS THOROUGH. CHECKED EVERY SINGLE RECORD. I SWEAR, MY TEAM WAS TIGHT! I'VE NEVER TRUSTED THE WRONG PEOPLE.
IT'S NOT ALL ON YOU, V. AS MUCH AS I'D LIKE THAT TO BE TRUE.
WE ACTUALLY BELIEVED THAT THIS CITY WOULDN'T REMEMBER OUR NAMES.
THEY'RE WRITTEN ALL OVER SILVER BAY. IT'S NOT GOING TO LET US FORGET WHO WE ARE.
I WIPED YOUR RECORD, MADE YOU GHOSTS. YOU'VE BEEN DEAD FOR THIRTEEN YEARS. THE ONLY ONES WHO REMEMBER ARE STANDING HERE IN THIS ROOM.
THE FOUR OF US. AND MY FAMILY. THEY KNOW, NOW.
YALE?
I SAW WHAT YOU DID BACK IN FROSTBROOK. WITH YOUR WANDS.
AND?
IT'S A DIFFERENT WORLD SINCE YOU LEFT. THERE WAS A PART OF ME THAT BELIEVED YOU TOOK A PIECE OF IT WITH YOU.
THE HELL ARE YOU TALKING ABOUT?
MAGIC'S DEAD. THOUGHT IT WAS, ANYWAY.
WHAT DO YOU MEAN, DEAD?

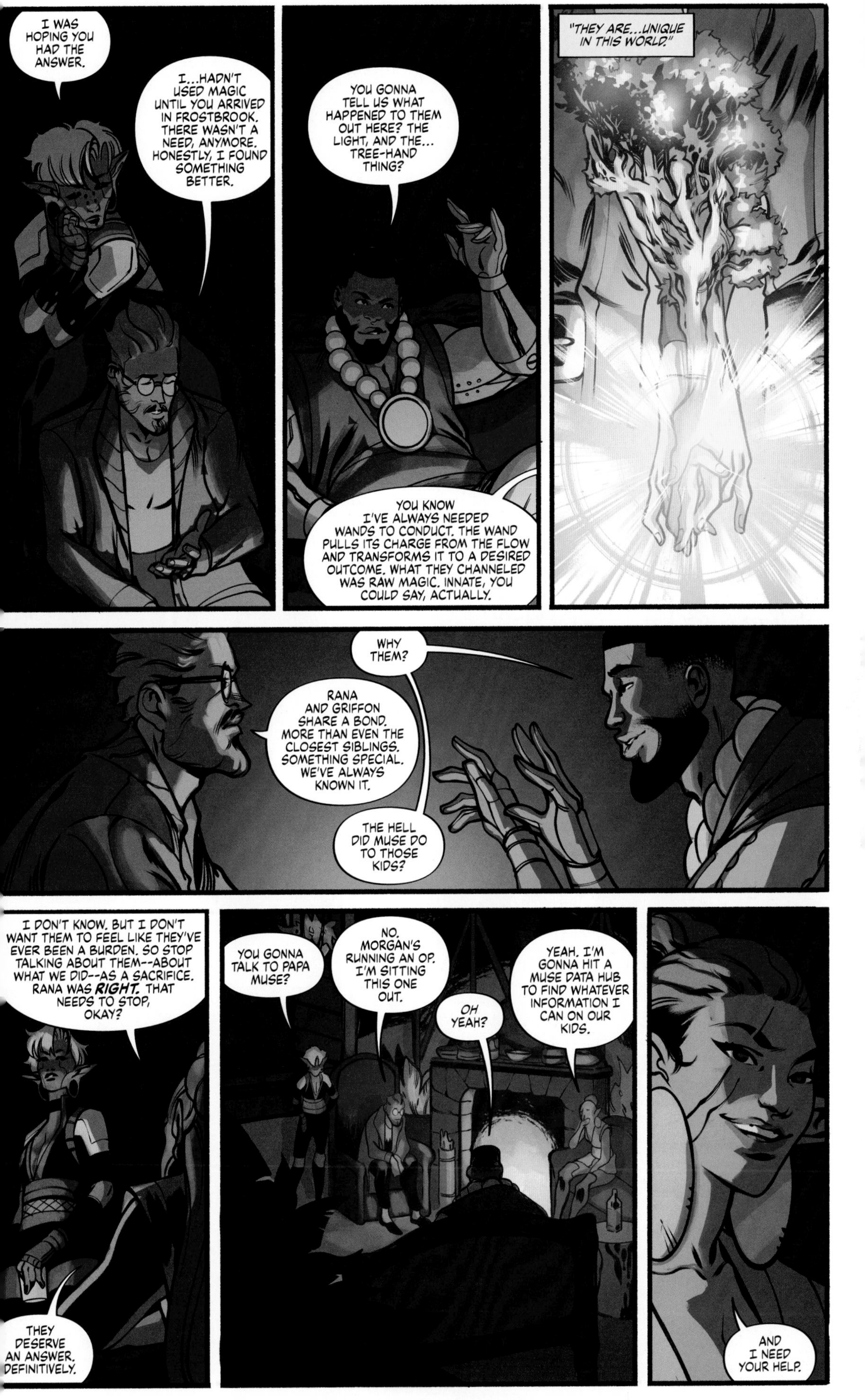

I WAS HOPING YOU HAD THE ANSWER.
I...HADN'T USED MAGIC UNTIL YOU ARRIVED IN FROSTBROOK. THERE WASN'T A NEED, ANYMORE. HONESTLY, I FOUND SOMETHING BETTER.
YOU GONNA TELL US WHAT HAPPENED TO THEM OUT HERE? THE LIGHT, AND THE... TREE-HAND THING?
YOU KNOW I'VE ALWAYS NEEDED WANDS TO CONDUCT. THE WAND PULLS ITS CHARGE FROM THE FLOW AND TRANSFORMS IT TO A DESIRED OUTCOME. WHAT THEY CHANNELED WAS RAW MAGIC. INNATE, YOU COULD SAY, ACTUALLY.
"THEY ARE...UNIQUE IN THIS WORLD."
WHY THEM?
RANA AND GRIFFON SHARE A BOND. MORE THAN EVEN THE CLOSEST SIBLINGS. SOMETHING SPECIAL. WE'VE ALWAYS KNOWN IT.
THE HELL DID MUSE DO TO THOSE KIDS?
I DON'T KNOW. BUT I DON'T WANT THEM TO FEEL LIKE THEY'VE EVER BEEN A BURDEN. SO STOP TALKING ABOUT THEM--ABOUT WHAT WE DID--AS A SACRIFICE. RANA WAS **RIGHT.** THAT NEEDS TO STOP, OKAY?
THEY DESERVE AN ANSWER. DEFINITIVELY.
YOU GONNA TALK TO PAPA MUSE?
NO. MORGAN'S RUNNING AN OP. I'M SITTING THIS ONE OUT.
OH YEAH?
YEAH. I'M GONNA HIT A MUSE DATA HUB TO FIND WHATEVER INFORMATION I CAN ON OUR KIDS.
AND I NEED YOUR HELP.

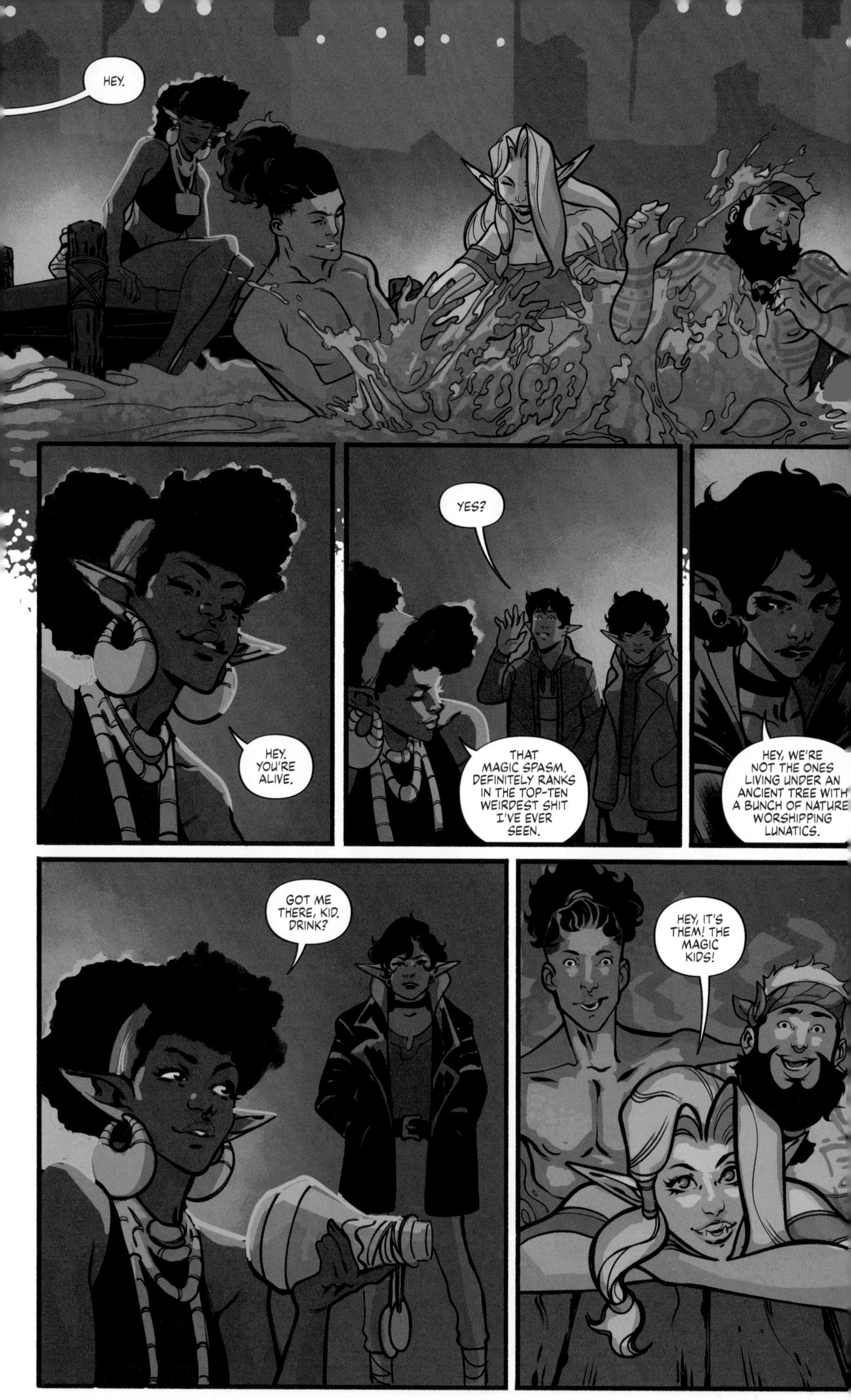
HEY.
HEY. YOU'RE ALIVE.
YES?
THAT MAGIC SPASM. DEFINITELY RANKS IN THE TOP-TEN WEIRDEST SHIT I'VE EVER SEEN.
HEY, WE'RE NOT THE ONES LIVING UNDER AN ANCIENT TREE WITH A BUNCH OF NATURE WORSHIPPING LUNATICS.
GOT ME THERE, KID. DRINK?
HEY, IT'S THEM! THE MAGIC KIDS!

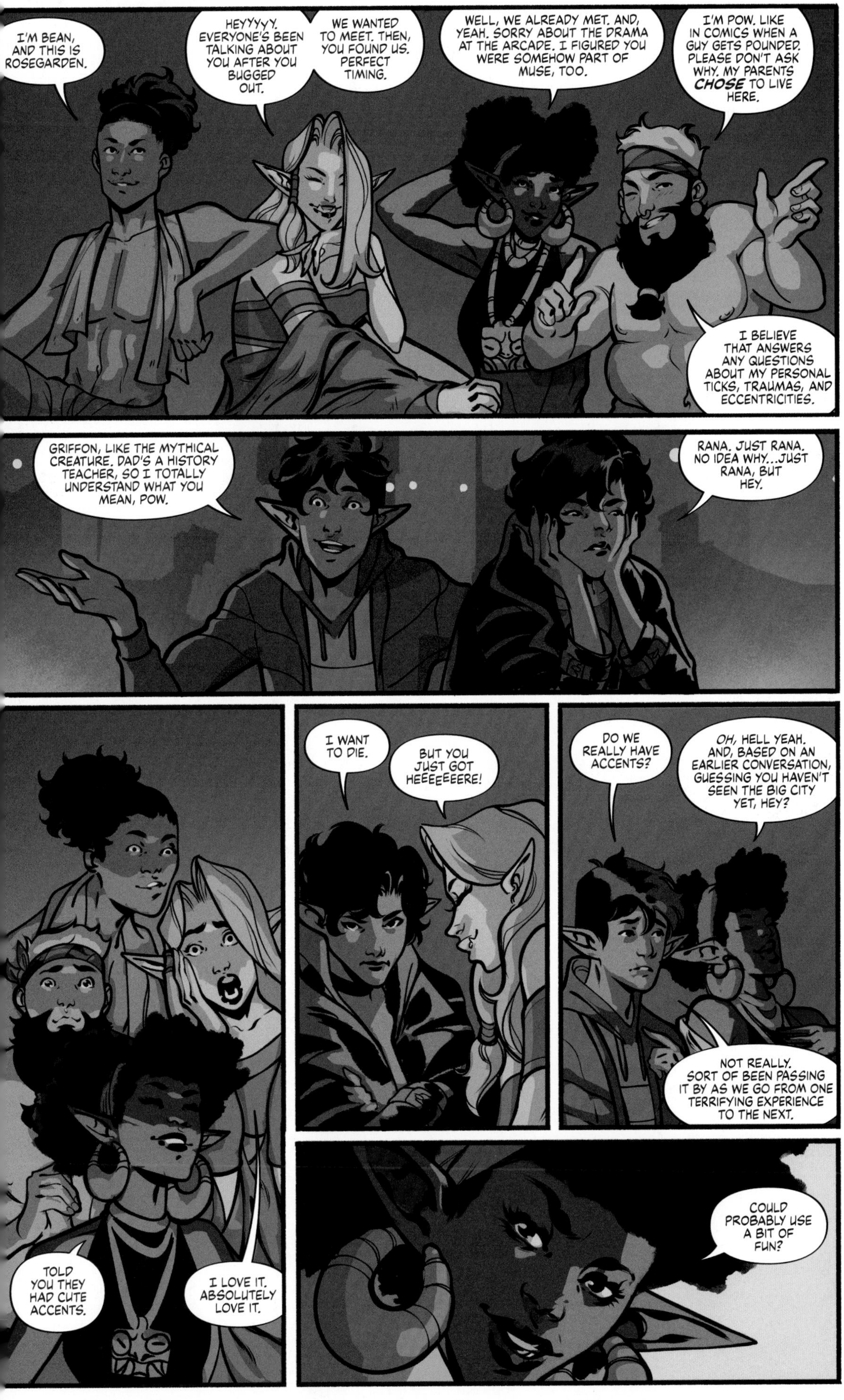
I'M BEAN, AND THIS IS ROSEGARDEN.
HEYYYYY. EVERYONE'S BEEN TALKING ABOUT YOU AFTER YOU BUGGED OUT.
WE WANTED TO MEET. THEN, YOU FOUND US. PERFECT TIMING.
WELL, WE ALREADY MET. AND, YEAH. SORRY ABOUT THE DRAMA AT THE ARCADE. I FIGURED YOU WERE SOMEHOW PART OF MUSE, TOO.
I'M POW. LIKE IN COMICS WHEN A GUY GETS POUNDED. PLEASE DON'T ASK WHY. MY PARENTS *CHOSE* TO LIVE HERE.
I BELIEVE THAT ANSWERS ANY QUESTIONS ABOUT MY PERSONAL TICKS, TRAUMAS, AND ECCENTRICITIES.
GRIFFON, LIKE THE MYTHICAL CREATURE. DAD'S A HISTORY TEACHER, SO I TOTALLY UNDERSTAND WHAT YOU MEAN, POW.
RANA. JUST RANA. NO IDEA WHY...JUST RANA, BUT HEY.
TOLD YOU THEY HAD CUTE ACCENTS.
I LOVE IT. ABSOLUTELY LOVE IT.
I WANT TO DIE.
BUT YOU JUST GOT HEEEEEEERE!
DO WE REALLY HAVE ACCENTS?
OH, HELL YEAH. AND, BASED ON AN EARLIER CONVERSATION, GUESSING YOU HAVEN'T SEEN THE BIG CITY YET, HEY?
NOT REALLY. SORT OF BEEN PASSING IT BY AS WE GO FROM ONE TERRIFYING EXPERIENCE TO THE NEXT.
COULD PROBABLY USE A BIT OF FUN?

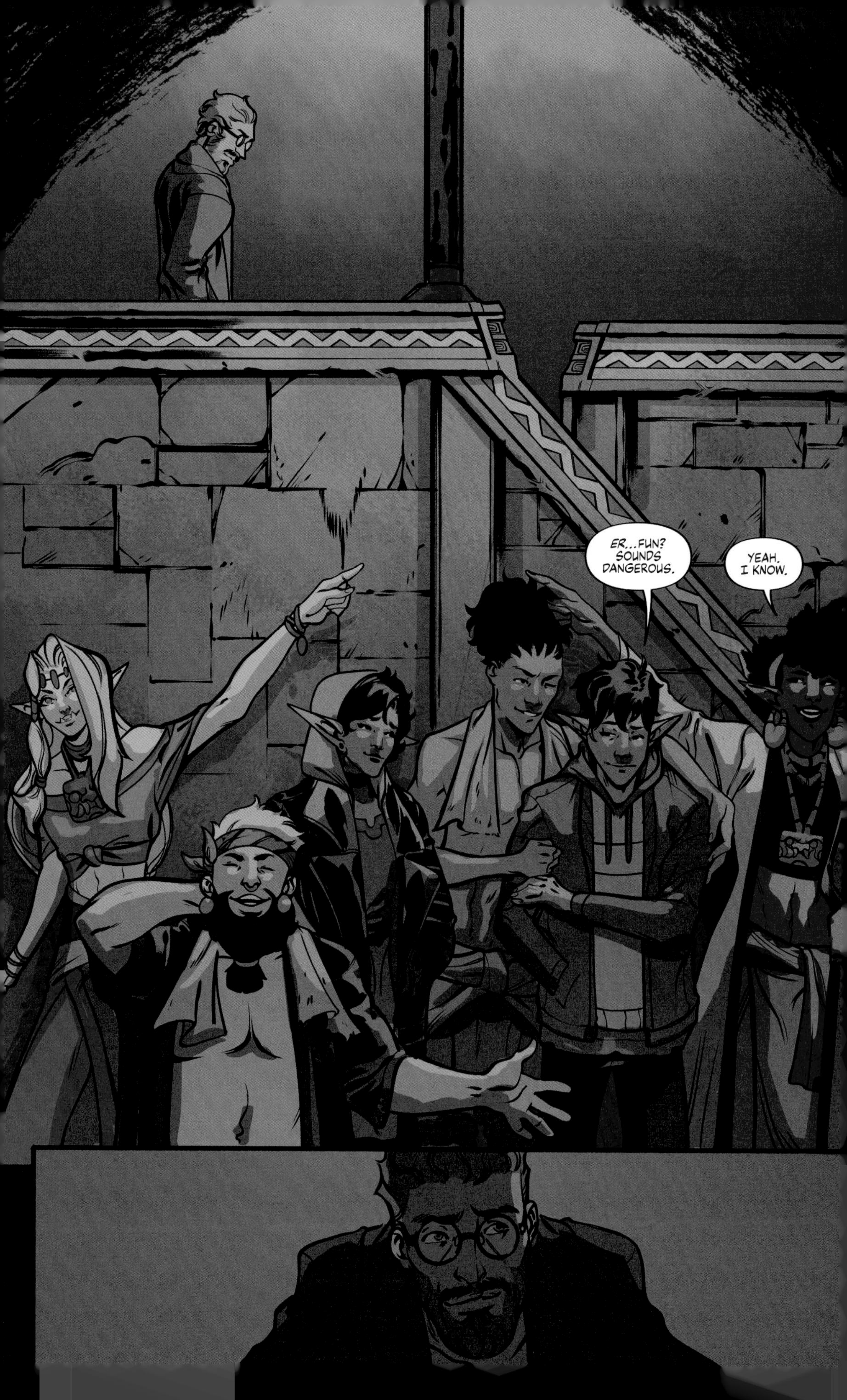
ER...FUN? SOUNDS DANGEROUS.
YEAH. I KNOW.

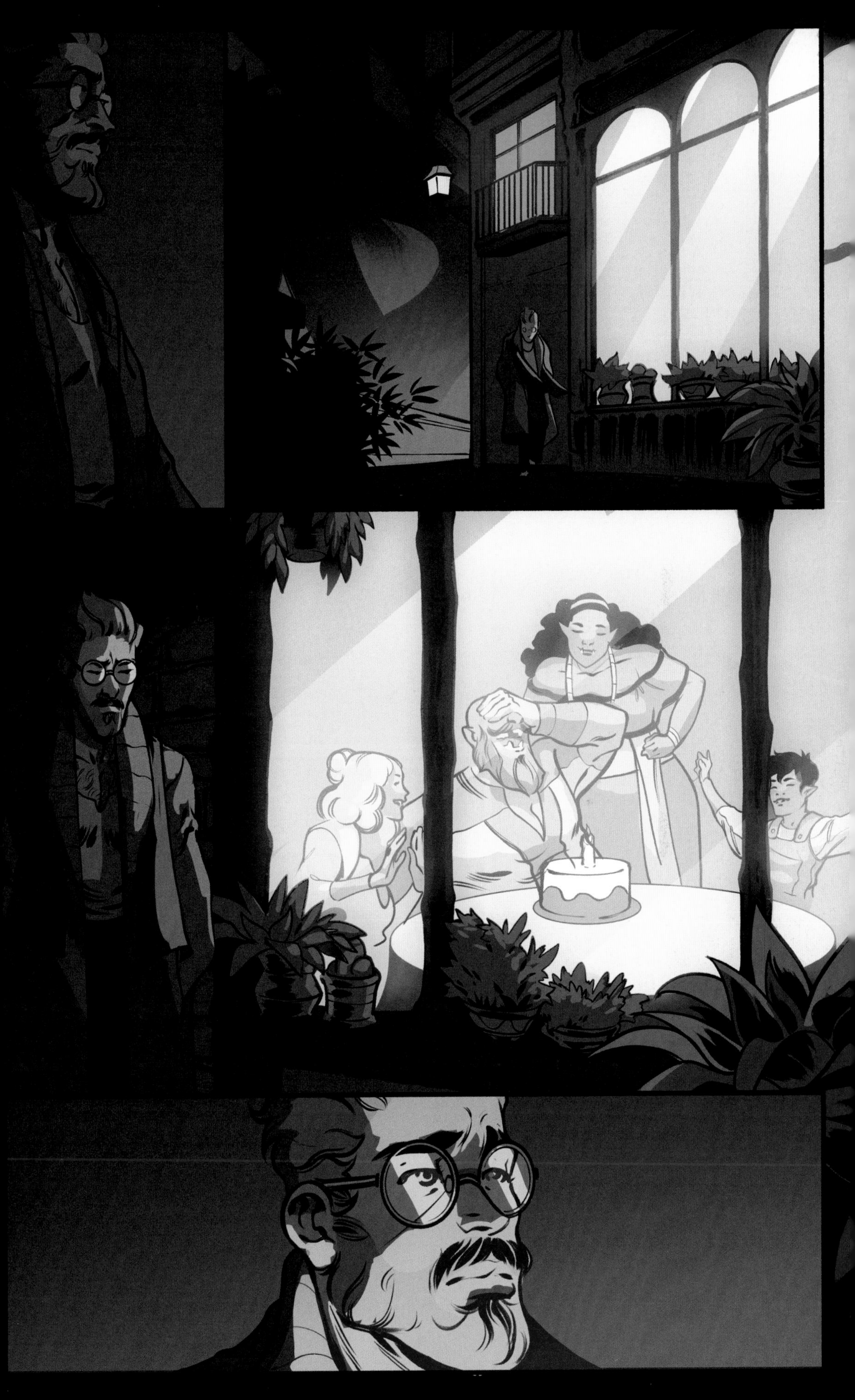

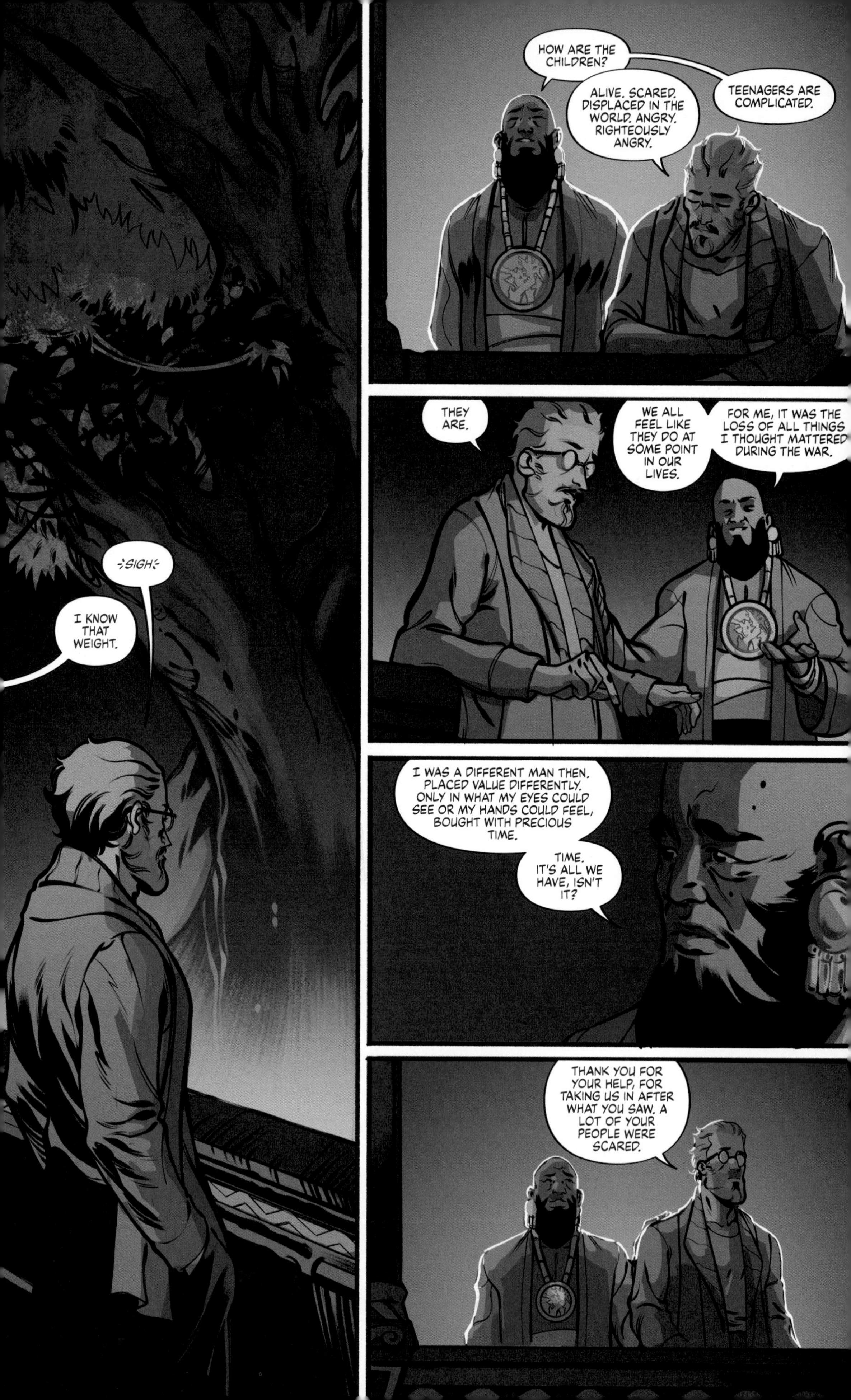

I KNOW THAT WEIGHT.
-SIGH-
HOW ARE THE CHILDREN?
ALIVE. SCARED. DISPLACED IN THE WORLD. ANGRY. RIGHTEOUSLY ANGRY.
TEENAGERS ARE COMPLICATED.
THEY ARE.
WE ALL FEEL LIKE THEY DO AT SOME POINT IN OUR LIVES.
FOR ME, IT WAS THE LOSS OF ALL THINGS I THOUGHT MATTERED DURING THE WAR.
I WAS A DIFFERENT MAN THEN. PLACED VALUE DIFFERENTLY. ONLY IN WHAT MY EYES COULD SEE OR MY HANDS COULD FEEL, BOUGHT WITH PRECIOUS TIME.
TIME. IT'S ALL WE HAVE, ISN'T IT?
THANK YOU FOR YOUR HELP, FOR TAKING US IN AFTER WHAT YOU SAW. A LOT OF YOUR PEOPLE WERE SCARED.

IN TIME, MORE FOLLOWED. THEY, TOO FOUND THEIR WAY HERE FOR ONE REASON OR ANOTHER. TO ESCAPE.

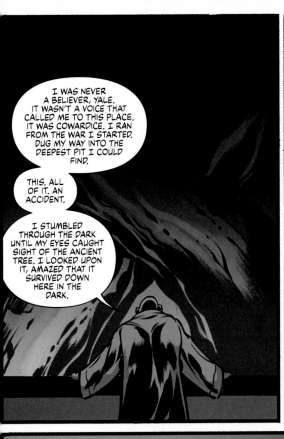

I WAS NEVER A BELIEVER, YALE. IT WASN'T A VOICE THAT CALLED ME TO THIS PLACE. IT WAS COWARDICE. I RAN FROM THE WAR I STARTED. DUG MY WAY INTO THE DEEPEST PIT I COULD FIND.

THIS. ALL OF IT. AN ACCIDENT.

I STUMBLED THROUGH THE DARK UNTIL MY EYES CAUGHT SIGHT OF THE ANCIENT TREE. I LOOKED UPON IT, AMAZED THAT IT SURVIVED DOWN HERE IN THE DARK.

THE SOWERS ARE A STORY, ONE WE KEEP TELLING OURSELVES TO MAKE THE WORLD A MORE MAGICAL PLACE.

OUR MAGIC IS A STORY.

YOUR STORY IS MAGIC.

I'M FIGHTING A WAR OF MY OWN, SIGIL. I'M CLAWING IN THE DARK. I DON'T KNOW HOW TO FIND MY WAY BACK SO FAR FROM THE PATH.

MAYBE NONE OF THIS IS CHANCE. MAYBE THERE WAS A VOICE ALL ALONG. SOMETHING CALLING US TOGETHER, DRAWING THOSE CHILDREN HOME.

YOU'RE SAFE HERE WITH US FOR THE DURATION OF YOUR SEARCH. WE WILL PROTECT YOU AND ANY YOU CALL FAMILY.

THANK YOU.

THERE'S ONE TRUTH WE CAN ALL HOLD TO IN TIMES LIKE THIS. THAT ALL PATHS WILL ONE DAY LEAD HOME.

GO BACK TO THE BEGINNING, YALE, TO WHERE YOU LOST THE WAY.

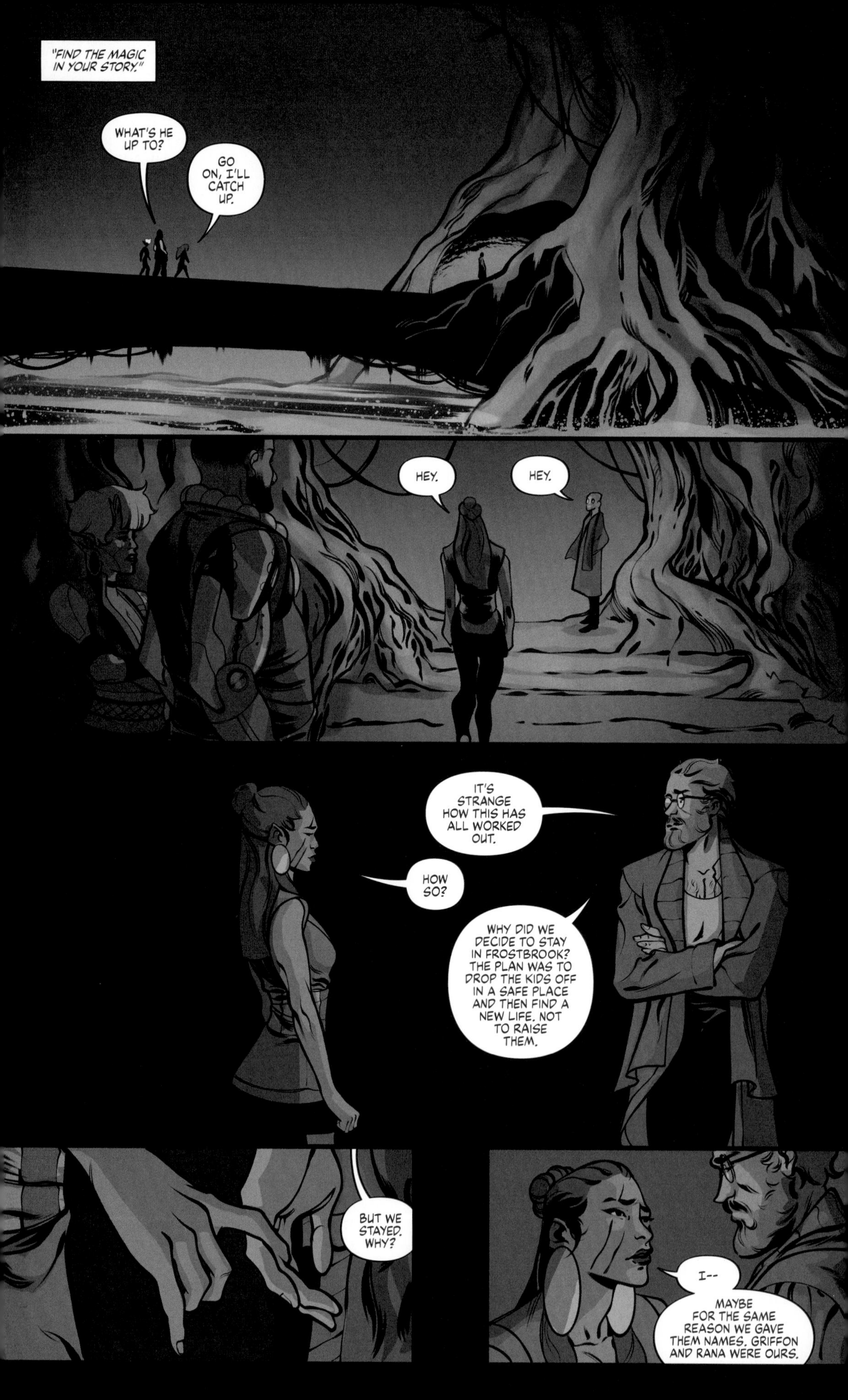
"FIND THE MAGIC IN YOUR STORY."
WHAT'S HE UP TO?
GO ON, I'LL CATCH UP.
HEY.
HEY.
IT'S STRANGE HOW THIS HAS ALL WORKED OUT.
HOW SO?
WHY DID WE DECIDE TO STAY IN FROSTBROOK? THE PLAN WAS TO DROP THE KIDS OFF IN A SAFE PLACE AND THEN FIND A NEW LIFE. NOT TO RAISE THEM.
BUT WE STAYED. WHY?
I--
MAYBE FOR THE SAME REASON WE GAVE THEM NAMES. GRIFFON AND RANA WERE OURS.

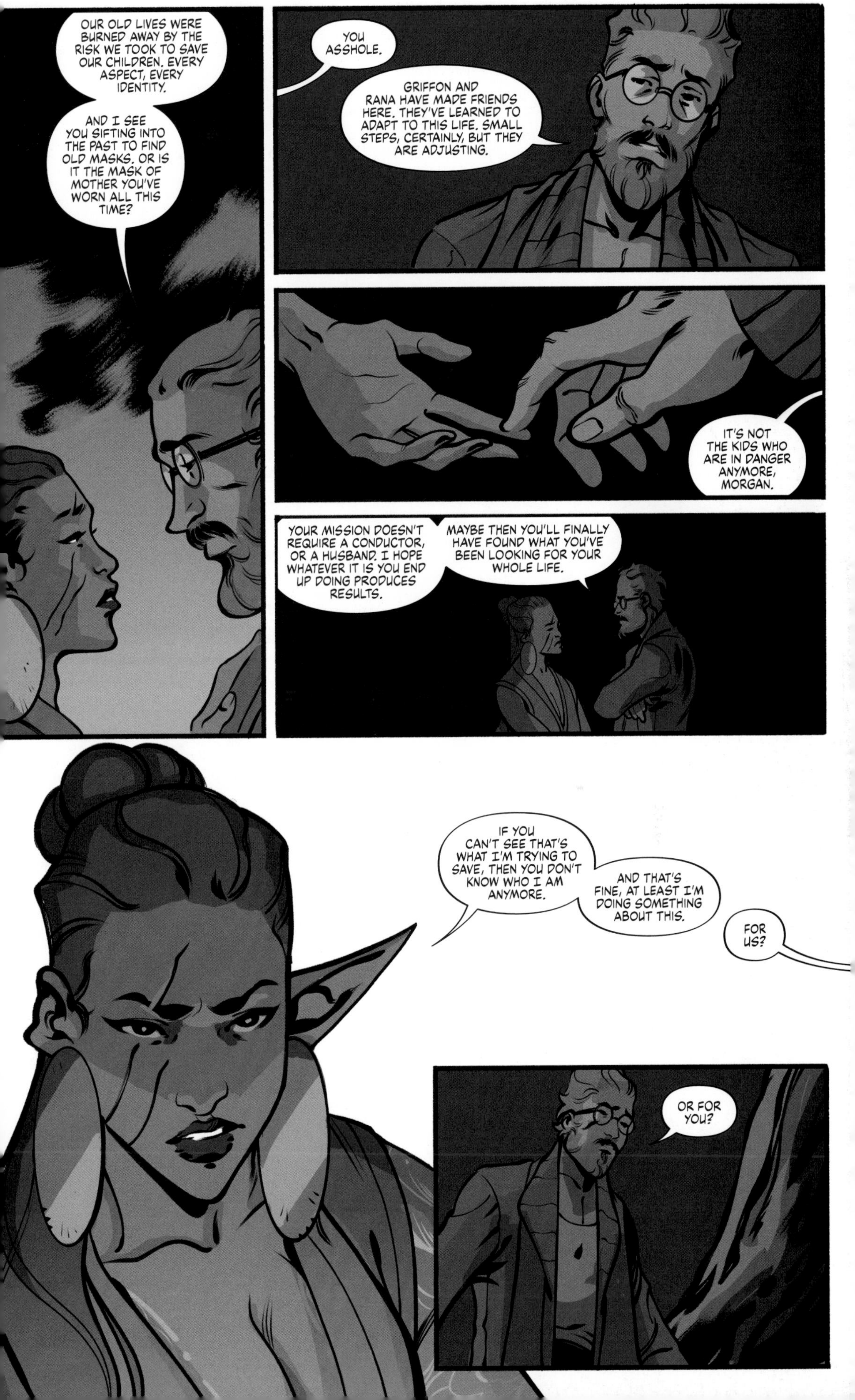
OUR OLD LIVES WERE BURNED AWAY BY THE RISK WE TOOK TO SAVE OUR CHILDREN. EVERY ASPECT, EVERY IDENTITY.
AND I SEE YOU SIFTING INTO THE PAST TO FIND OLD MASKS. OR IS IT THE MASK OF MOTHER YOU'VE WORN ALL THIS TIME?
YOU ASSHOLE.
GRIFFON AND RANA HAVE MADE FRIENDS HERE. THEY'VE LEARNED TO ADAPT TO THIS LIFE. SMALL STEPS, CERTAINLY, BUT THEY ARE ADJUSTING.
IT'S NOT THE KIDS WHO ARE IN DANGER ANYMORE, MORGAN.
YOUR MISSION DOESN'T REQUIRE A CONDUCTOR, OR A HUSBAND. I HOPE WHATEVER IT IS YOU END UP DOING PRODUCES RESULTS.
MAYBE THEN YOU'LL FINALLY HAVE FOUND WHAT YOU'VE BEEN LOOKING FOR YOUR WHOLE LIFE.
IF YOU CAN'T SEE THAT'S WHAT I'M TRYING TO SAVE, THEN YOU DON'T KNOW WHO I AM ANYMORE.
AND THAT'S FINE, AT LEAST I'M DOING SOMETHING ABOUT THIS.
FOR US?
OR FOR YOU?

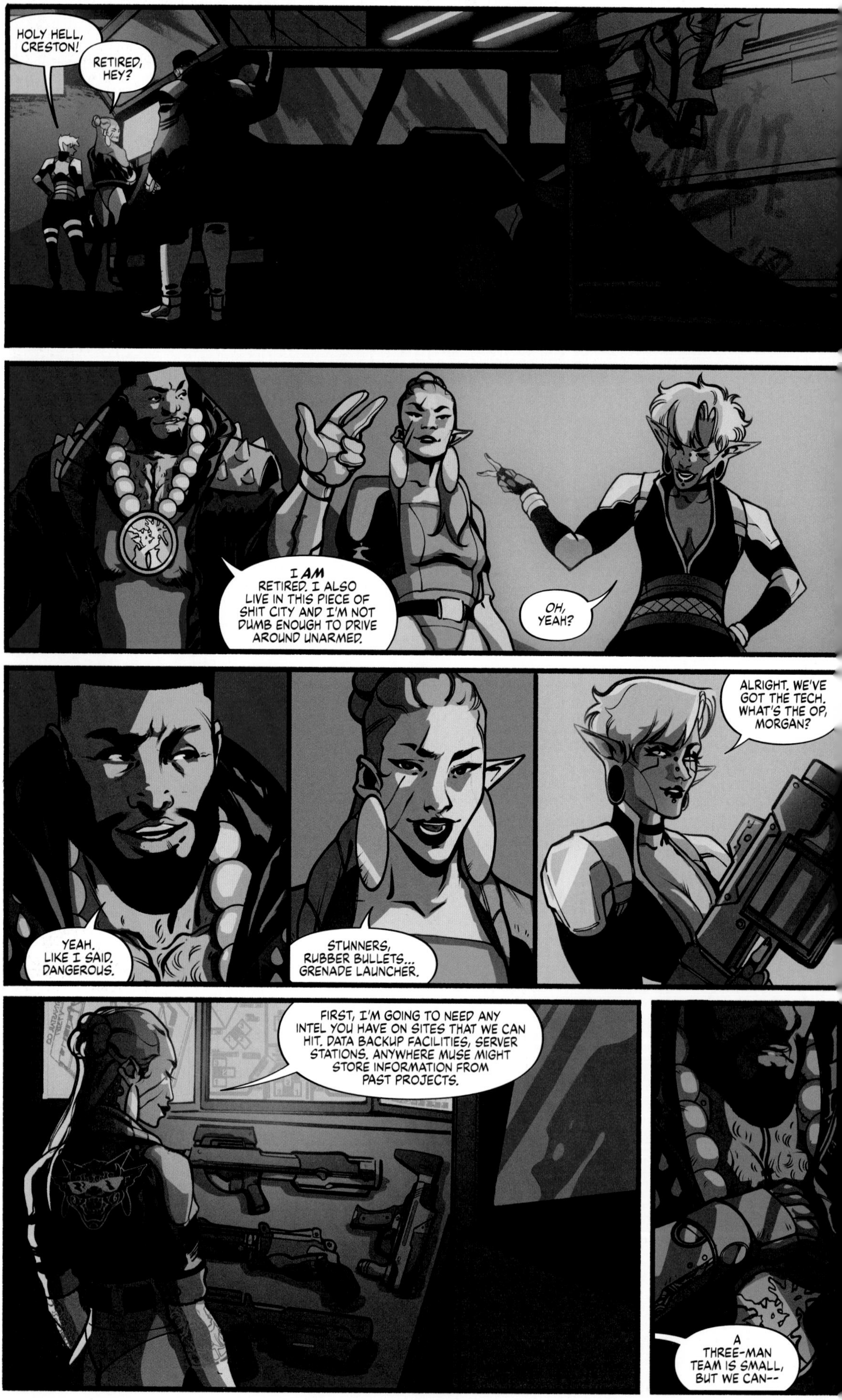
HOLY HELL, CRESTON!
RETIRED, HEY?
I *AM* RETIRED. I ALSO LIVE IN THIS PIECE OF SHIT CITY AND I'M NOT DUMB ENOUGH TO DRIVE AROUND UNARMED.
OH, YEAH?
YEAH. LIKE I SAID. DANGEROUS.
STUNNERS, RUBBER BULLETS... GRENADE LAUNCHER.
ALRIGHT. WE'VE GOT THE TECH. WHAT'S THE OP, MORGAN?
FIRST, I'M GOING TO NEED ANY INTEL YOU HAVE ON SITES THAT WE CAN HIT. DATA BACKUP FACILITIES, SERVER STATIONS. ANYWHERE MUSE MIGHT STORE INFORMATION FROM PAST PROJECTS.
A THREE-MAN TEAM IS SMALL, BUT WE CAN--

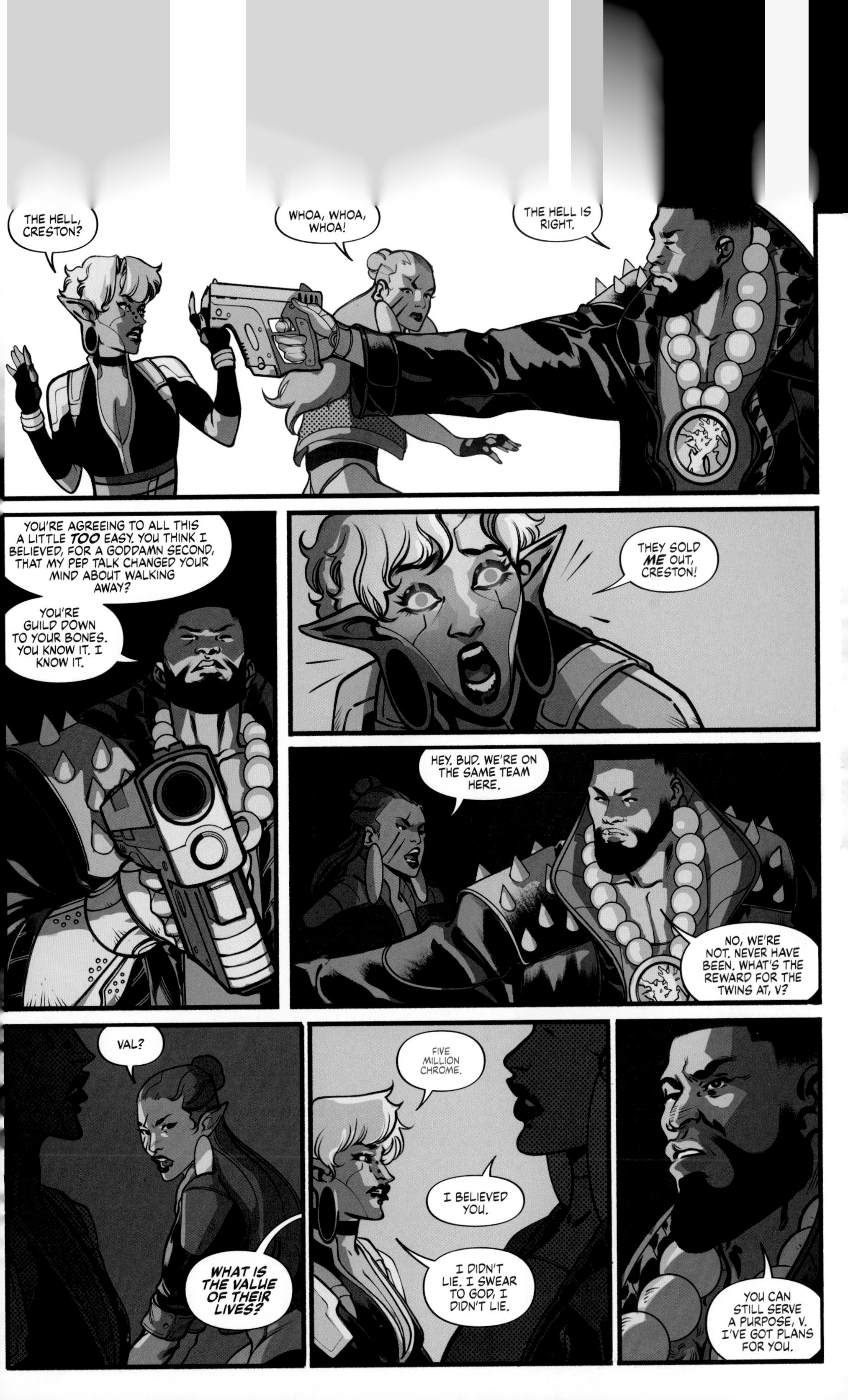
THE HELL, CRESTON?
WHOA, WHOA, WHOA!
THE HELL IS RIGHT.
YOU'RE AGREEING TO ALL THIS A LITTLE TOO EASY. YOU THINK I BELIEVED, FOR A GODDAMN SECOND, THAT MY PEP TALK CHANGED YOUR MIND ABOUT WALKING AWAY?
YOU'RE GUILD DOWN TO YOUR BONES. YOU KNOW IT. I KNOW IT.
THEY SOLD ME OUT, CRESTON!
HEY. BUD. WE'RE ON THE SAME TEAM HERE.
NO, WE'RE NOT. NEVER HAVE BEEN. WHAT'S THE REWARD FOR THE TWINS AT, V?
VAL?
WHAT IS THE VALUE OF THEIR LIVES?
FIVE MILLION CHROME.
I BELIEVED YOU.
I DIDN'T LIE. I SWEAR TO GOD, I DIDN'T LIE.
YOU CAN STILL SERVE A PURPOSE, V. I'VE GOT PLANS FOR YOU.

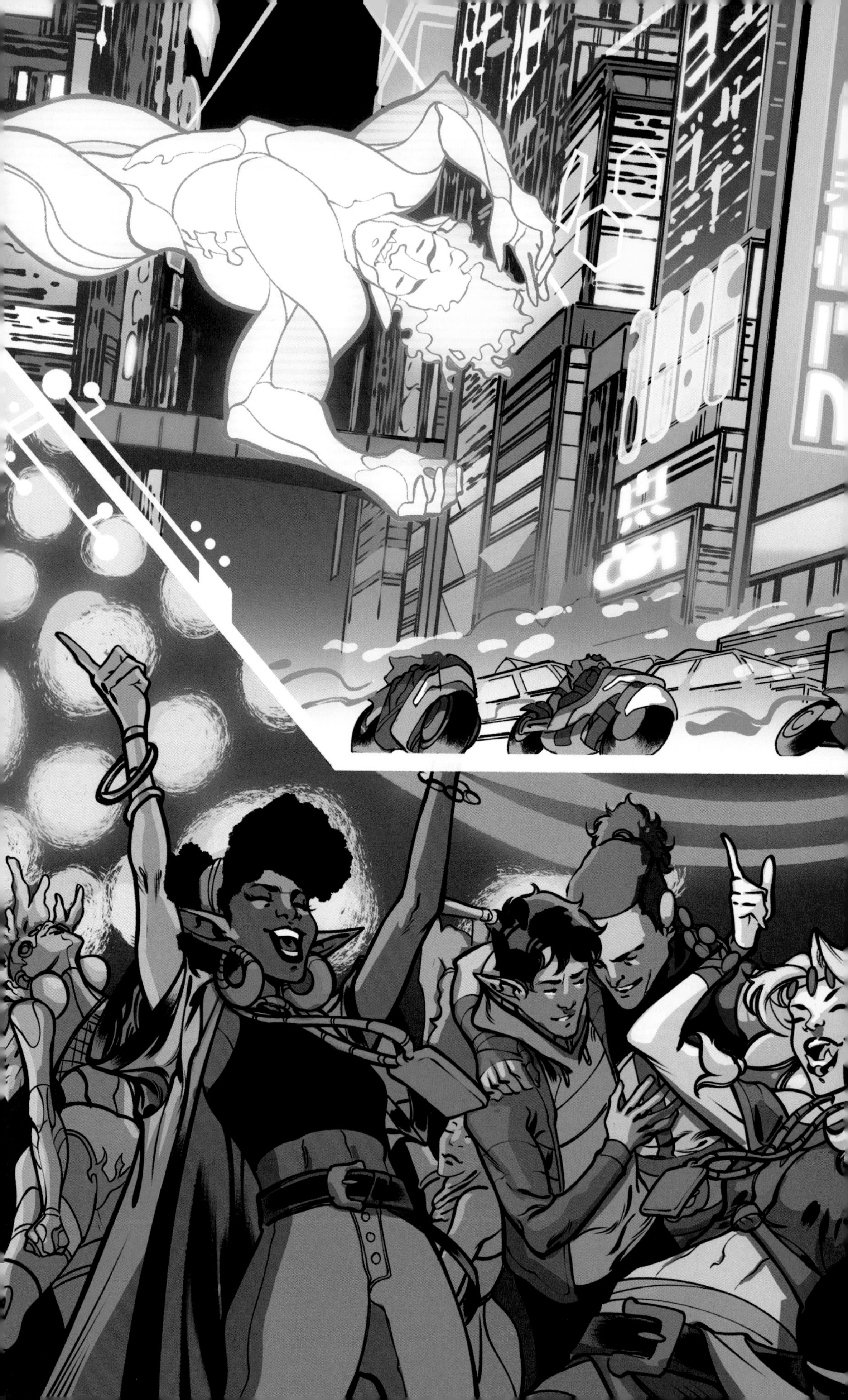

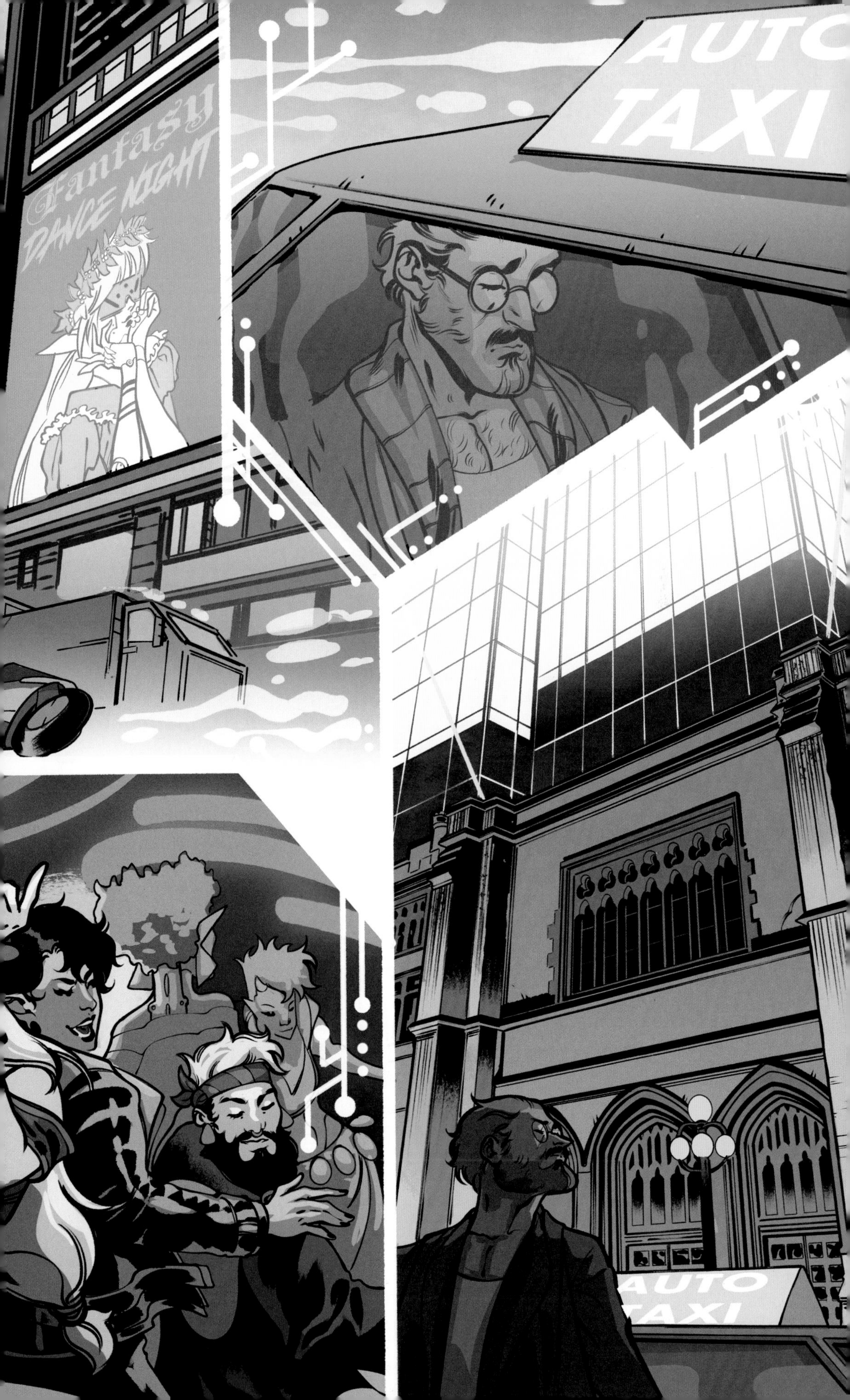
Fantasy
DANCE NIGHT
AUTO
TAXI
AUTO
TAXI

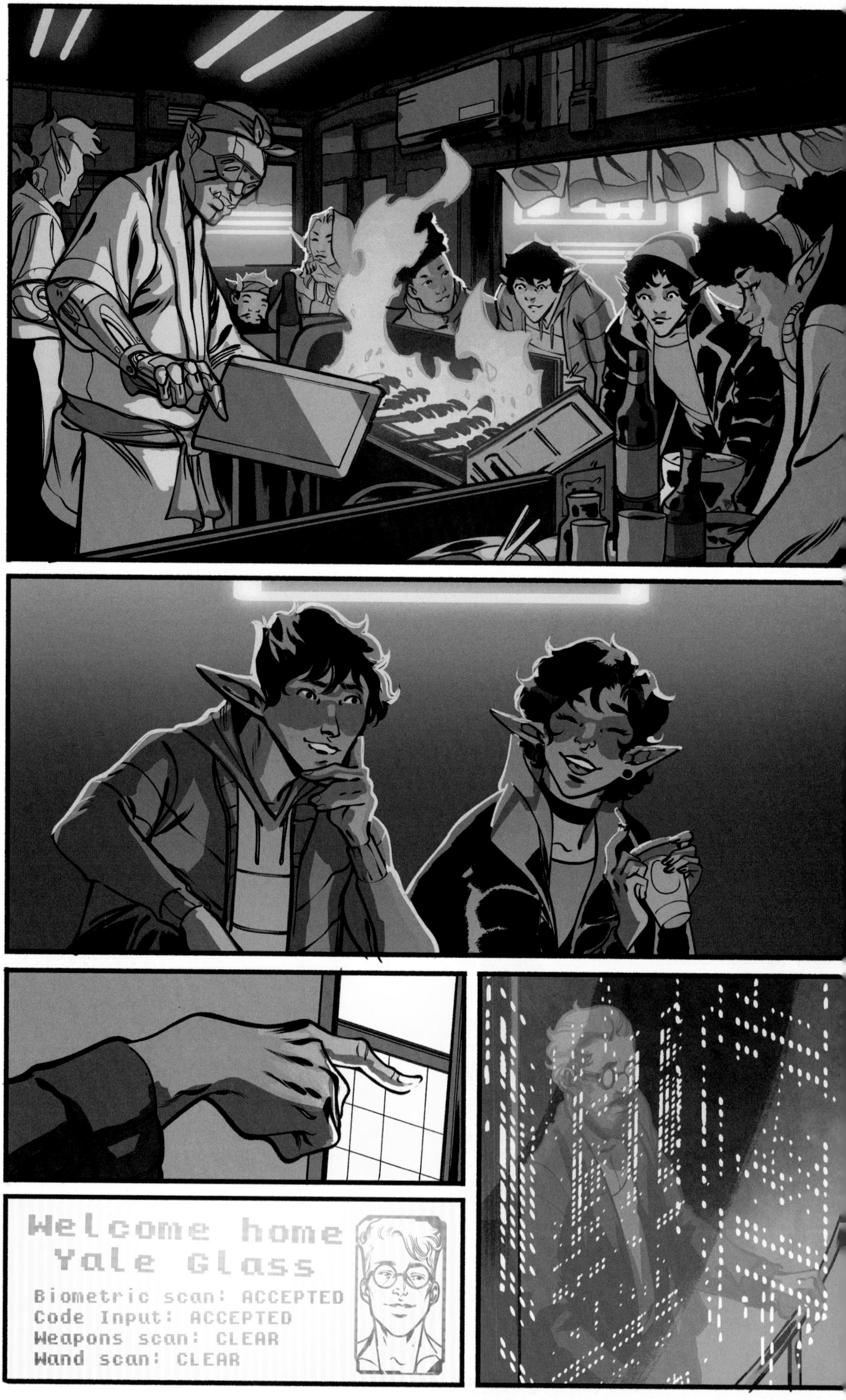
Welcome home
Yale Glass
Biometric scan: ACCEPTED
Code Input: ACCEPTED
Weapons scan: CLEAR
Wand scan: CLEAR

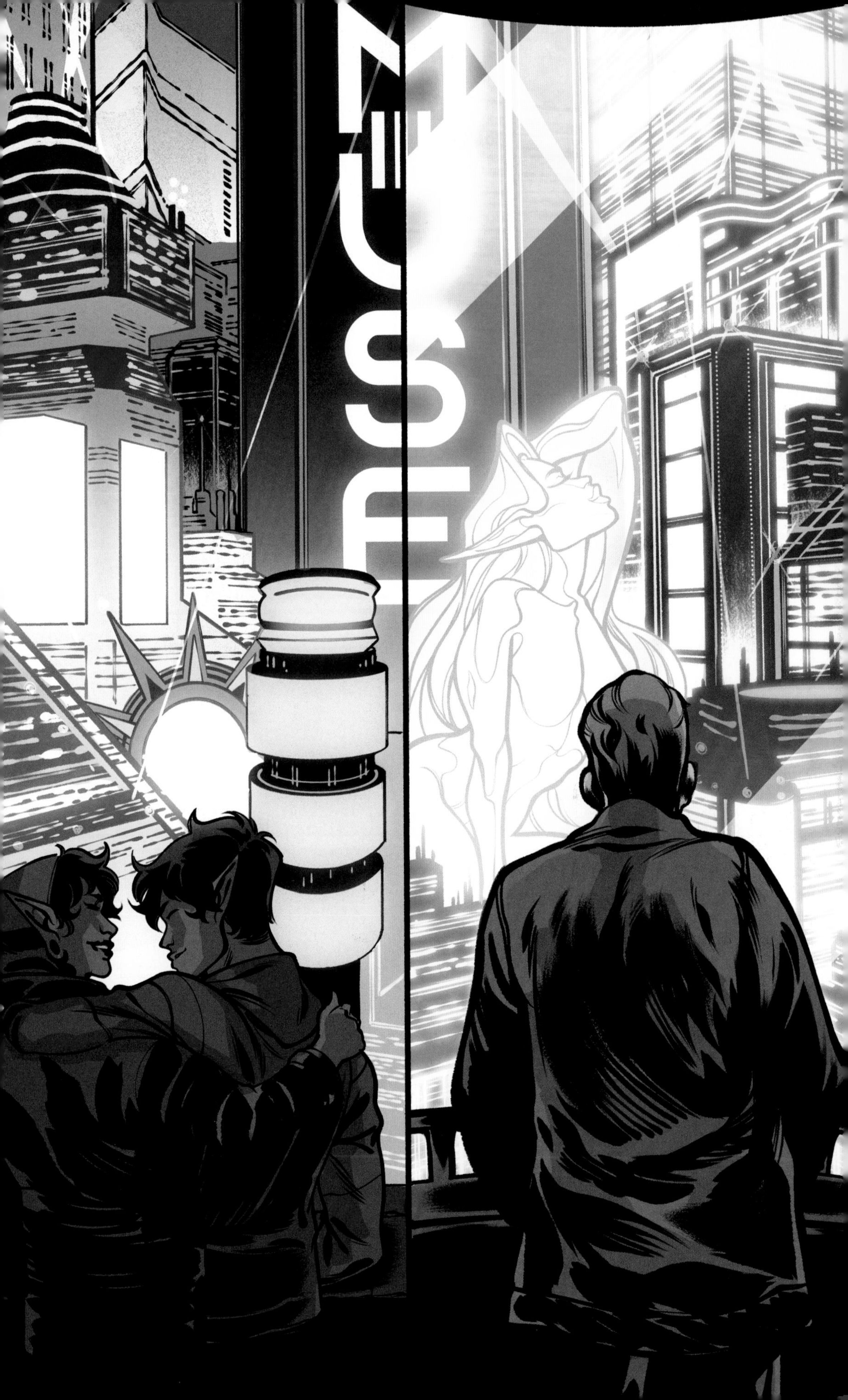

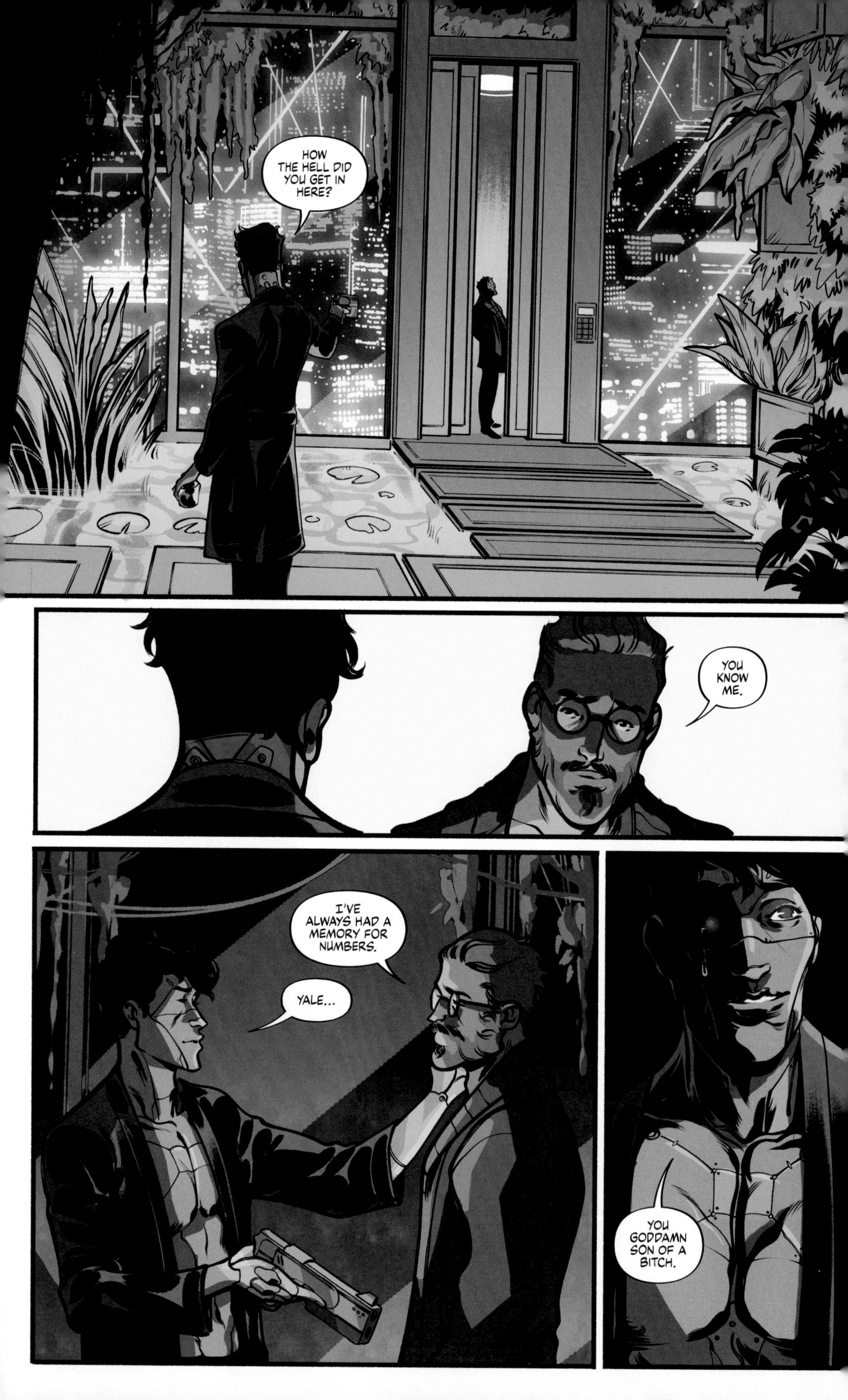
HOW THE HELL DID YOU GET IN HERE?
YOU KNOW ME.
I'VE ALWAYS HAD A MEMORY FOR NUMBERS.
YALE...
YOU GODDAMN SON OF A BITCH.

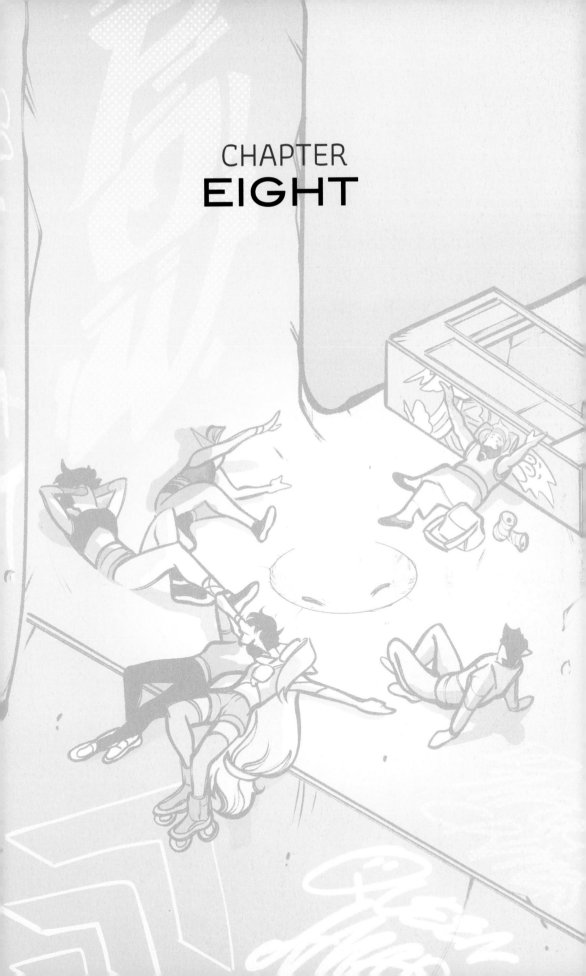

CHAPTER
EIGHT

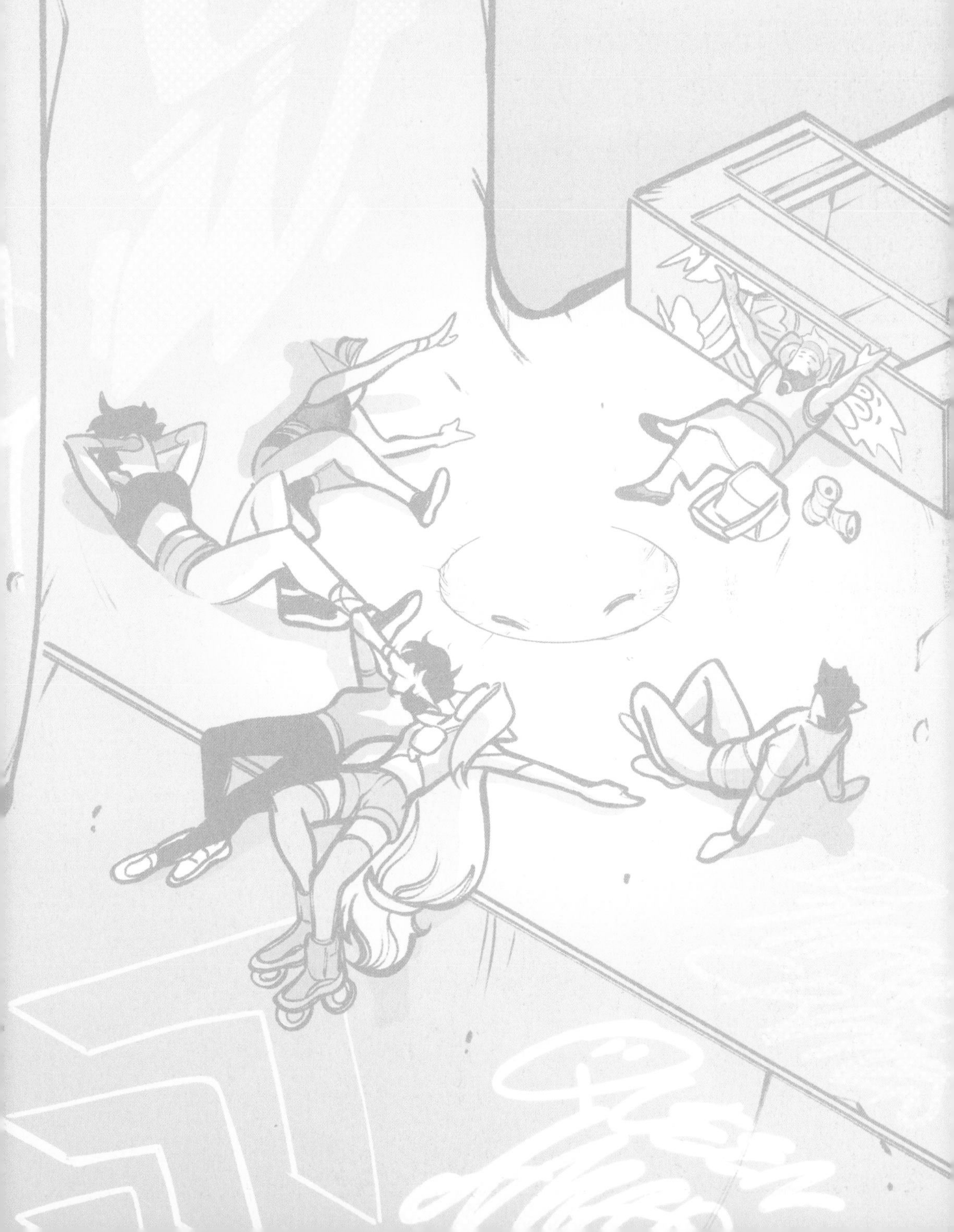

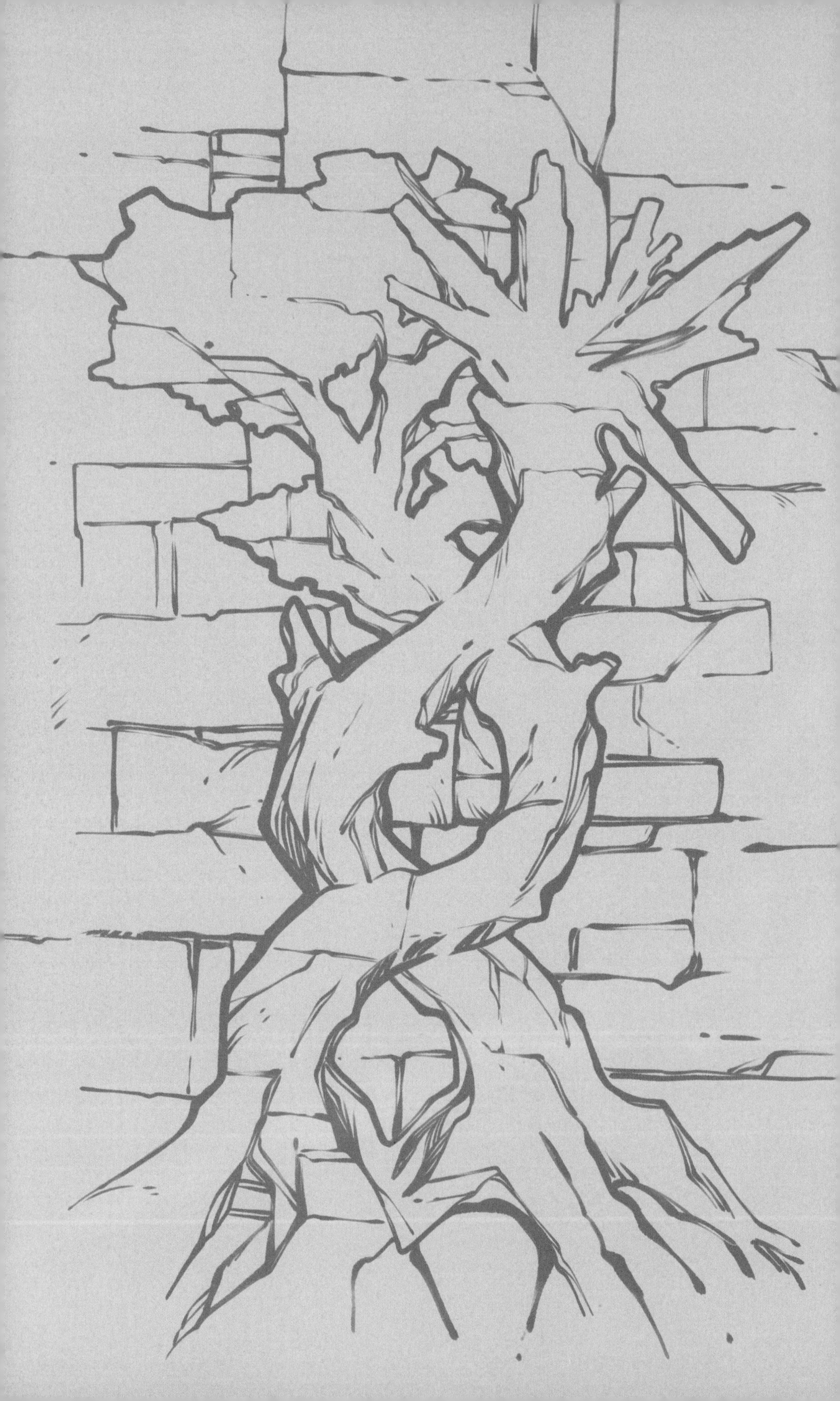

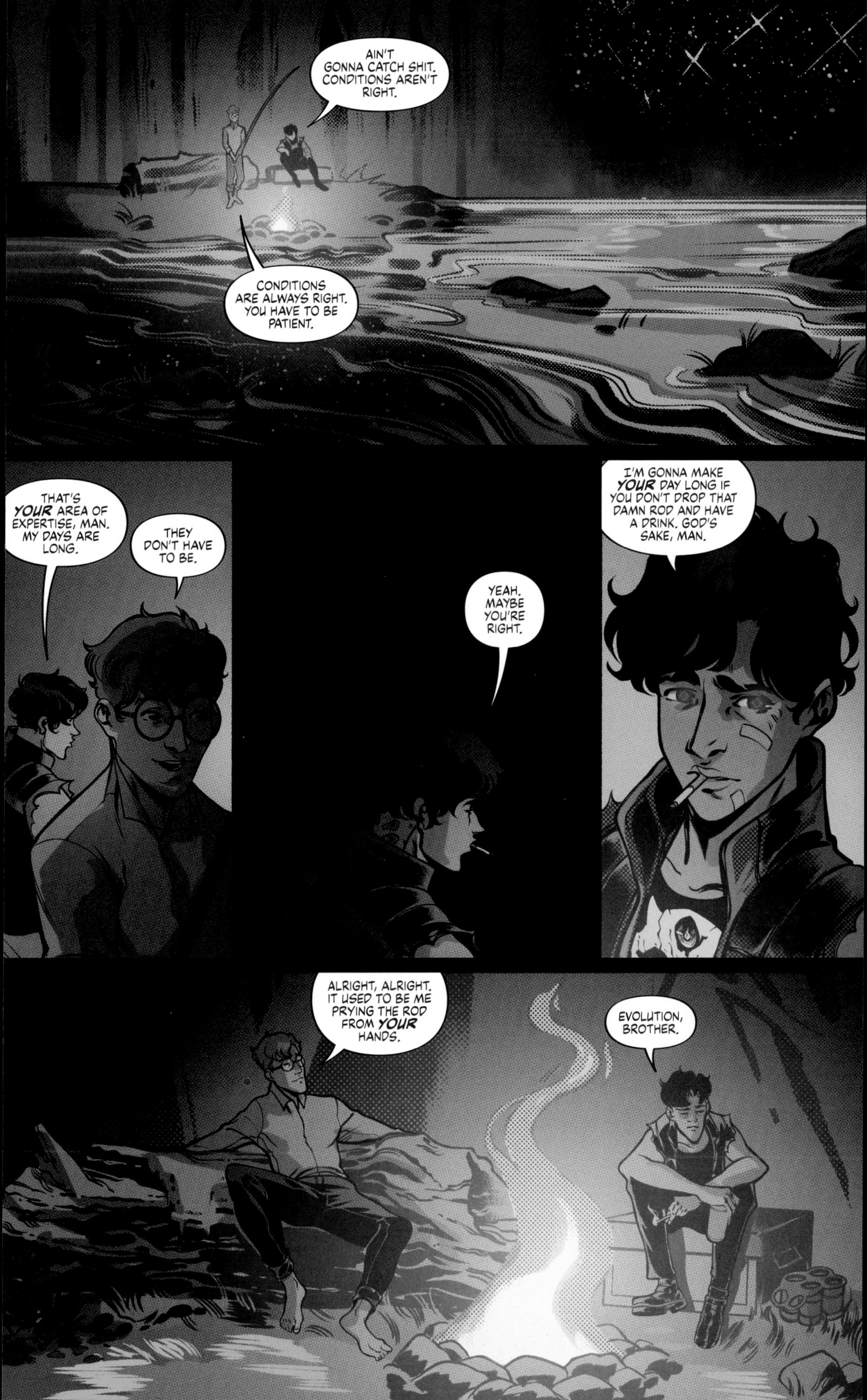
AIN'T GONNA CATCH SHIT. CONDITIONS AREN'T RIGHT.
CONDITIONS ARE ALWAYS RIGHT. YOU HAVE TO BE PATIENT.
THAT'S *YOUR* AREA OF EXPERTISE, MAN. MY DAYS ARE LONG.
THEY DON'T HAVE TO BE.
YEAH. MAYBE YOU'RE RIGHT.
I'M GONNA MAKE *YOUR* DAY LONG IF YOU DON'T DROP THAT DAMN ROD AND HAVE A DRINK. GOD'S SAKE, MAN.
ALRIGHT, ALRIGHT. IT USED TO BE ME PRYING THE ROD FROM *YOUR* HANDS.
EVOLUTION, BROTHER.

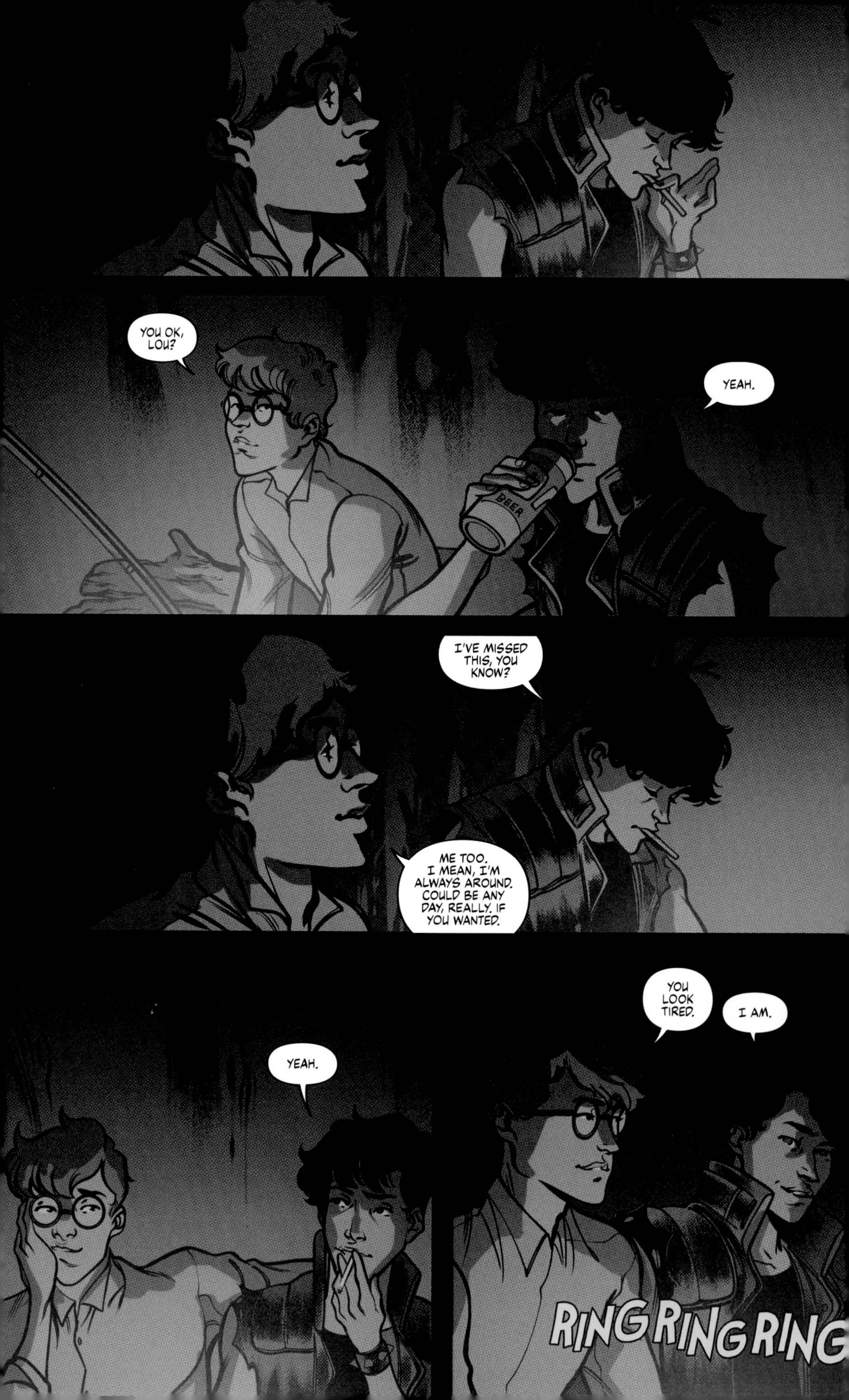
YOU OK, LOU?
YEAH.
I'VE MISSED THIS, YOU KNOW?
ME TOO. I MEAN, I'M ALWAYS AROUND. COULD BE ANY DAY, REALLY. IF YOU WANTED.
YEAH.
YOU LOOK TIRED.
I AM.
RING RING RING

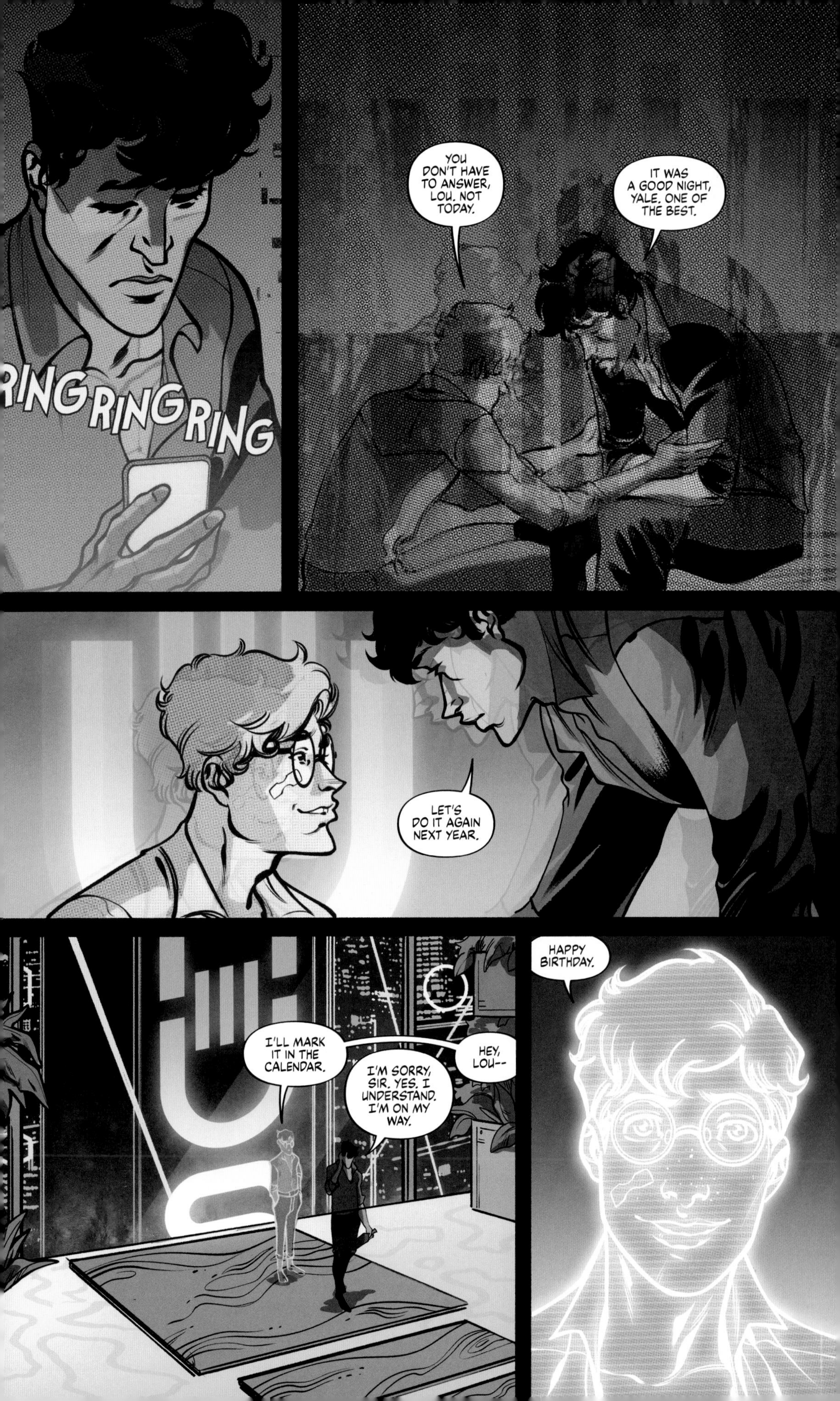
RINGRINGRING
YOU DON'T HAVE TO ANSWER, LOU. NOT TODAY.
IT WAS A GOOD NIGHT, YALE. ONE OF THE BEST.
LET'S DO IT AGAIN NEXT YEAR.
I'LL MARK IT IN THE CALENDAR.
HEY, LOU--
I'M SORRY, SIR. YES. I UNDERSTAND. I'M ON MY WAY.
HAPPY BIRTHDAY.

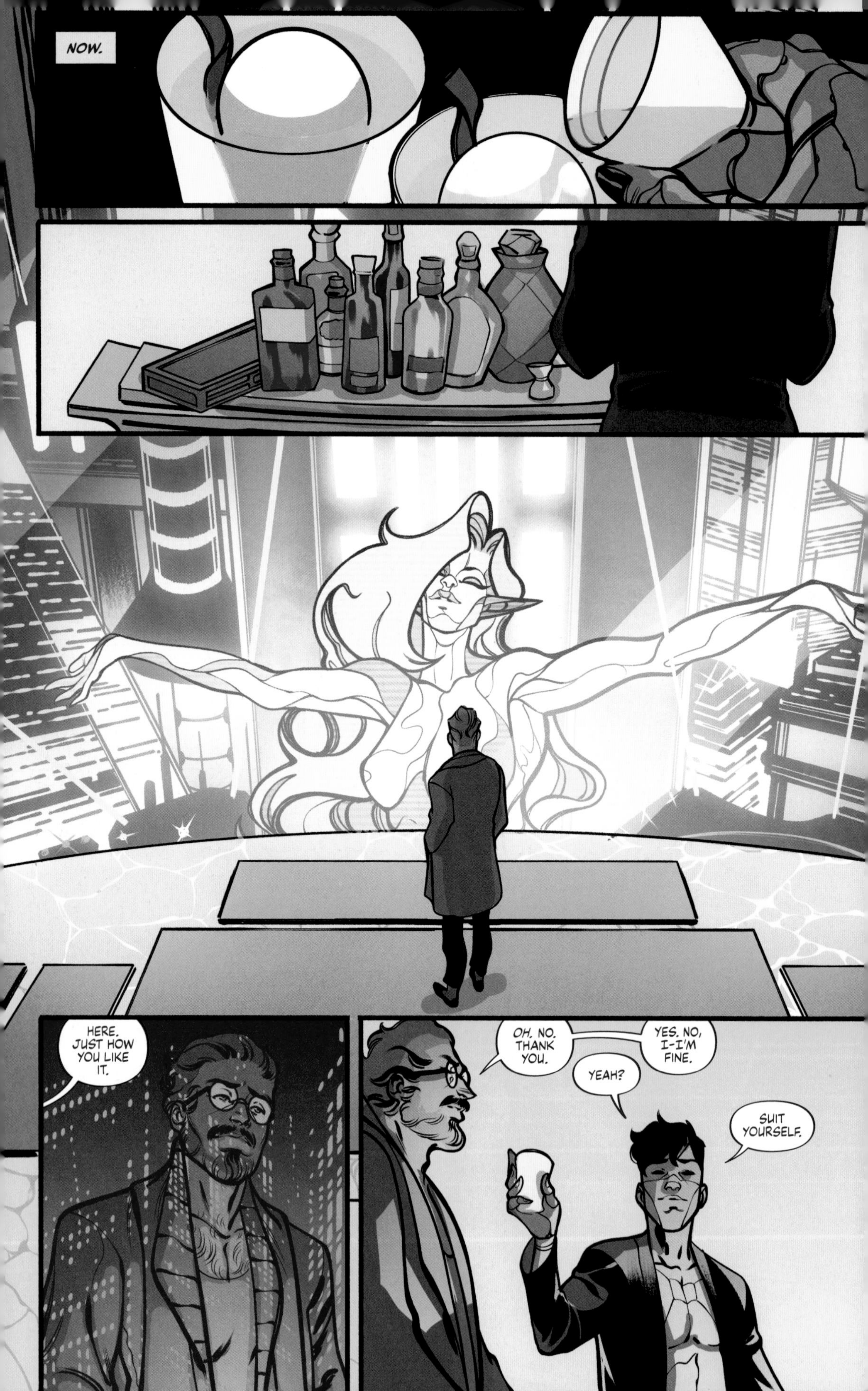
NOW.
HERE. JUST HOW YOU LIKE IT.
OH. NO. THANK YOU.
YES. NO, I-I'M FINE.
YEAH?
SUIT YOURSELF.

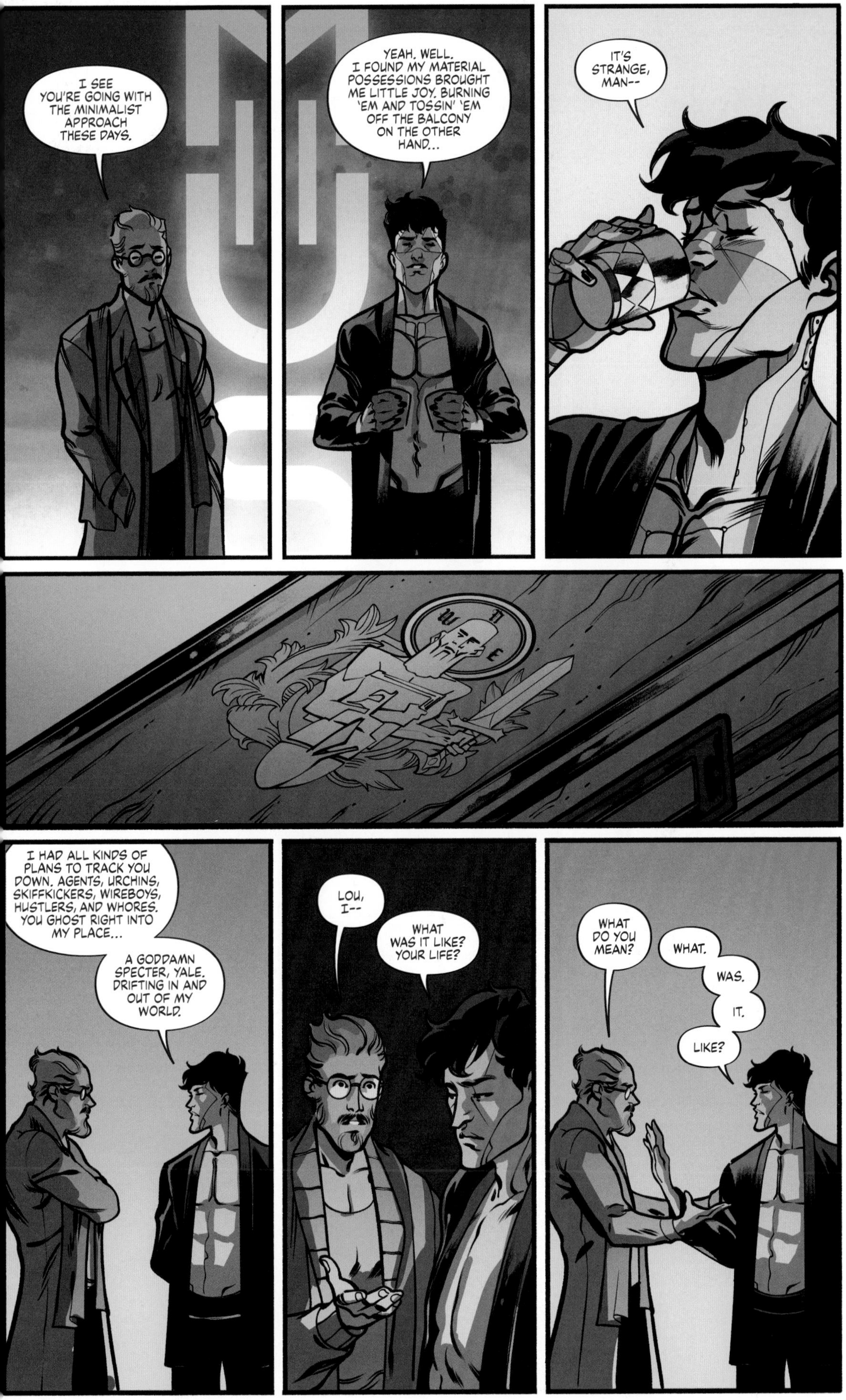
I SEE YOU'RE GOING WITH THE MINIMALIST APPROACH THESE DAYS.
YEAH. WELL. I FOUND MY MATERIAL POSSESSIONS BROUGHT ME LITTLE JOY. BURNING 'EM AND TOSSIN' 'EM OFF THE BALCONY ON THE OTHER HAND...
IT'S STRANGE, MAN--
I HAD ALL KINDS OF PLANS TO TRACK YOU DOWN. AGENTS, URCHINS, SKIFFKICKERS, WIREBOYS, HUSTLERS, AND WHORES. YOU GHOST RIGHT INTO MY PLACE...
A GODDAMN SPECTER, YALE. DRIFTING IN AND OUT OF MY WORLD.
LOU, I--
WHAT WAS IT LIKE? YOUR LIFE?
WHAT DO YOU MEAN?
WHAT.
WAS.
IT.
LIKE?

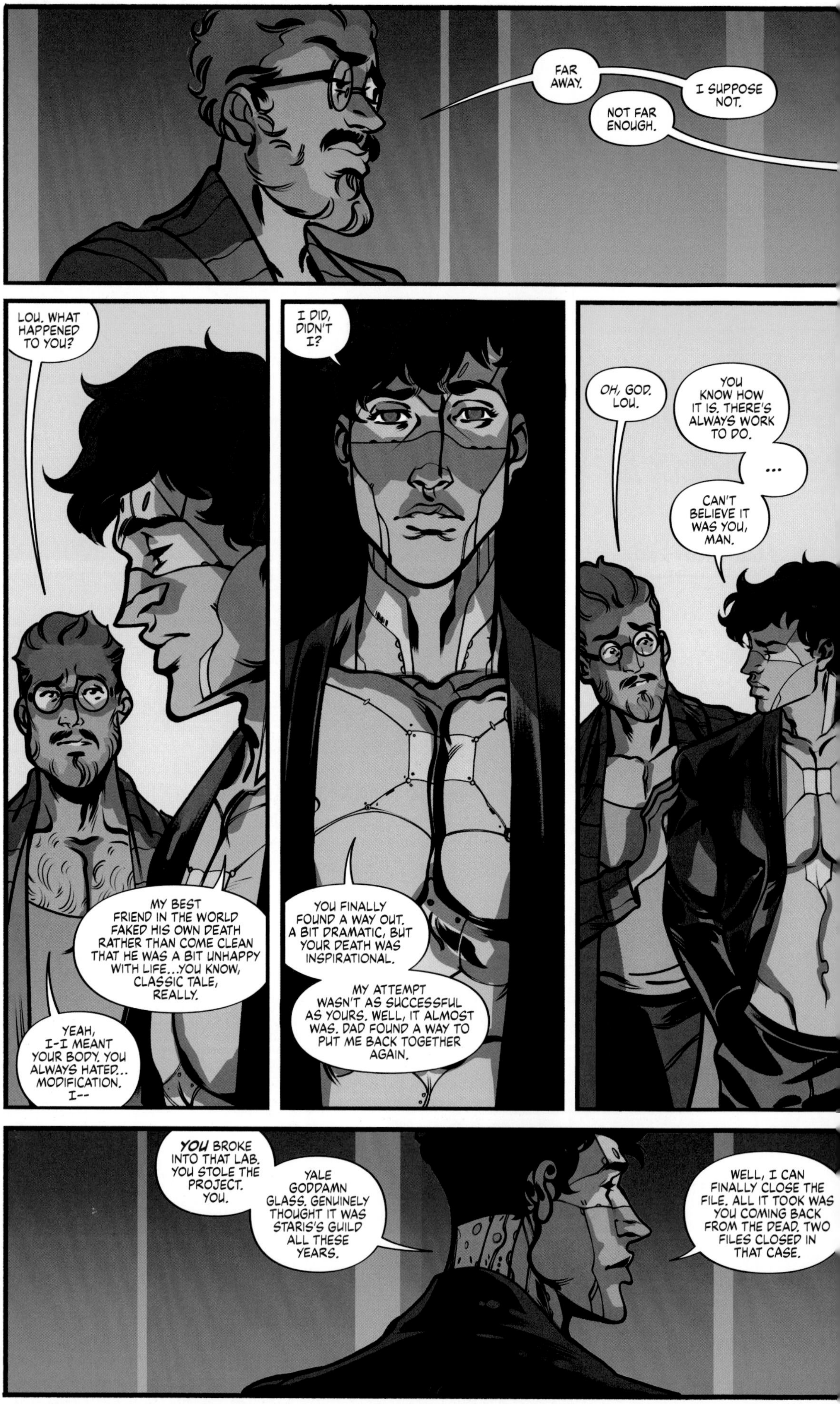
FAR AWAY.
I SUPPOSE NOT.
NOT FAR ENOUGH.
LOU. WHAT HAPPENED TO YOU?
MY BEST FRIEND IN THE WORLD FAKED HIS OWN DEATH RATHER THAN COME CLEAN THAT HE WAS A BIT UNHAPPY WITH LIFE...YOU KNOW, CLASSIC TALE, REALLY.
YEAH, I-I MEANT YOUR BODY. YOU ALWAYS HATED... MODIFICATION. I--
I DID, DIDN'T I?
YOU FINALLY FOUND A WAY OUT. A BIT DRAMATIC, BUT YOUR DEATH WAS INSPIRATIONAL.
MY ATTEMPT WASN'T AS SUCCESSFUL AS YOURS. WELL, IT ALMOST WAS. DAD FOUND A WAY TO PUT ME BACK TOGETHER AGAIN.
OH, GOD. LOU.
YOU KNOW HOW IT IS. THERE'S ALWAYS WORK TO DO.
...
CAN'T BELIEVE IT WAS YOU, MAN.
YOU BROKE INTO THAT LAB. YOU STOLE THE PROJECT. YOU.
YALE GODDAMN GLASS. GENUINELY THOUGHT IT WAS STARIS'S GUILD ALL THESE YEARS.
WELL, I CAN FINALLY CLOSE THE FILE. ALL IT TOOK WAS YOU COMING BACK FROM THE DEAD. TWO FILES CLOSED IN THAT CASE.

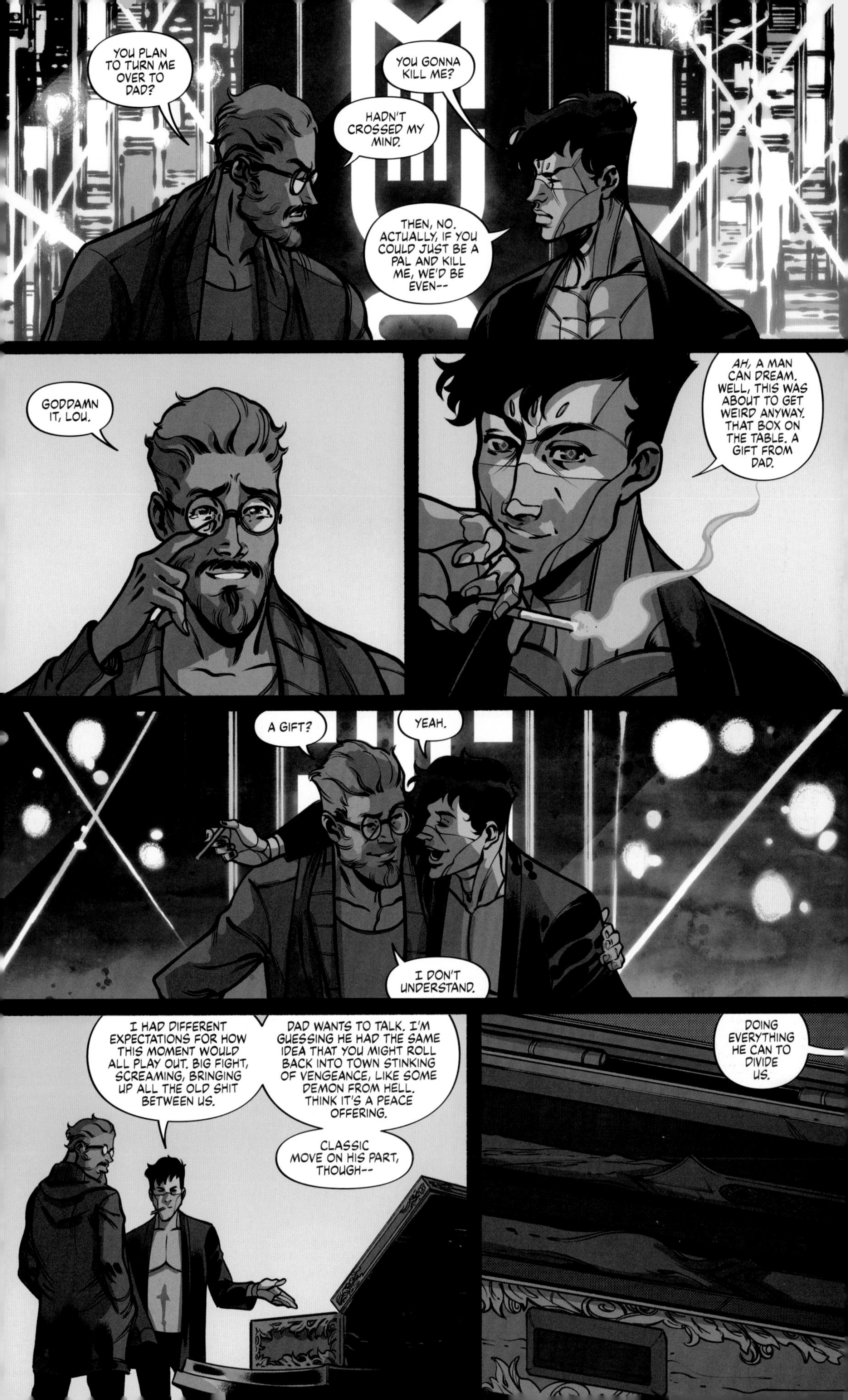
YOU PLAN TO TURN ME OVER TO DAD?
HADN'T CROSSED MY MIND.
YOU GONNA KILL ME?
THEN, NO. ACTUALLY, IF YOU COULD JUST BE A PAL AND KILL ME, WE'D BE EVEN--
GODDAMN IT, LOU.
AH, A MAN CAN DREAM. WELL, THIS WAS ABOUT TO GET WEIRD ANYWAY. THAT BOX ON THE TABLE. A GIFT FROM DAD.
A GIFT?
YEAH.
I DON'T UNDERSTAND.
I HAD DIFFERENT EXPECTATIONS FOR HOW THIS MOMENT WOULD ALL PLAY OUT. BIG FIGHT, SCREAMING, BRINGING UP ALL THE OLD SHIT BETWEEN US.
DAD WANTS TO TALK. I'M GUESSING HE HAD THE SAME IDEA THAT YOU MIGHT ROLL BACK INTO TOWN STINKING OF VENGEANCE, LIKE SOME DEMON FROM HELL. THINK IT'S A PEACE OFFERING.
CLASSIC MOVE ON HIS PART, THOUGH--
DOING EVERYTHING HE CAN TO DIVIDE US.

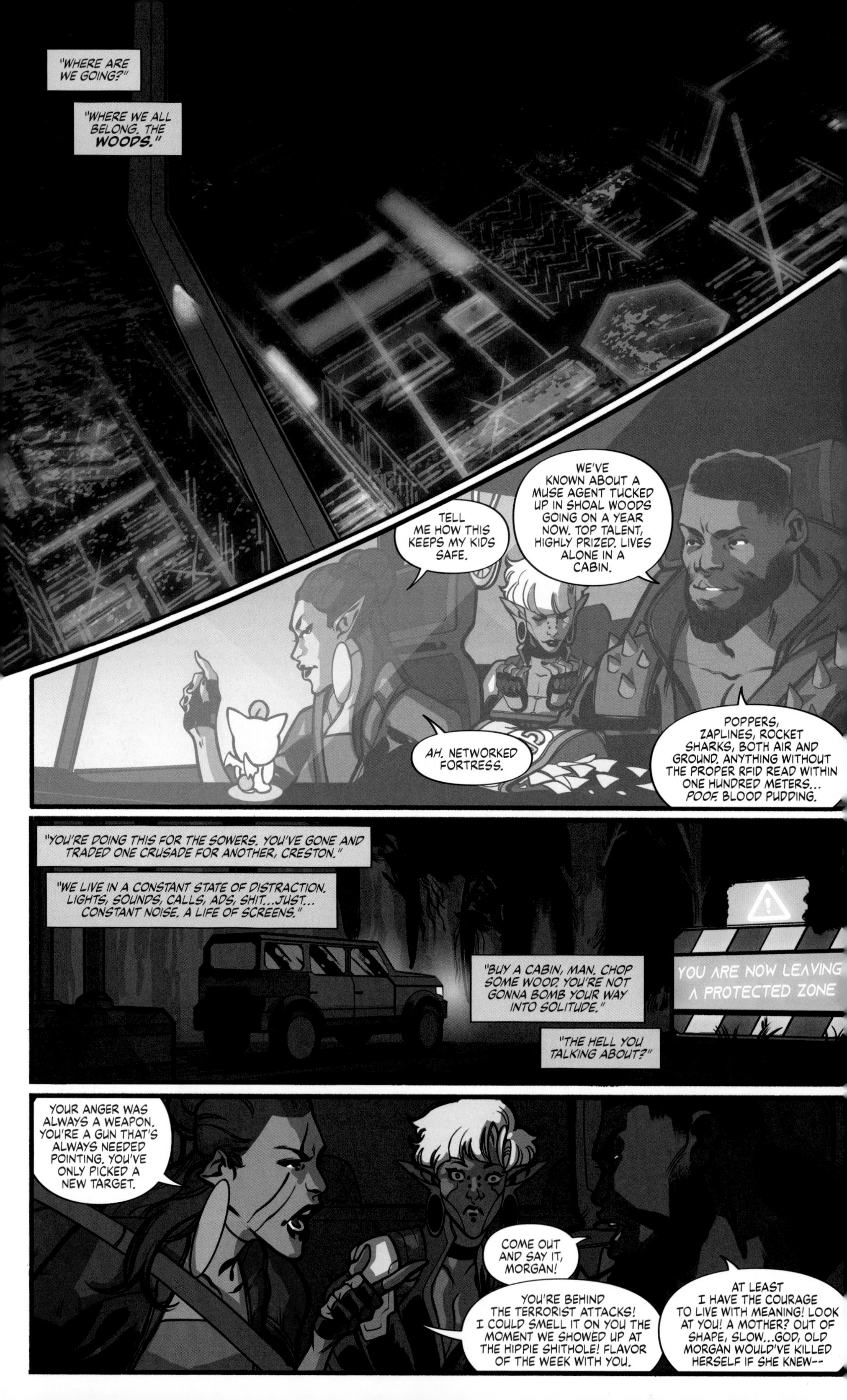
"WHERE ARE WE GOING?"
"WHERE WE ALL BELONG. THE WOODS."
TELL ME HOW THIS KEEPS MY KIDS SAFE.
WE'VE KNOWN ABOUT A MUSE AGENT TUCKED UP IN SHOAL WOODS GOING ON A YEAR NOW. TOP TALENT, HIGHLY PRIZED. LIVES ALONE IN A CABIN.
AH. NETWORKED FORTRESS.
POPPERS, ZAPLINES, ROCKET SHARKS, BOTH AIR AND GROUND. ANYTHING WITHOUT THE PROPER RFID READ WITHIN ONE HUNDRED METERS... POOF. BLOOD PUDDING.
"YOU'RE DOING THIS FOR THE SOWERS. YOU'VE GONE AND TRADED ONE CRUSADE FOR ANOTHER, CRESTON."
"WE LIVE IN A CONSTANT STATE OF DISTRACTION. LIGHTS, SOUNDS, CALLS, ADS, SHIT...JUST... CONSTANT NOISE. A LIFE OF SCREENS."
YOU ARE NOW LEAVING A PROTECTED ZONE
"BUY A CABIN, MAN. CHOP SOME WOOD. YOU'RE NOT GONNA BOMB YOUR WAY INTO SOLITUDE."
"THE HELL YOU TALKING ABOUT?"
YOUR ANGER WAS ALWAYS A WEAPON. YOU'RE A GUN THAT'S ALWAYS NEEDED POINTING. YOU'VE ONLY PICKED A NEW TARGET.
COME OUT AND SAY IT, MORGAN!
YOU'RE BEHIND THE TERRORIST ATTACKS! I COULD SMELL IT ON YOU THE MOMENT WE SHOWED UP AT THE HIPPIE SHITHOLE! FLAVOR OF THE WEEK WITH YOU.
AT LEAST I HAVE THE COURAGE TO LIVE WITH MEANING! LOOK AT YOU! A MOTHER? OUT OF SHAPE, SLOW...GOD, OLD MORGAN WOULD'VE KILLED HERSELF IF SHE KNEW--

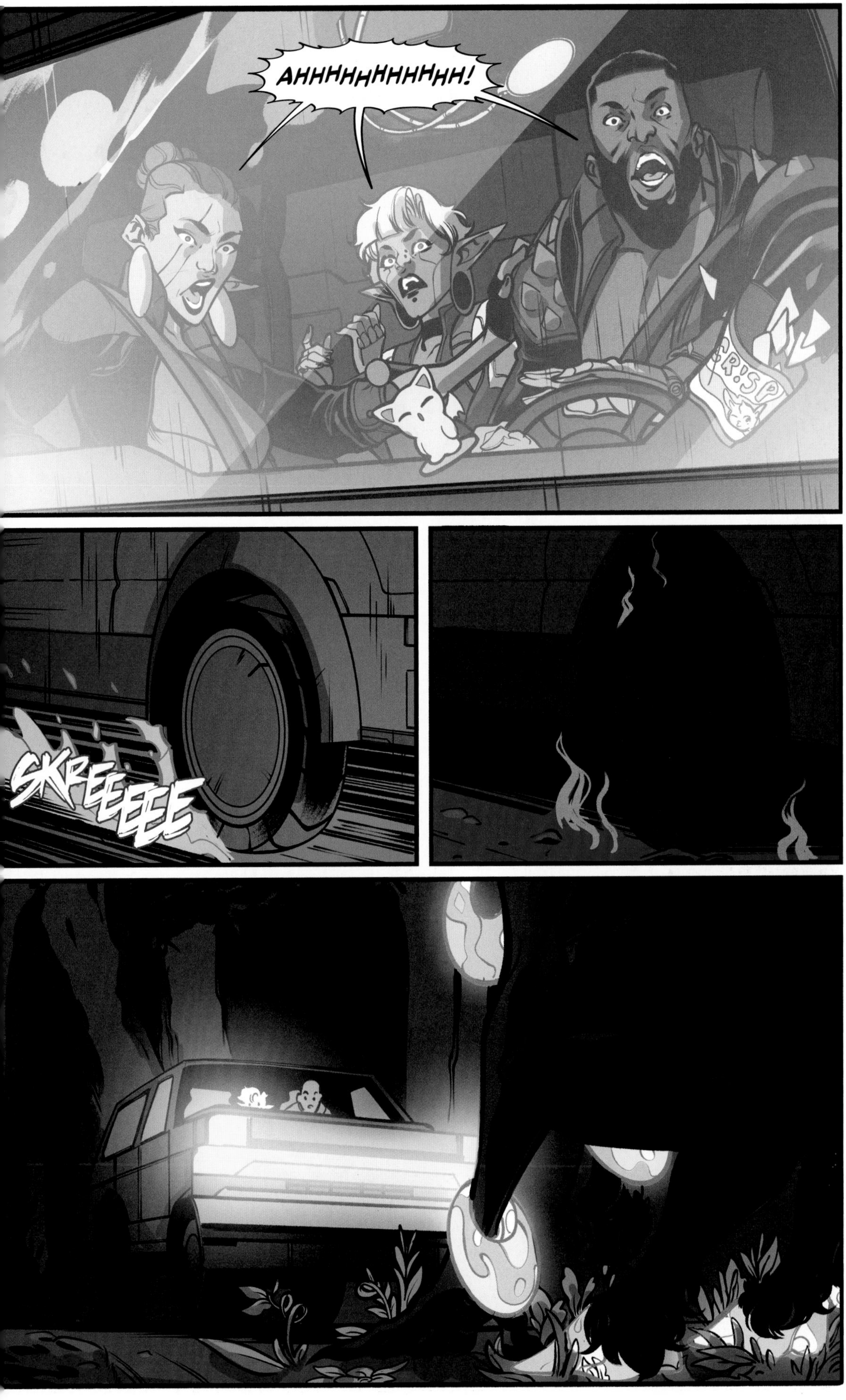
AHHHHHHHHHHHH!
CR!SP
SKREEEEEE

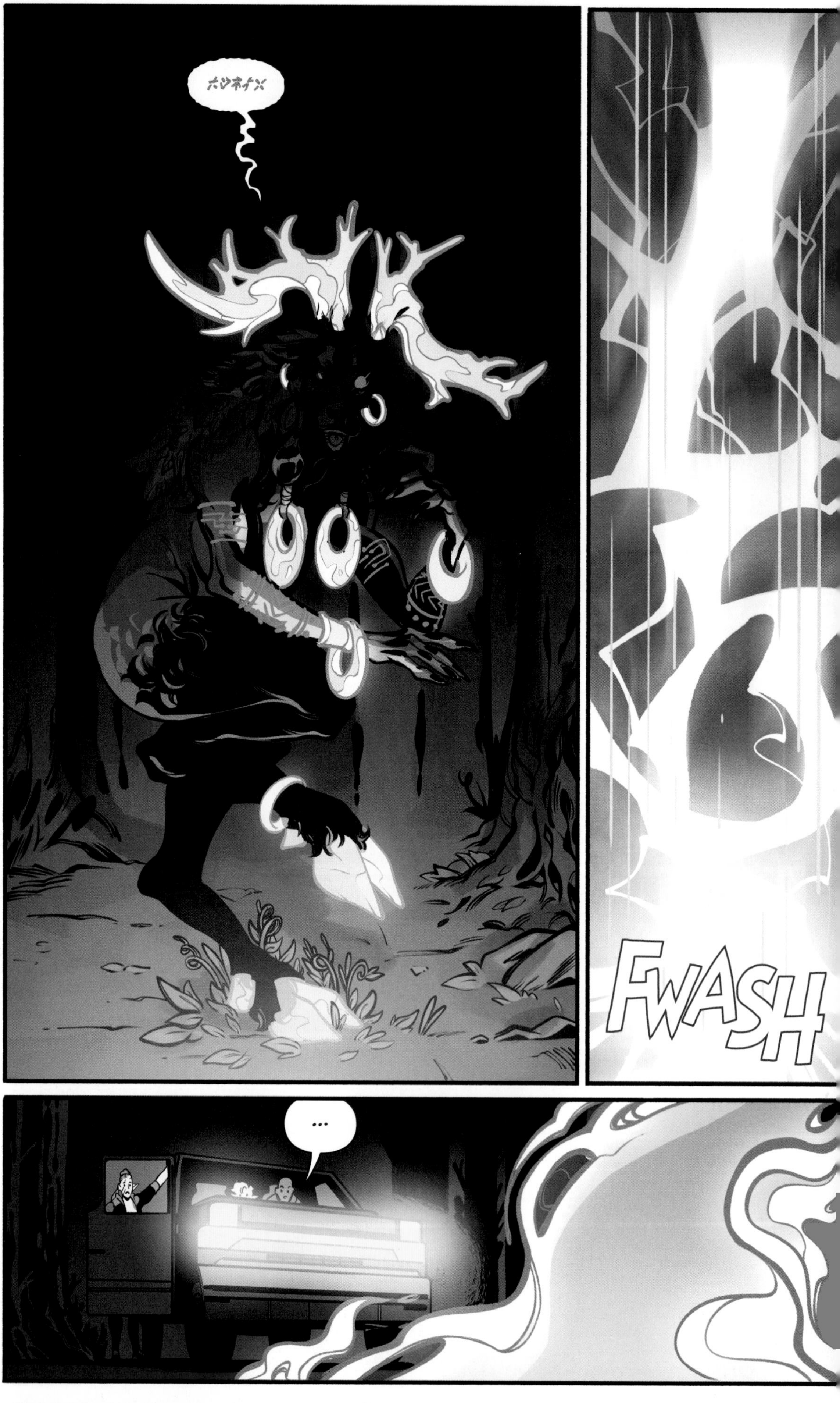
FWASH
...

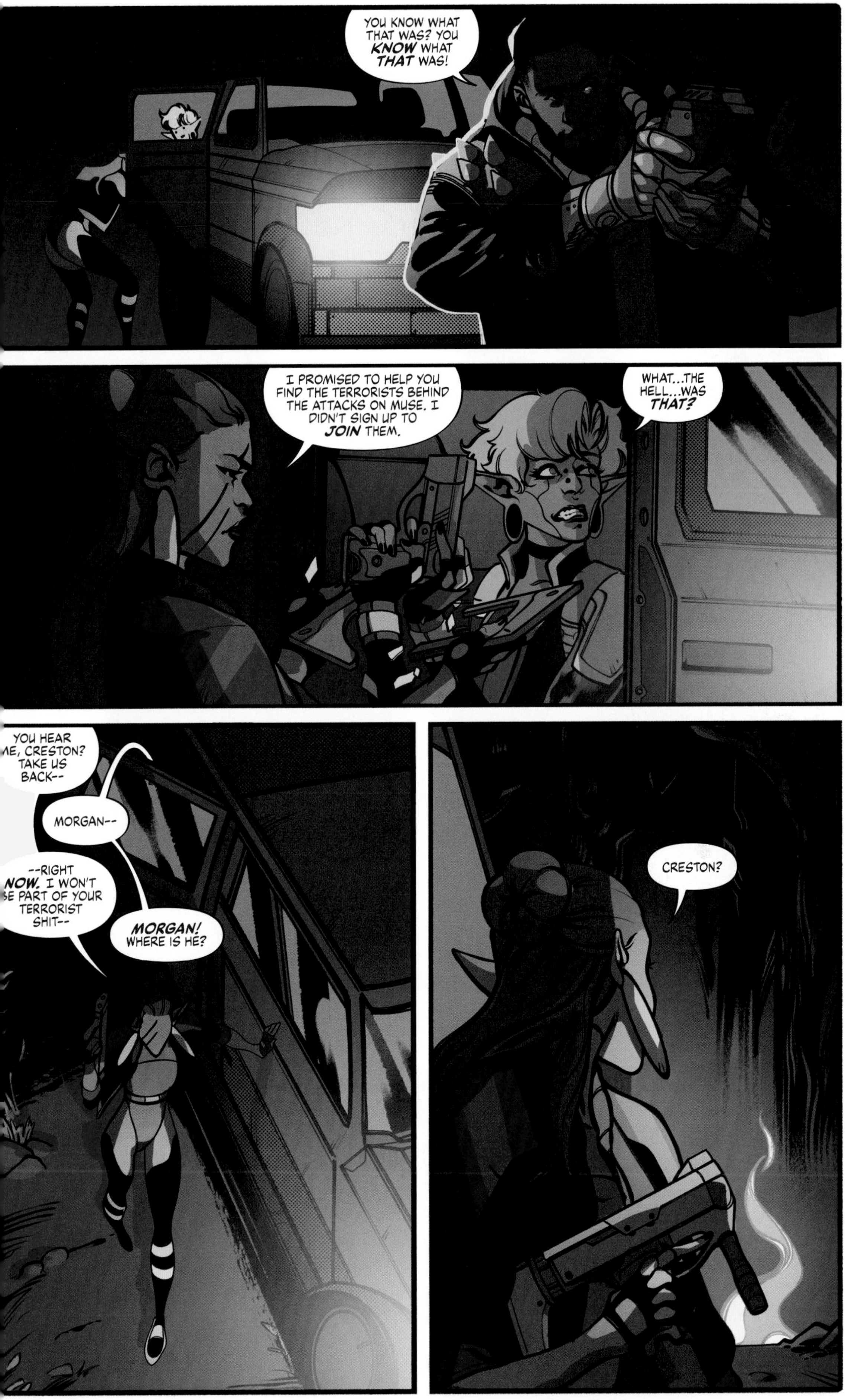
YOU KNOW WHAT THAT WAS? YOU KNOW WHAT THAT WAS!
I PROMISED TO HELP YOU FIND THE TERRORISTS BEHIND THE ATTACKS ON MUSE. I DIDN'T SIGN UP TO JOIN THEM.
WHAT...THE HELL...WAS THAT?
YOU HEAR ME, CRESTON? TAKE US BACK--
MORGAN--
--RIGHT NOW. I WON'T BE PART OF YOUR TERRORIST SHIT--
MORGAN! WHERE IS HE?
CRESTON?

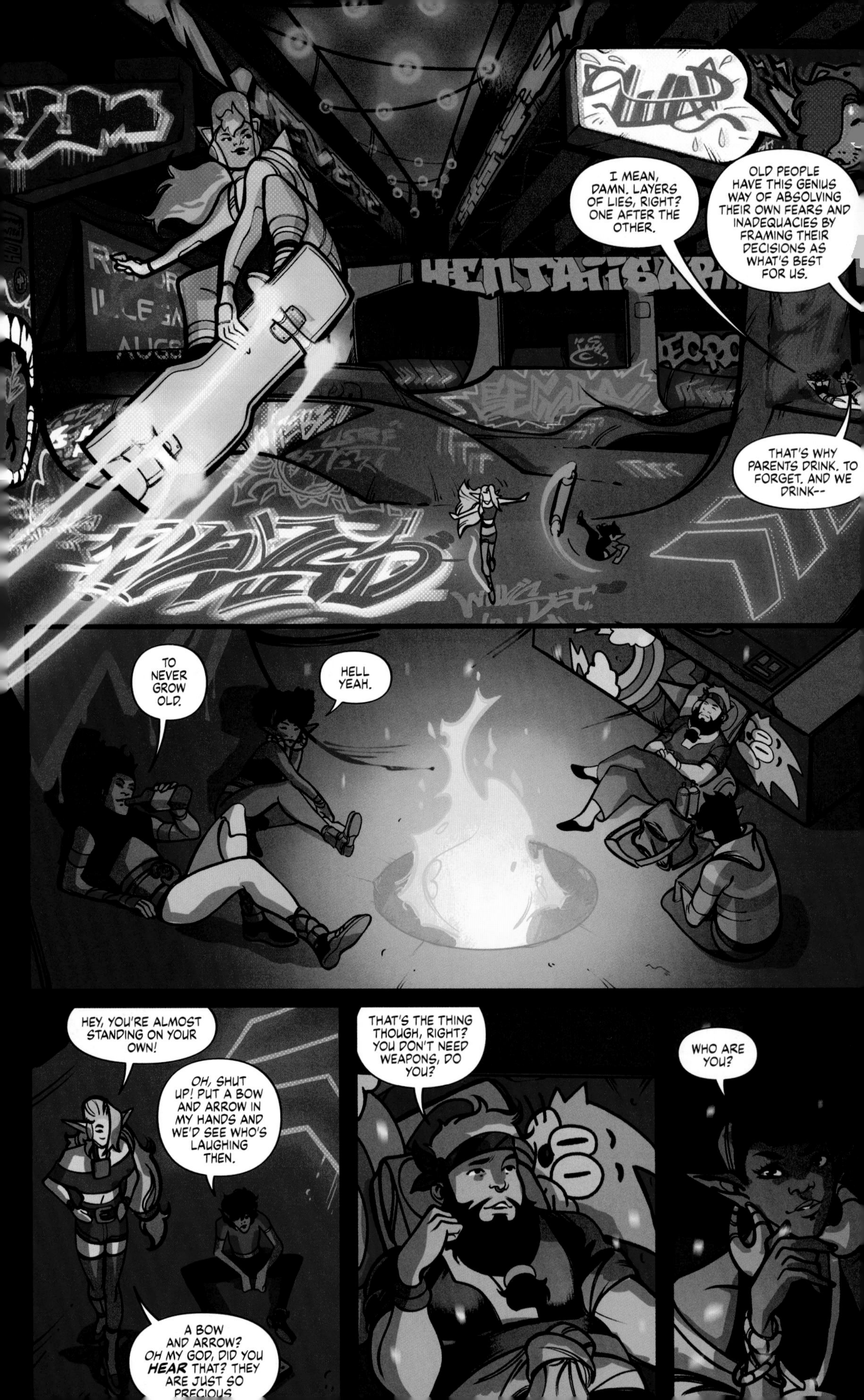
I MEAN, DAMN. LAYERS OF LIES, RIGHT? ONE AFTER THE OTHER.
OLD PEOPLE HAVE THIS GENIUS WAY OF ABSOLVING THEIR OWN FEARS AND INADEQUACIES BY FRAMING THEIR DECISIONS AS WHAT'S BEST FOR US.
THAT'S WHY PARENTS DRINK. TO FORGET. AND WE DRINK--
TO NEVER GROW OLD.
HELL YEAH.
HEY, YOU'RE ALMOST STANDING ON YOUR OWN!
OH, SHUT UP! PUT A BOW AND ARROW IN MY HANDS AND WE'D SEE WHO'S LAUGHING THEN.
A BOW AND ARROW? OH MY GOD, DID YOU HEAR THAT? THEY ARE JUST SO PRECIOUS
THAT'S THE THING THOUGH, RIGHT? YOU DON'T NEED WEAPONS, DO YOU?
WHO ARE YOU?

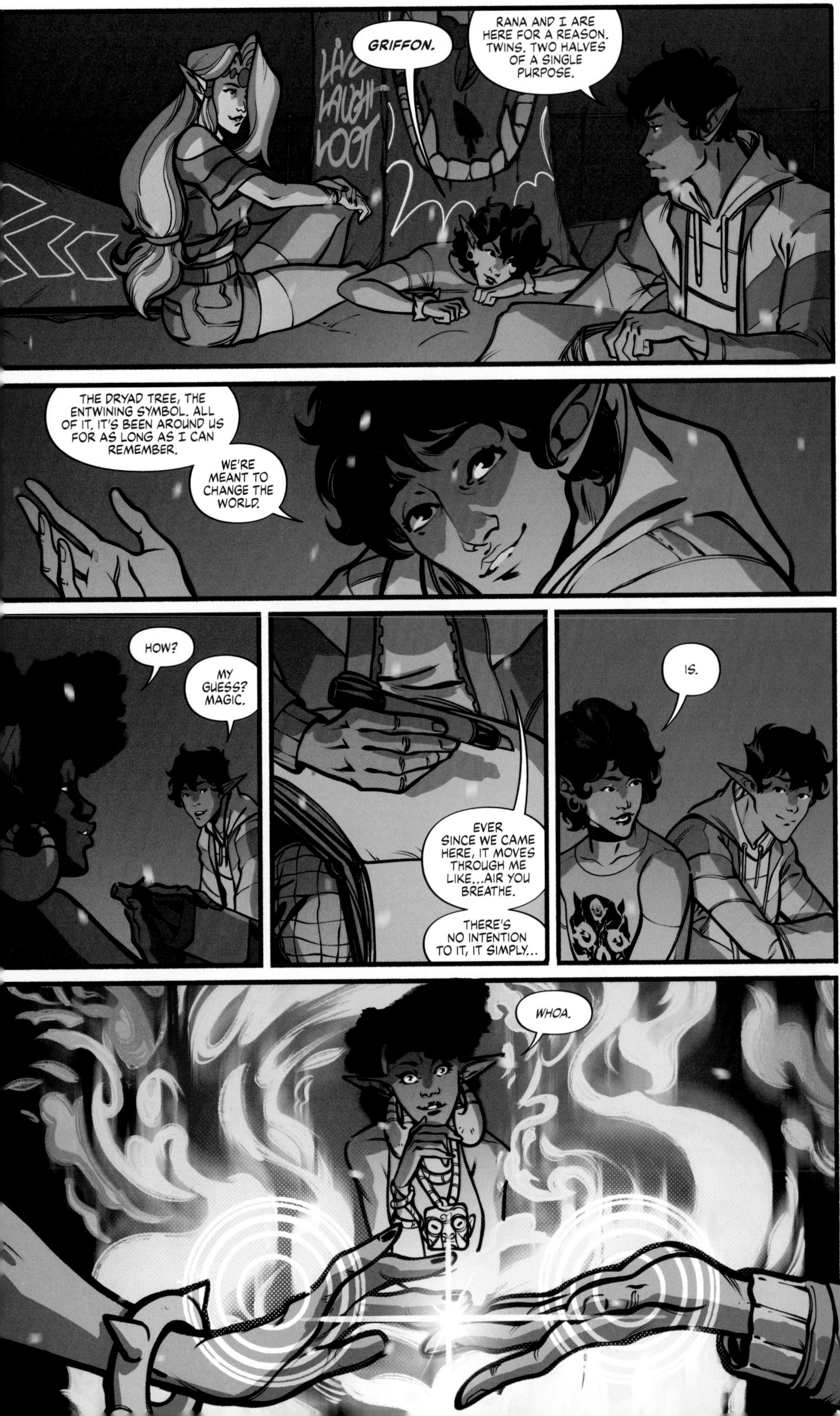
GRIFFON.
RANA AND I ARE HERE FOR A REASON. TWINS. TWO HALVES OF A SINGLE PURPOSE.
THE DRYAD TREE, THE ENTWINING SYMBOL. ALL OF IT. IT'S BEEN AROUND US FOR AS LONG AS I CAN REMEMBER.
WE'RE MEANT TO CHANGE THE WORLD.
HOW?
MY GUESS? MAGIC.
EVER SINCE WE CAME HERE, IT MOVES THROUGH ME LIKE...AIR YOU BREATHE.
THERE'S NO INTENTION TO IT, IT SIMPLY...
IS.
WHOA.

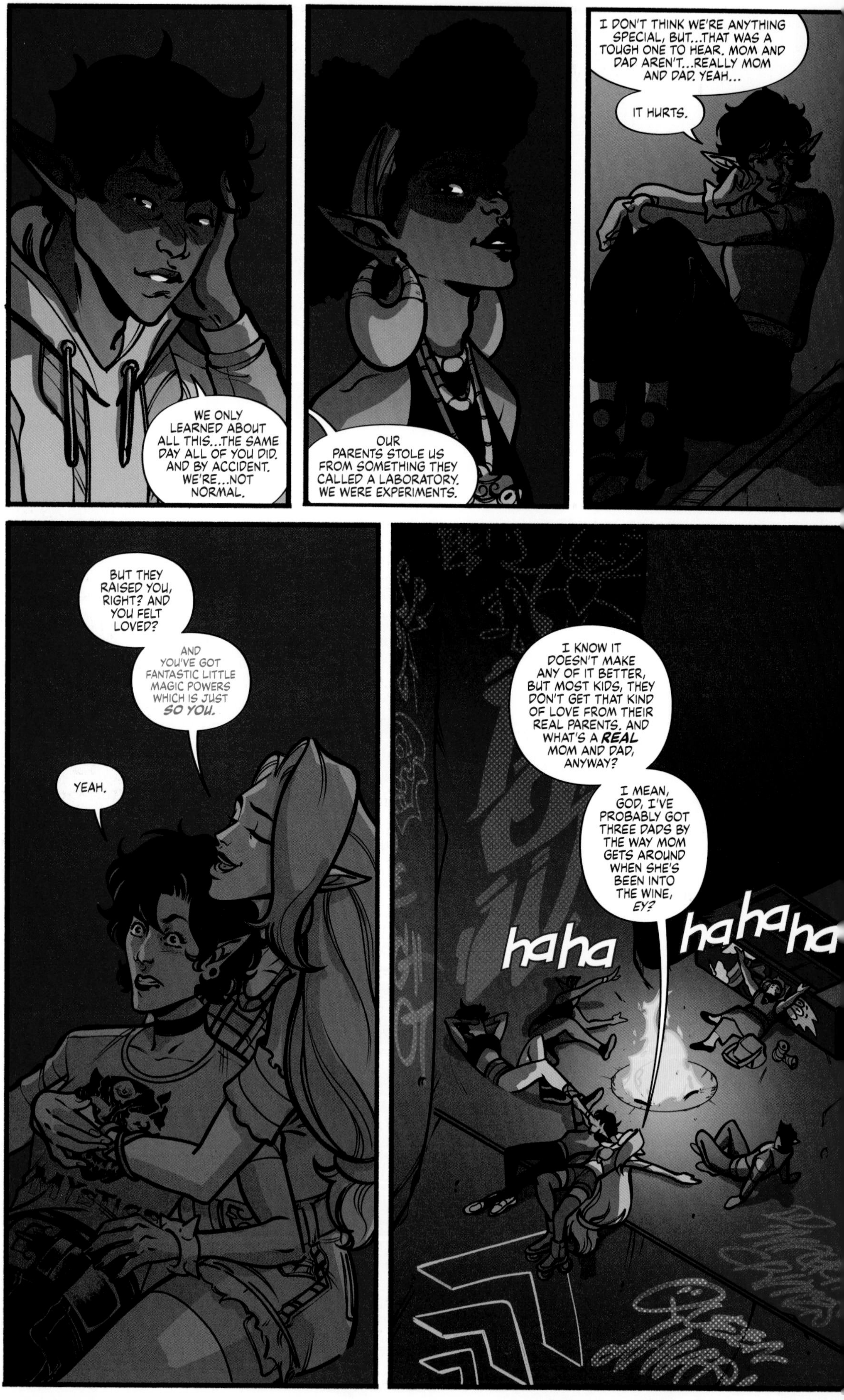
WE ONLY LEARNED ABOUT ALL THIS...THE SAME DAY ALL OF YOU DID. AND BY ACCIDENT. WE'RE...NOT NORMAL.
OUR PARENTS STOLE US FROM SOMETHING THEY CALLED A LABORATORY. WE WERE EXPERIMENTS.
I DON'T THINK WE'RE ANYTHING SPECIAL, BUT...THAT WAS A TOUGH ONE TO HEAR. MOM AND DAD AREN'T...REALLY MOM AND DAD. YEAH...
IT HURTS.
BUT THEY RAISED YOU, RIGHT? AND YOU FELT LOVED?
AND YOU'VE GOT FANTASTIC LITTLE MAGIC POWERS WHICH IS JUST *SO YOU.*
YEAH.
I KNOW IT DOESN'T MAKE ANY OF IT BETTER, BUT MOST KIDS, THEY DON'T GET THAT KIND OF LOVE FROM THEIR REAL PARENTS. AND WHAT'S A ***REAL*** MOM AND DAD, ANYWAY?
I MEAN, GOD, I'VE PROBABLY GOT THREE DADS BY THE WAY MOM GETS AROUND WHEN SHE'S BEEN INTO THE WINE, *EY?*
haha
hahaha

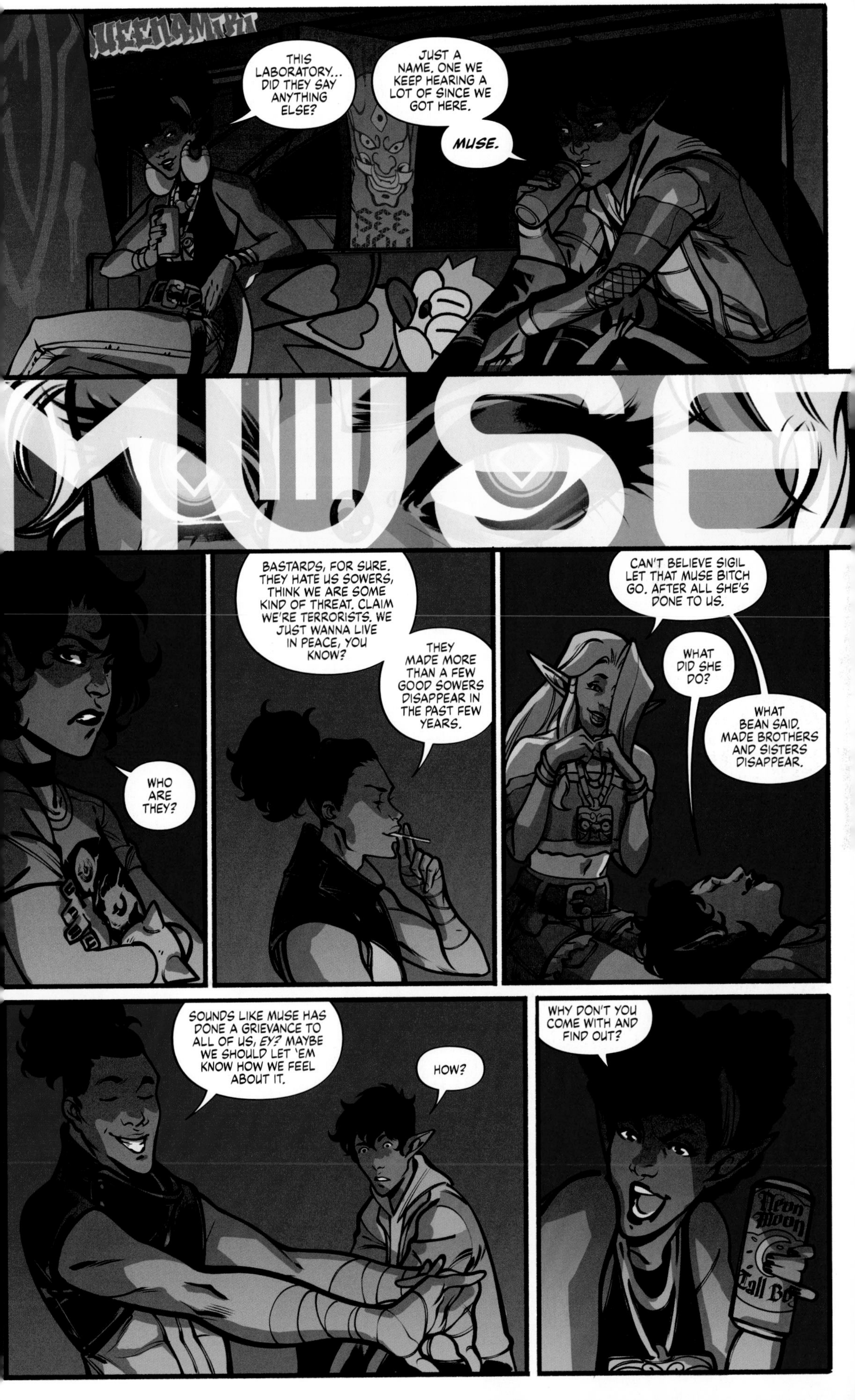

QUEENAMIBII
THIS LABORATORY... DID THEY SAY ANYTHING ELSE?
JUST A NAME. ONE WE KEEP HEARING A LOT OF SINCE WE GOT HERE.
MUSE.
MUSE
WHO ARE THEY?
BASTARDS, FOR SURE. THEY HATE US SOWERS, THINK WE ARE SOME KIND OF THREAT. CLAIM WE'RE TERRORISTS. WE JUST WANNA LIVE IN PEACE, YOU KNOW?
THEY MADE MORE THAN A FEW GOOD SOWERS DISAPPEAR IN THE PAST FEW YEARS.
CAN'T BELIEVE SIGIL LET THAT MUSE BITCH GO. AFTER ALL SHE'S DONE TO US.
WHAT DID SHE DO?
WHAT BEAN SAID. MADE BROTHERS AND SISTERS DISAPPEAR.
SOUNDS LIKE MUSE HAS DONE A GRIEVANCE TO ALL OF US, *EY?* MAYBE WE SHOULD LET 'EM KNOW HOW WE FEEL ABOUT IT.
HOW?
WHY DON'T YOU COME WITH AND FIND OUT?
Neon Moon
Tall Boy

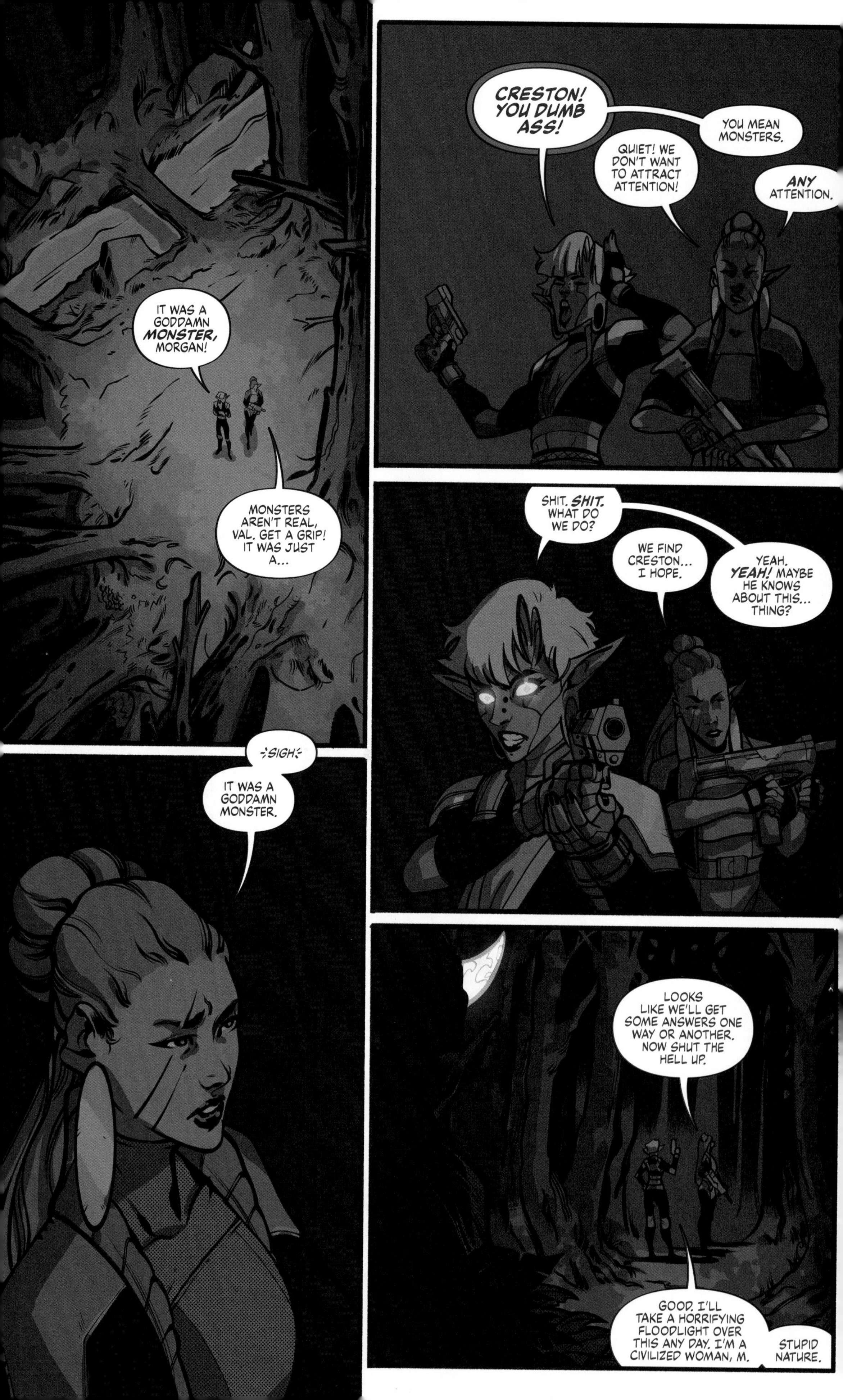
IT WAS A GODDAMN MONSTER, MORGAN!
MONSTERS AREN'T REAL, VAL. GET A GRIP! IT WAS JUST A...
CRESTON! YOU DUMB ASS!
QUIET! WE DON'T WANT TO ATTRACT ATTENTION!
YOU MEAN MONSTERS.
ANY ATTENTION.
SIGH
IT WAS A GODDAMN MONSTER.
SHIT. SHIT. WHAT DO WE DO?
WE FIND CRESTON... I HOPE.
YEAH. YEAH! MAYBE HE KNOWS ABOUT THIS... THING?
LOOKS LIKE WE'LL GET SOME ANSWERS ONE WAY OR ANOTHER. NOW SHUT THE HELL UP.
GOOD. I'LL TAKE A HORRIFYING FLOODLIGHT OVER THIS ANY DAY. I'M A CIVILIZED WOMAN, M.
STUPID NATURE.

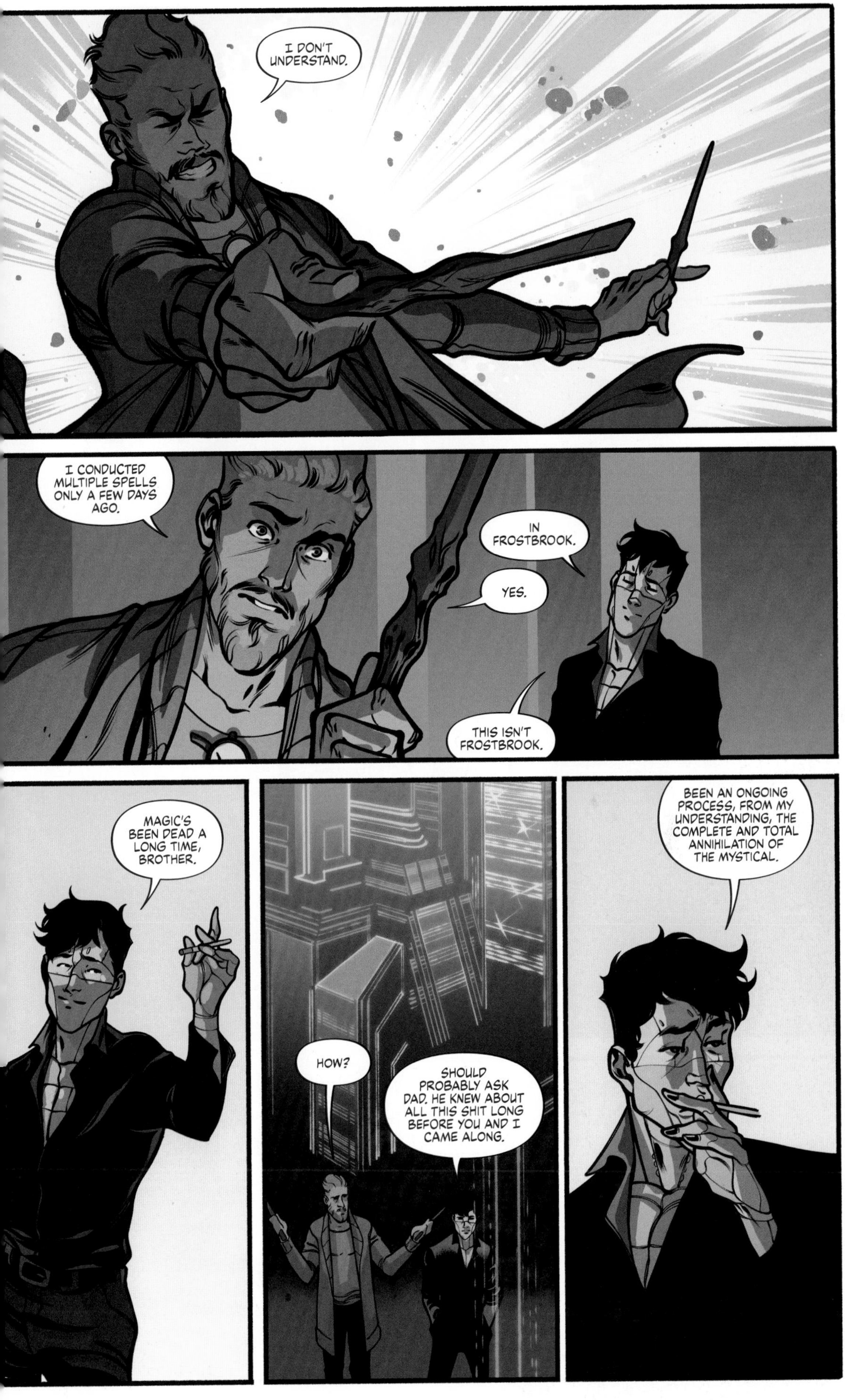
I DON'T UNDERSTAND.
I CONDUCTED MULTIPLE SPELLS ONLY A FEW DAYS AGO.
IN FROSTBROOK.
YES.
THIS ISN'T FROSTBROOK.
MAGIC'S BEEN DEAD A LONG TIME, BROTHER.
HOW?
SHOULD PROBABLY ASK DAD. HE KNEW ABOUT ALL THIS SHIT LONG BEFORE YOU AND I CAME ALONG.
BEEN AN ONGOING PROCESS, FROM MY UNDERSTANDING, THE COMPLETE AND TOTAL ANNIHILATION OF THE MYSTICAL.

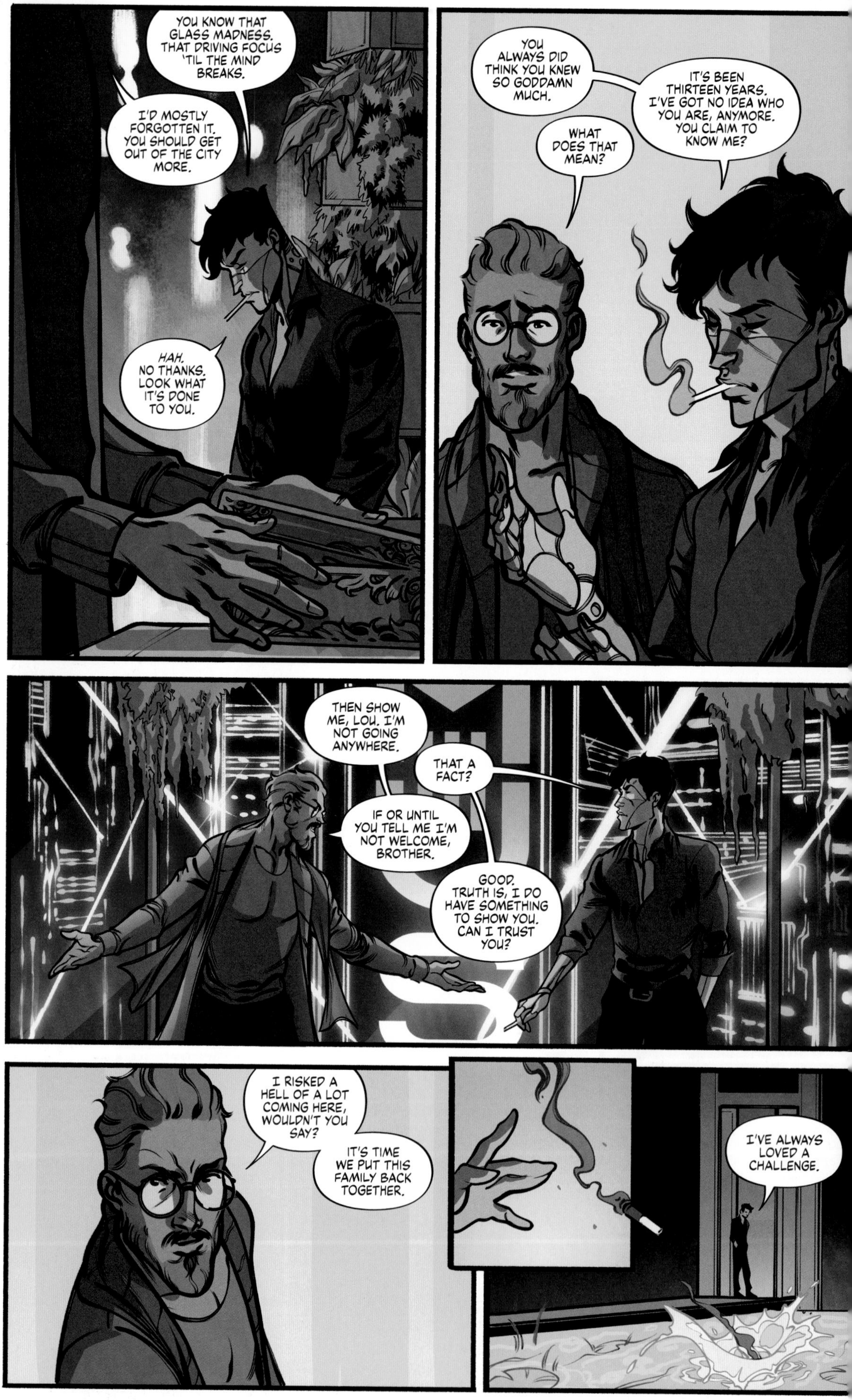
YOU KNOW THAT GLASS MADNESS. THAT DRIVING FOCUS 'TIL THE MIND BREAKS.
I'D MOSTLY FORGOTTEN IT. YOU SHOULD GET OUT OF THE CITY MORE.
HAH. NO THANKS. LOOK WHAT IT'S DONE TO YOU.
YOU ALWAYS DID THINK YOU KNEW SO GODDAMN MUCH.
WHAT DOES THAT MEAN?
IT'S BEEN THIRTEEN YEARS. I'VE GOT NO IDEA WHO YOU ARE, ANYMORE. YOU CLAIM TO KNOW ME?
THEN SHOW ME, LOU. I'M NOT GOING ANYWHERE.
THAT A FACT?
IF OR UNTIL YOU TELL ME I'M NOT WELCOME, BROTHER.
GOOD. TRUTH IS, I DO HAVE SOMETHING TO SHOW YOU. CAN I TRUST YOU?
I RISKED A HELL OF A LOT COMING HERE, WOULDN'T YOU SAY?
IT'S TIME WE PUT THIS FAMILY BACK TOGETHER.
I'VE ALWAYS LOVED A CHALLENGE.

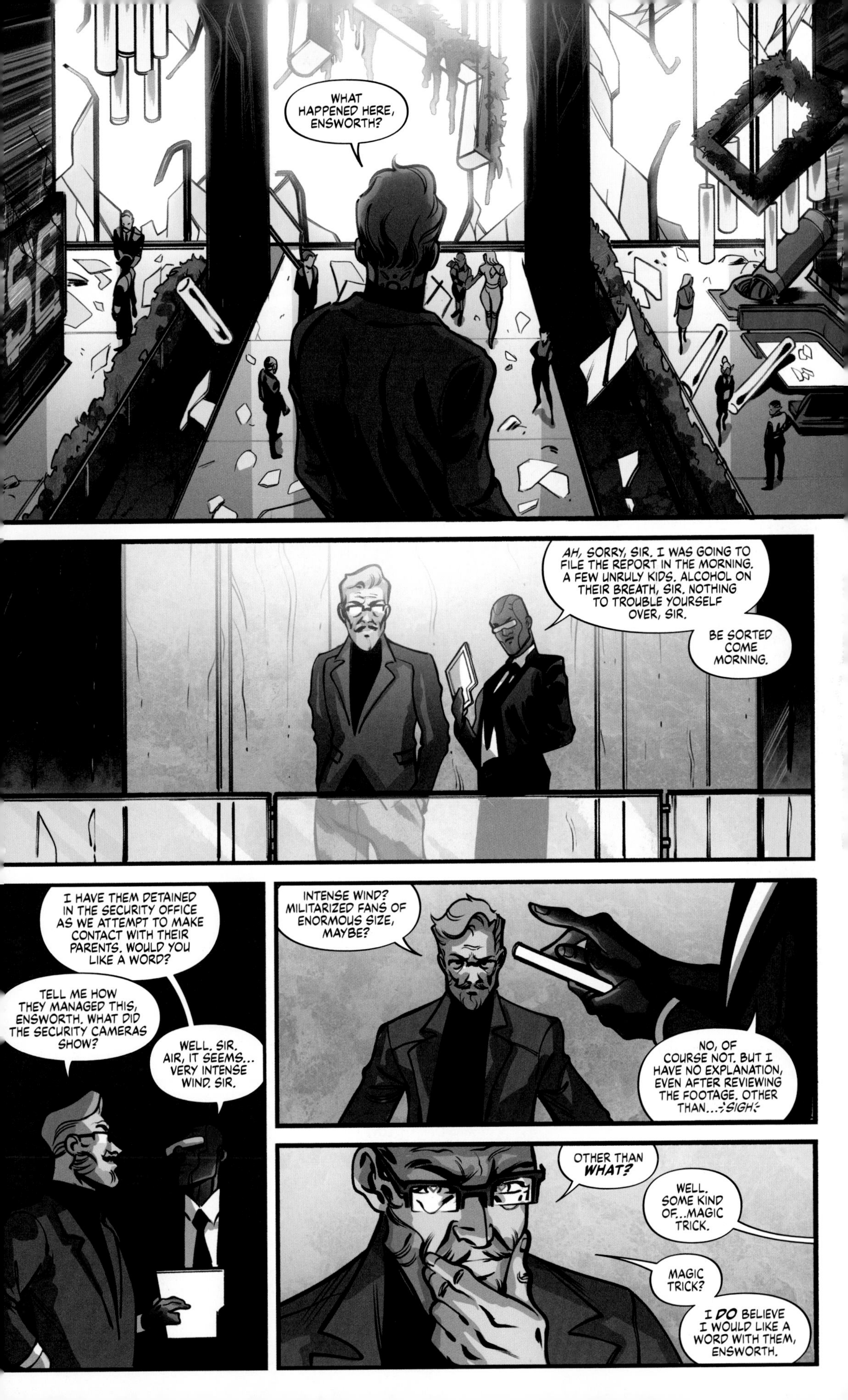
WHAT HAPPENED HERE, ENSWORTH?
AH, SORRY, SIR. I WAS GOING TO FILE THE REPORT IN THE MORNING. A FEW UNRULY KIDS. ALCOHOL ON THEIR BREATH, SIR. NOTHING TO TROUBLE YOURSELF OVER, SIR.
BE SORTED COME MORNING.
I HAVE THEM DETAINED IN THE SECURITY OFFICE AS WE ATTEMPT TO MAKE CONTACT WITH THEIR PARENTS. WOULD YOU LIKE A WORD?
TELL ME HOW THEY MANAGED THIS, ENSWORTH. WHAT DID THE SECURITY CAMERAS SHOW?
WELL, SIR. AIR, IT SEEMS... VERY INTENSE WIND, SIR.
INTENSE WIND? MILITARIZED FANS OF ENORMOUS SIZE, MAYBE?
NO, OF COURSE NOT. BUT I HAVE NO EXPLANATION, EVEN AFTER REVIEWING THE FOOTAGE. OTHER THAN... SIGH
OTHER THAN *WHAT?*
WELL. SOME KIND OF...MAGIC TRICK.
MAGIC TRICK?
I *DO* BELIEVE I WOULD LIKE A WORD WITH THEM, ENSWORTH.

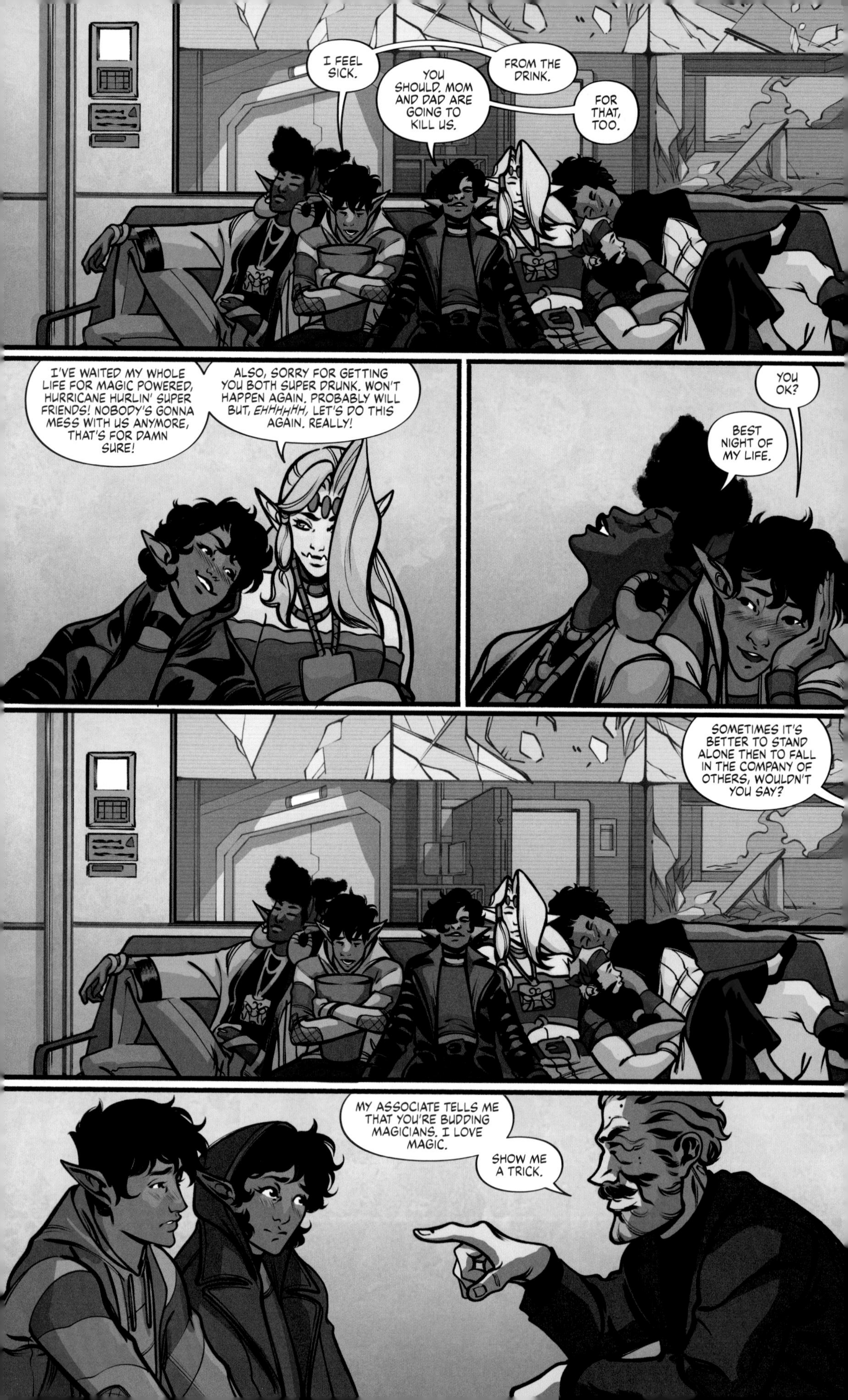
I FEEL SICK.
YOU SHOULD. MOM AND DAD ARE GOING TO KILL US.
FROM THE DRINK.
FOR THAT, TOO.
I'VE WAITED MY WHOLE LIFE FOR MAGIC POWERED, HURRICANE HURLIN' SUPER FRIENDS! NOBODY'S GONNA MESS WITH US ANYMORE, THAT'S FOR DAMN SURE!
ALSO, SORRY FOR GETTING YOU BOTH SUPER DRUNK. WON'T HAPPEN AGAIN. PROBABLY WILL BUT, *EHHHHHH,* LET'S DO THIS AGAIN. REALLY!
YOU OK?
BEST NIGHT OF MY LIFE.
SOMETIMES IT'S BETTER TO STAND ALONE THEN TO FALL IN THE COMPANY OF OTHERS, WOULDN'T YOU SAY?
MY ASSOCIATE TELLS ME THAT YOU'RE BUDDING MAGICIANS. I LOVE MAGIC.
SHOW ME A TRICK.

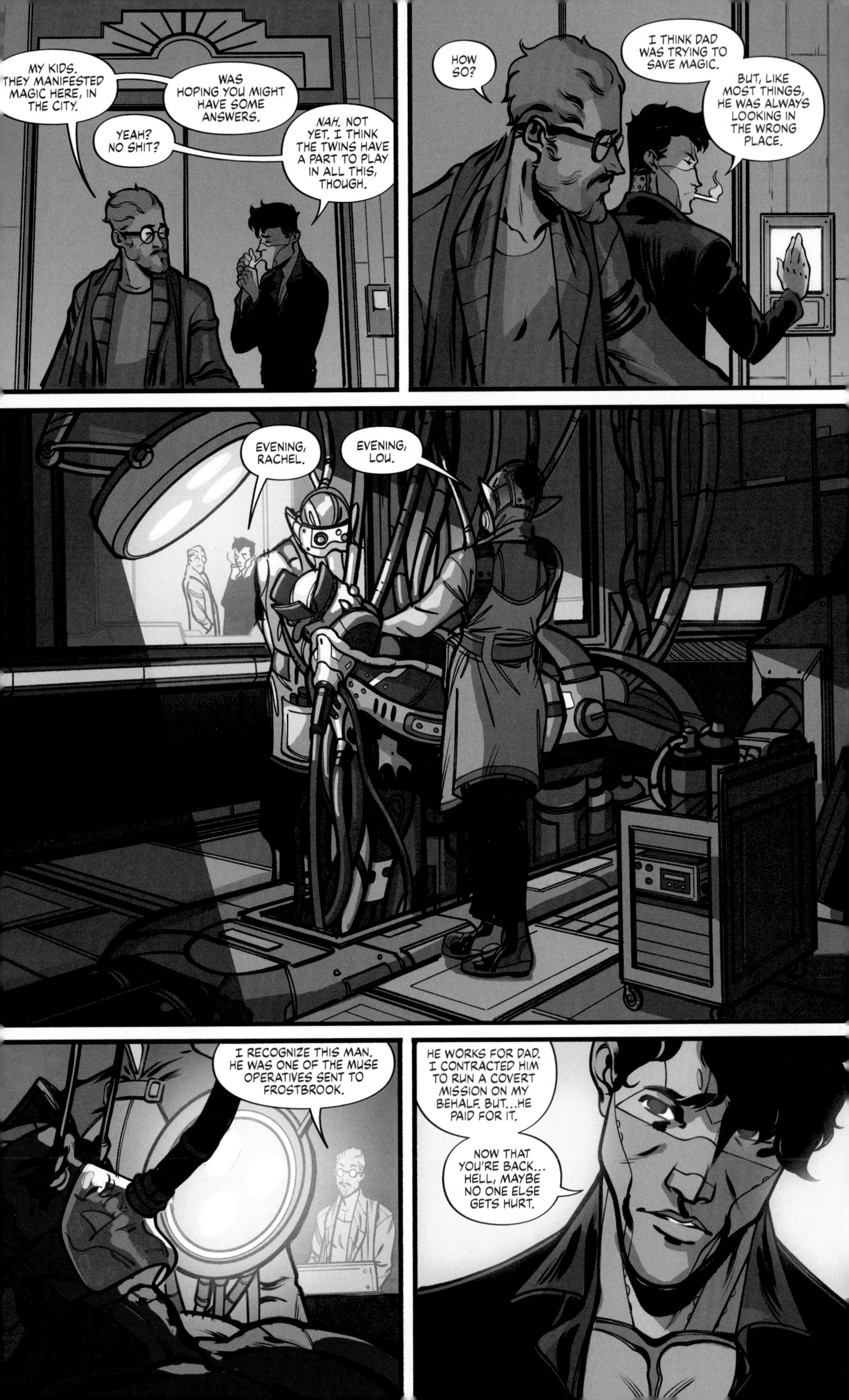
MY KIDS. THEY MANIFESTED MAGIC HERE, IN THE CITY.
WAS HOPING YOU MIGHT HAVE SOME ANSWERS.
YEAH? NO SHIT?
NAH. NOT YET. I THINK THE TWINS HAVE A PART TO PLAY IN ALL THIS, THOUGH.
HOW SO?
I THINK DAD WAS TRYING TO SAVE MAGIC.
BUT, LIKE MOST THINGS, HE WAS ALWAYS LOOKING IN THE WRONG PLACE.
EVENING, RACHEL.
EVENING, LOU.
I RECOGNIZE THIS MAN. HE WAS ONE OF THE MUSE OPERATIVES SENT TO FROSTBROOK.
HE WORKS FOR DAD. I CONTRACTED HIM TO RUN A COVERT MISSION ON MY BEHALF. BUT...HE PAID FOR IT.
NOW THAT YOU'RE BACK... HELL, MAYBE NO ONE ELSE GETS HURT.

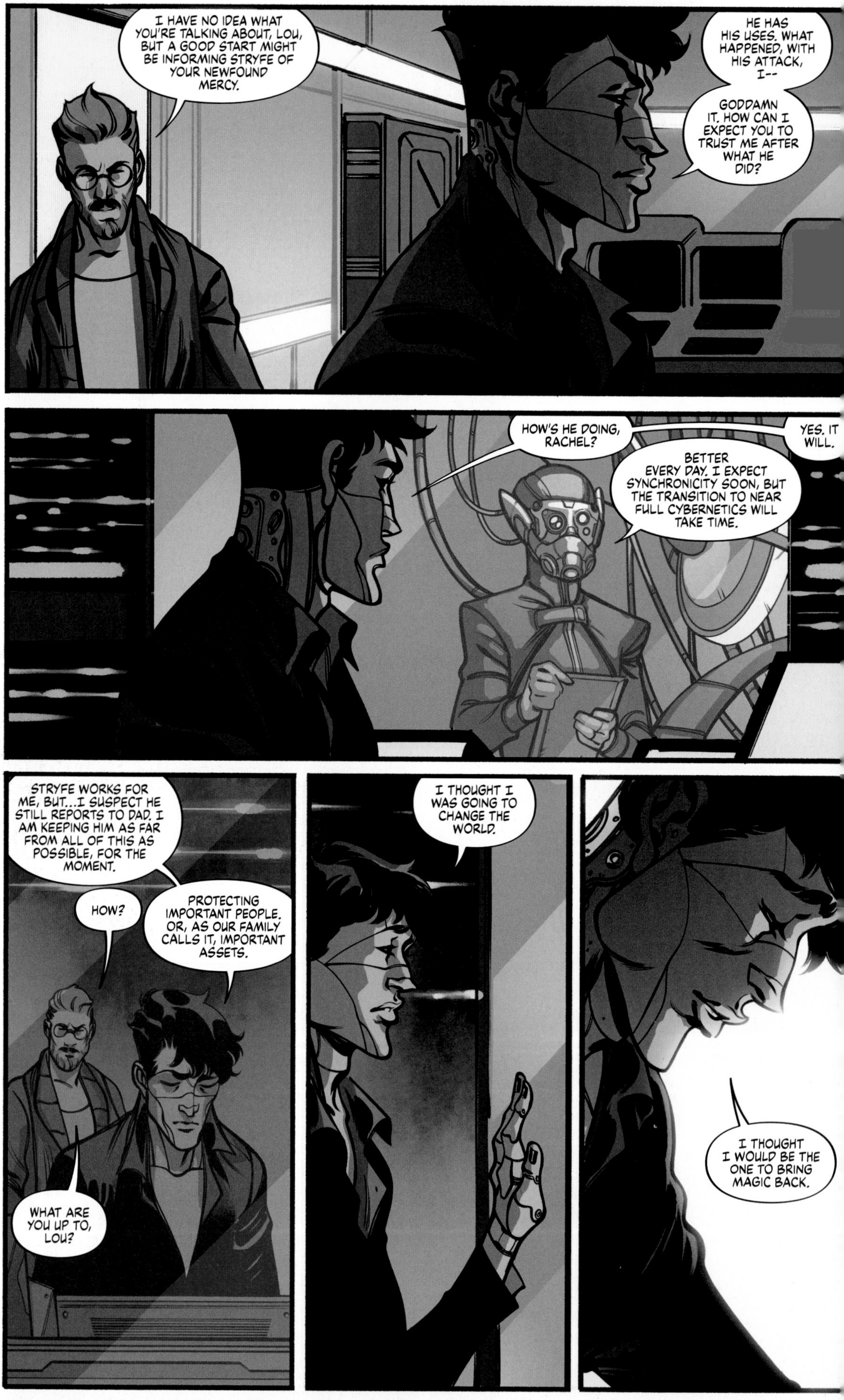
I HAVE NO IDEA WHAT YOU'RE TALKING ABOUT, LOU, BUT A GOOD START MIGHT BE INFORMING STRYFE OF YOUR NEWFOUND MERCY.
HE HAS HIS USES. WHAT HAPPENED, WITH HIS ATTACK, I--
GODDAMN IT. HOW CAN I EXPECT YOU TO TRUST ME AFTER WHAT HE DID?
HOW'S HE DOING, RACHEL?
BETTER EVERY DAY. I EXPECT SYNCHRONICITY SOON, BUT THE TRANSITION TO NEAR FULL CYBERNETICS WILL TAKE TIME.
YES. IT WILL.
STRYFE WORKS FOR ME, BUT...I SUSPECT HE STILL REPORTS TO DAD. I AM KEEPING HIM AS FAR FROM ALL OF THIS AS POSSIBLE, FOR THE MOMENT.
HOW?
PROTECTING IMPORTANT PEOPLE. OR, AS OUR FAMILY CALLS IT, IMPORTANT ASSETS.
WHAT ARE YOU UP TO, LOU?
I THOUGHT I WAS GOING TO CHANGE THE WORLD.
I THOUGHT I WOULD BE THE ONE TO BRING MAGIC BACK.

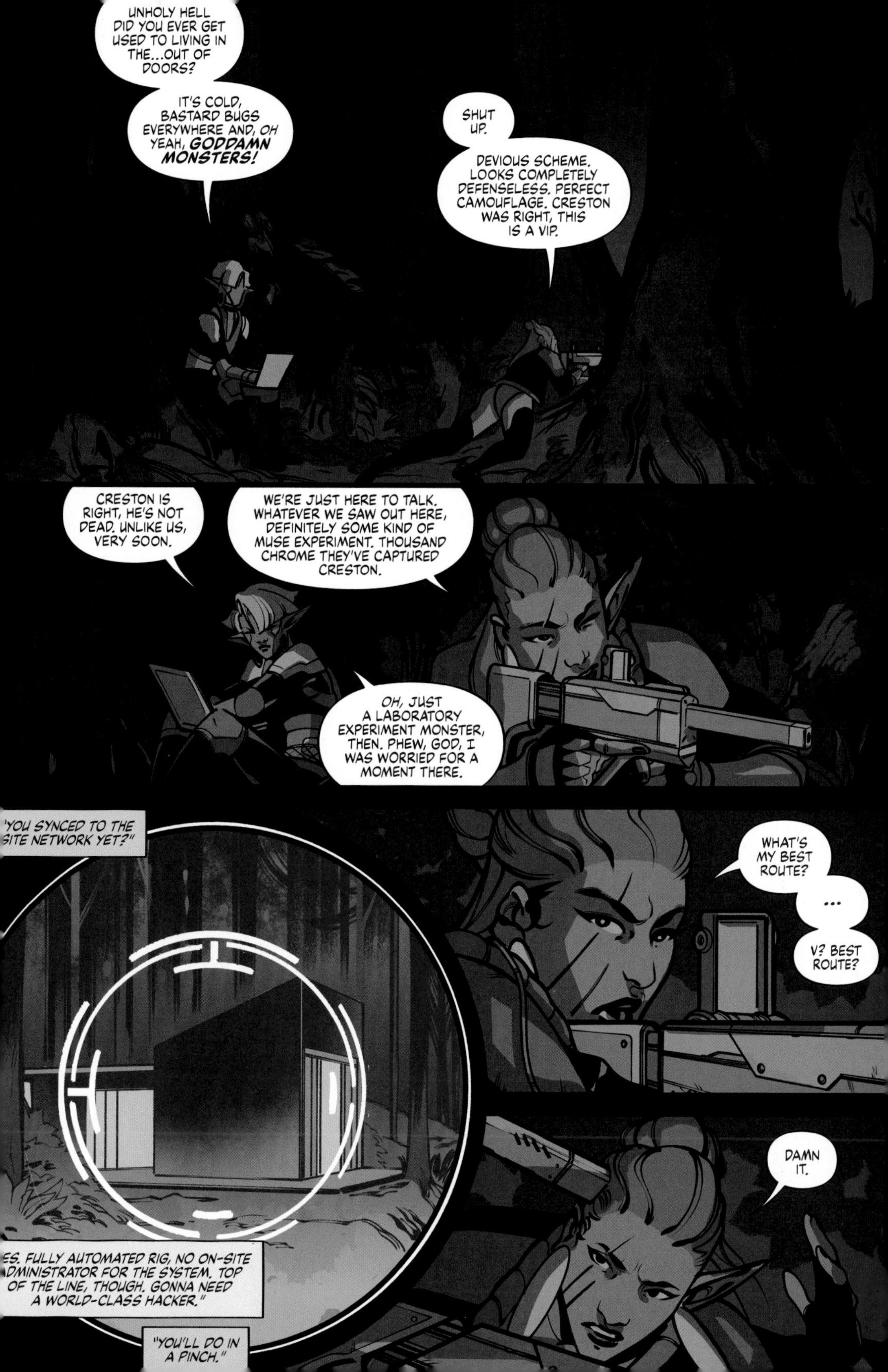
UNHOLY HELL DID YOU EVER GET USED TO LIVING IN THE...OUT OF DOORS?
IT'S COLD, BASTARD BUGS EVERYWHERE AND, OH YEAH, GODDAMN MONSTERS!
SHUT UP.
DEVIOUS SCHEME. LOOKS COMPLETELY DEFENSELESS. PERFECT CAMOUFLAGE. CRESTON WAS RIGHT, THIS IS A VIP.
CRESTON IS RIGHT, HE'S NOT DEAD. UNLIKE US, VERY SOON.
WE'RE JUST HERE TO TALK. WHATEVER WE SAW OUT HERE, DEFINITELY SOME KIND OF MUSE EXPERIMENT. THOUSAND CHROME THEY'VE CAPTURED CRESTON.
OH, JUST A LABORATORY EXPERIMENT MONSTER, THEN. PHEW, GOD, I WAS WORRIED FOR A MOMENT THERE.
"YOU SYNCED TO THE SITE NETWORK YET?"
WHAT'S MY BEST ROUTE?
...
V? BEST ROUTE?
ES. FULLY AUTOMATED RIG, NO ON-SITE DMINISTRATOR FOR THE SYSTEM. TOP OF THE LINE, THOUGH. GONNA NEED A WORLD-CLASS HACKER."
DAMN IT.
"YOU'LL DO IN A PINCH."

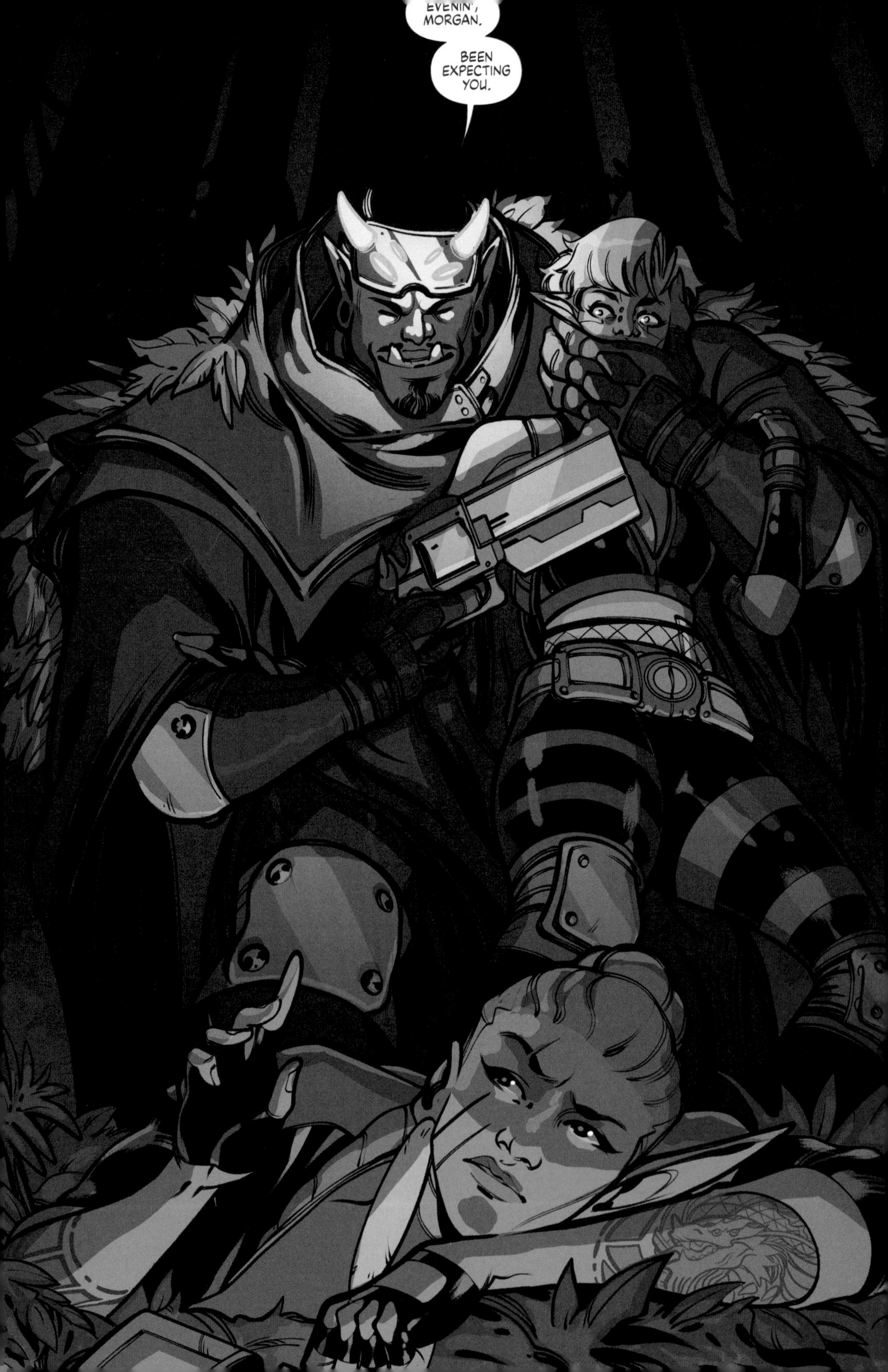
EVENIN', MORGAN.
BEEN EXPECTING YOU.

CHAPTER NINE

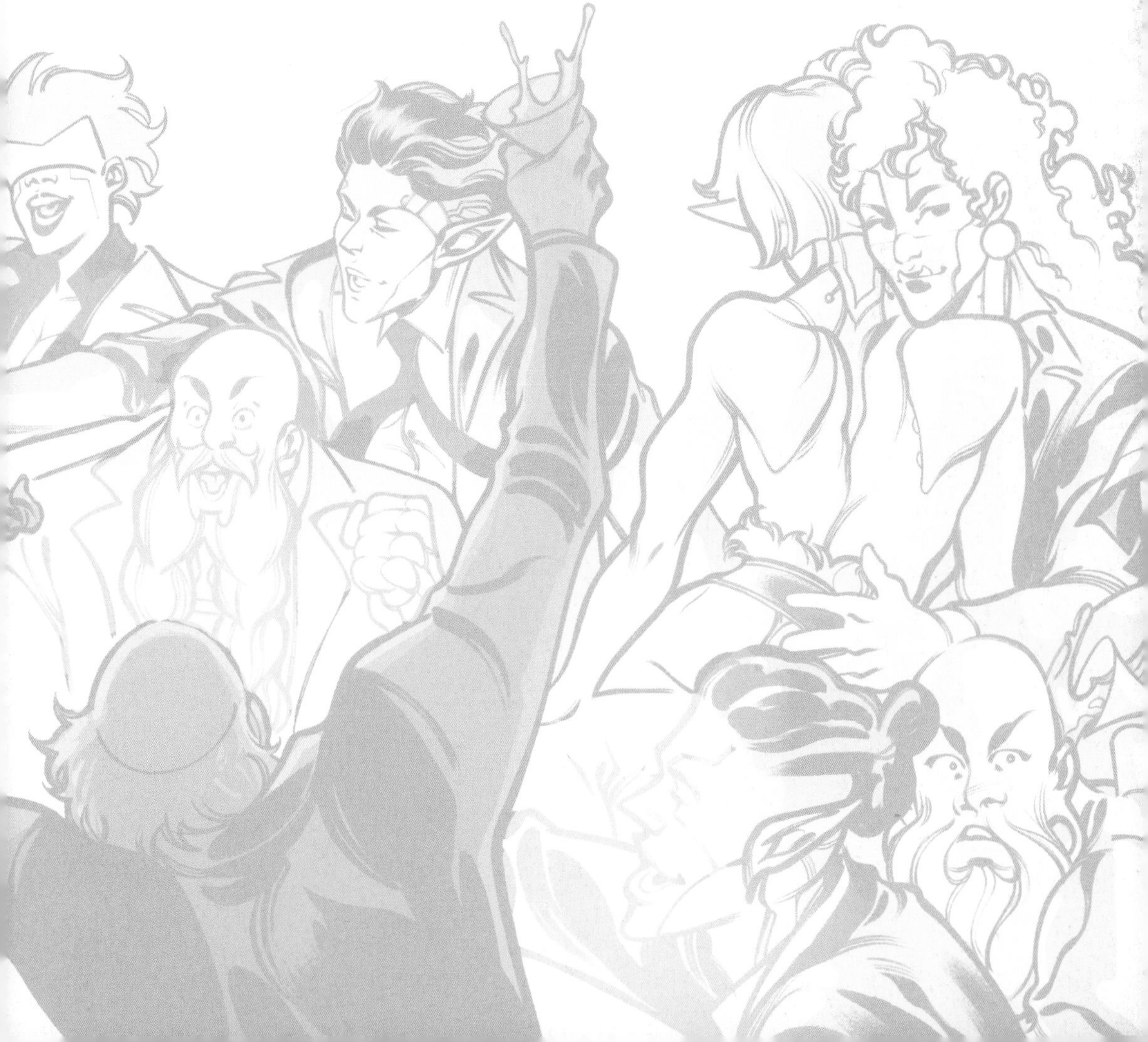

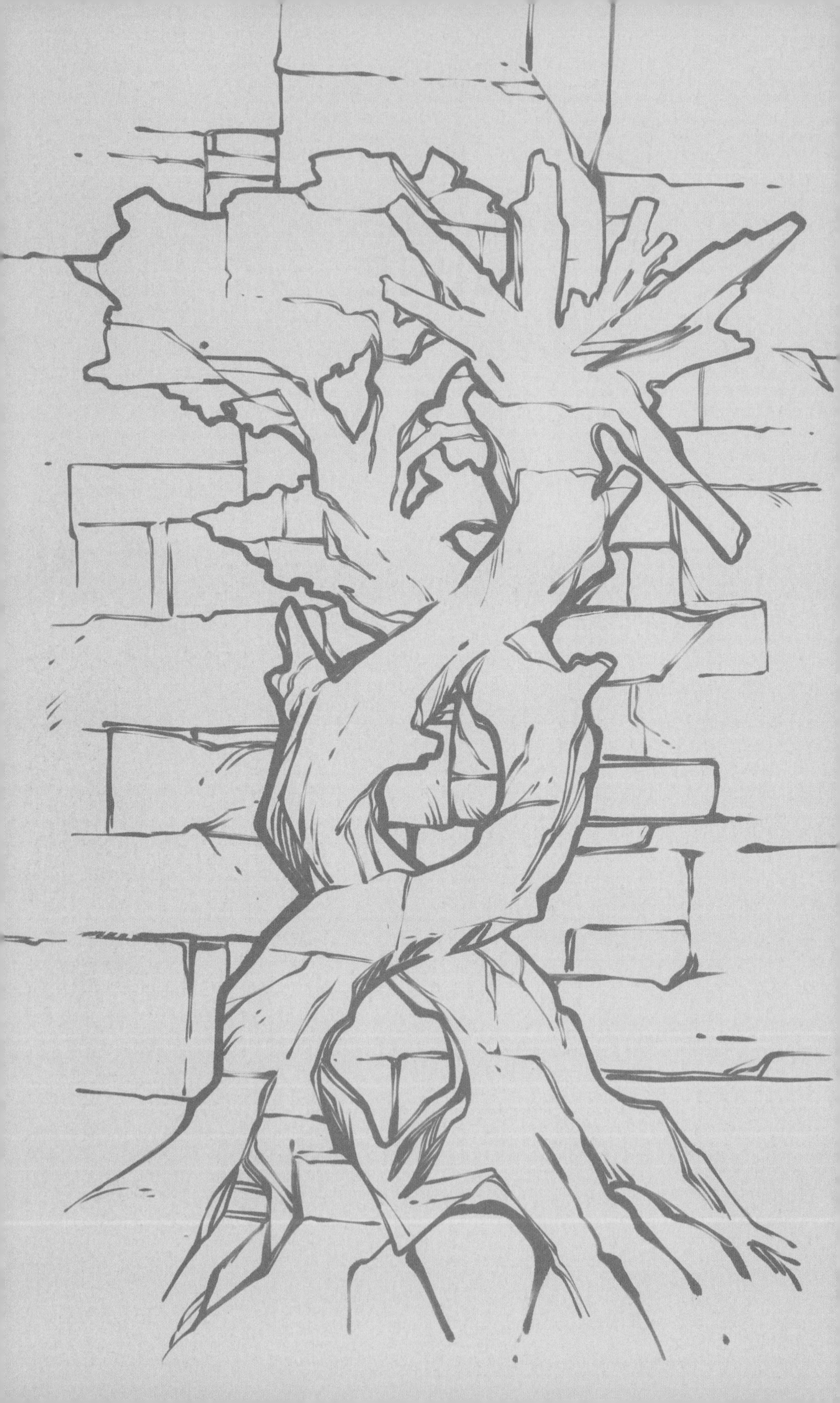

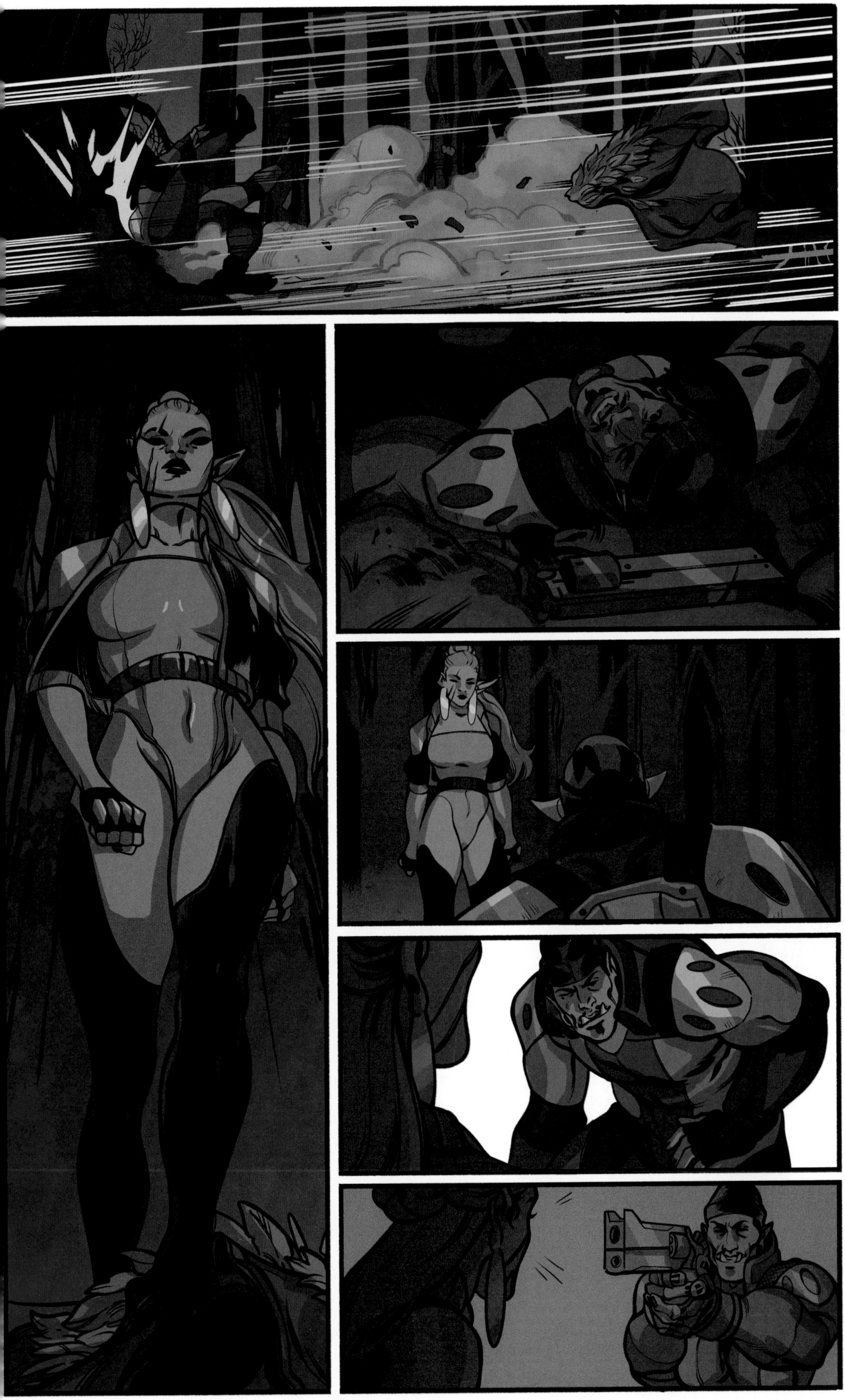

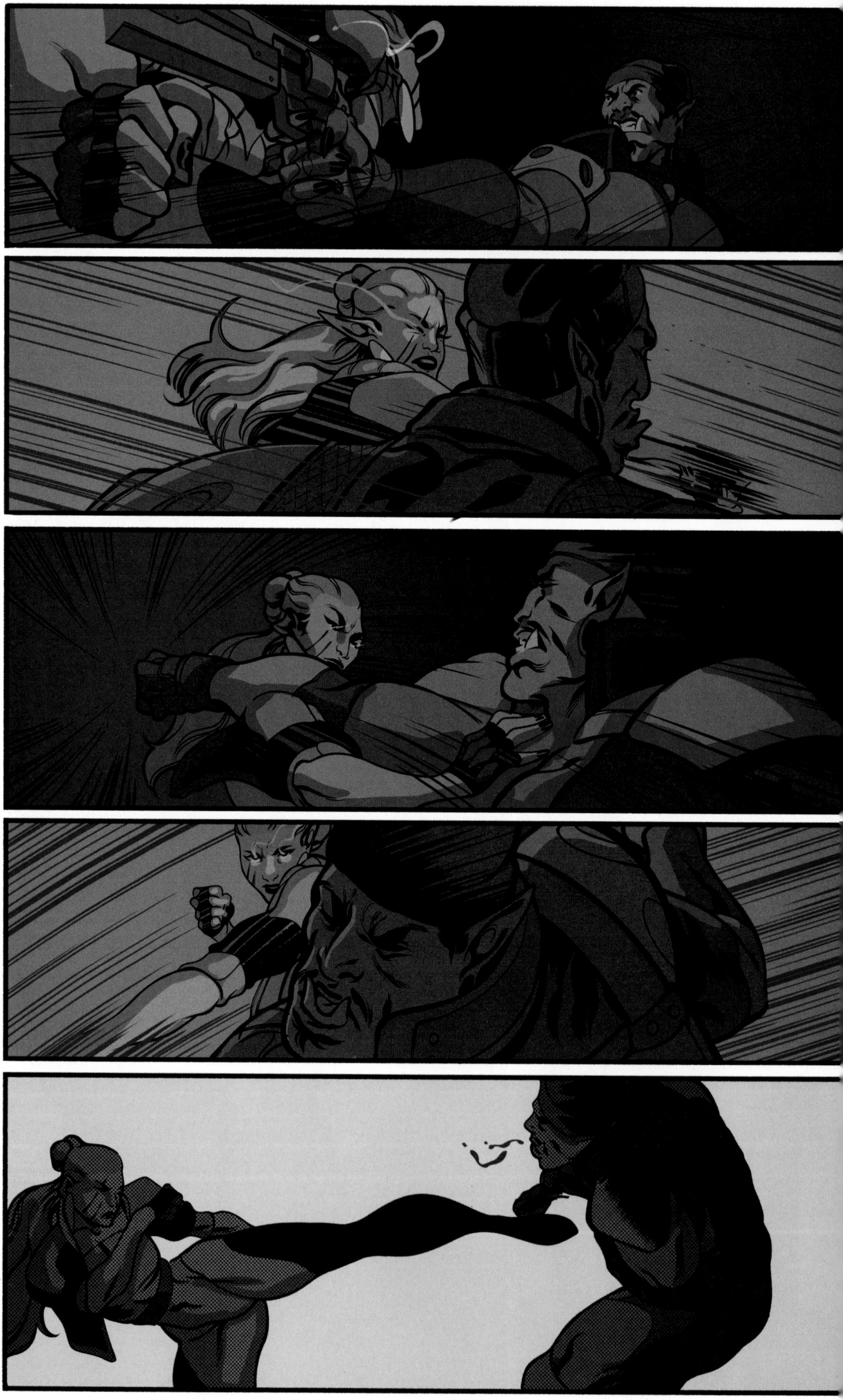

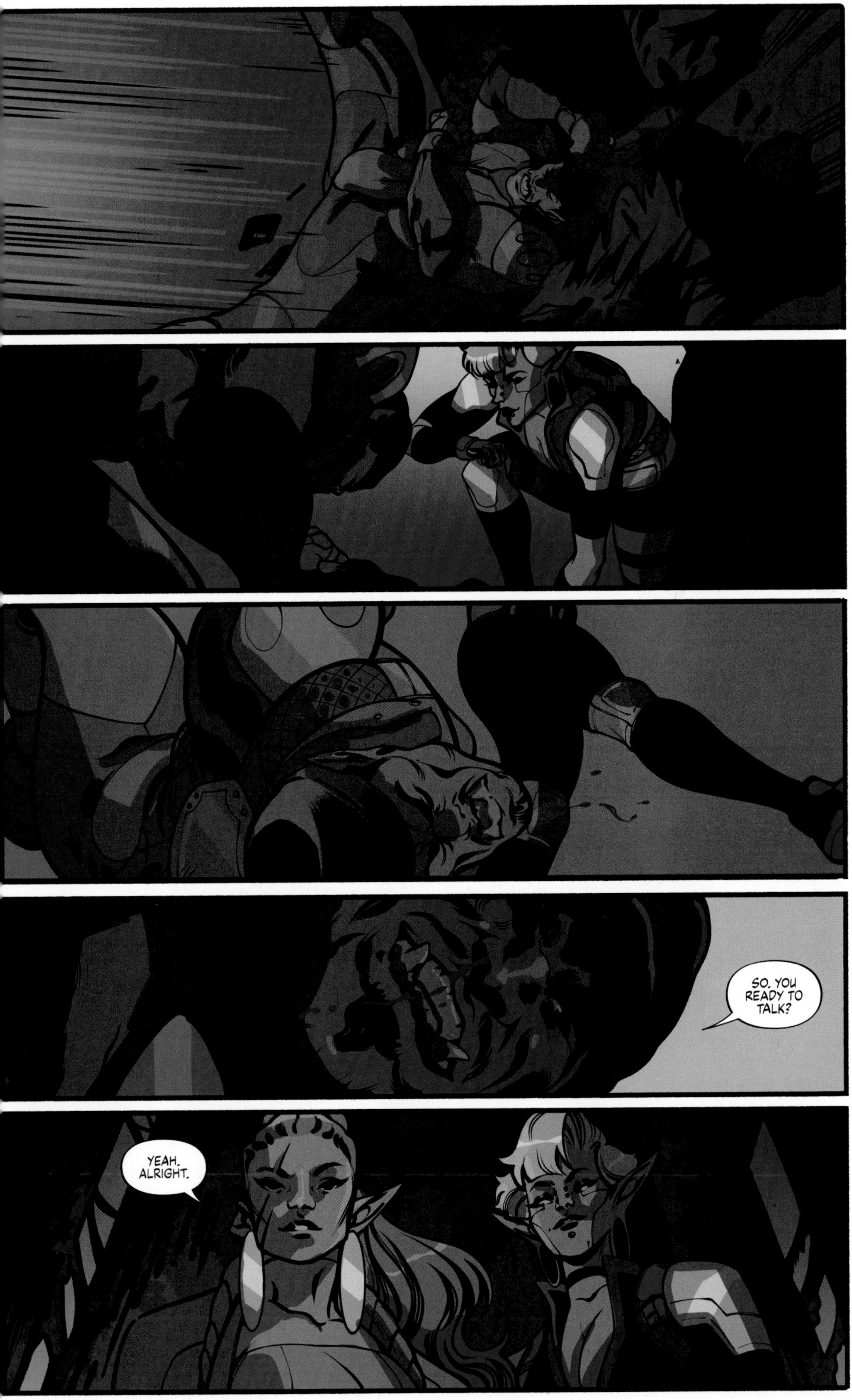
SO. YOU READY TO TALK?
YEAH. ALRIGHT.

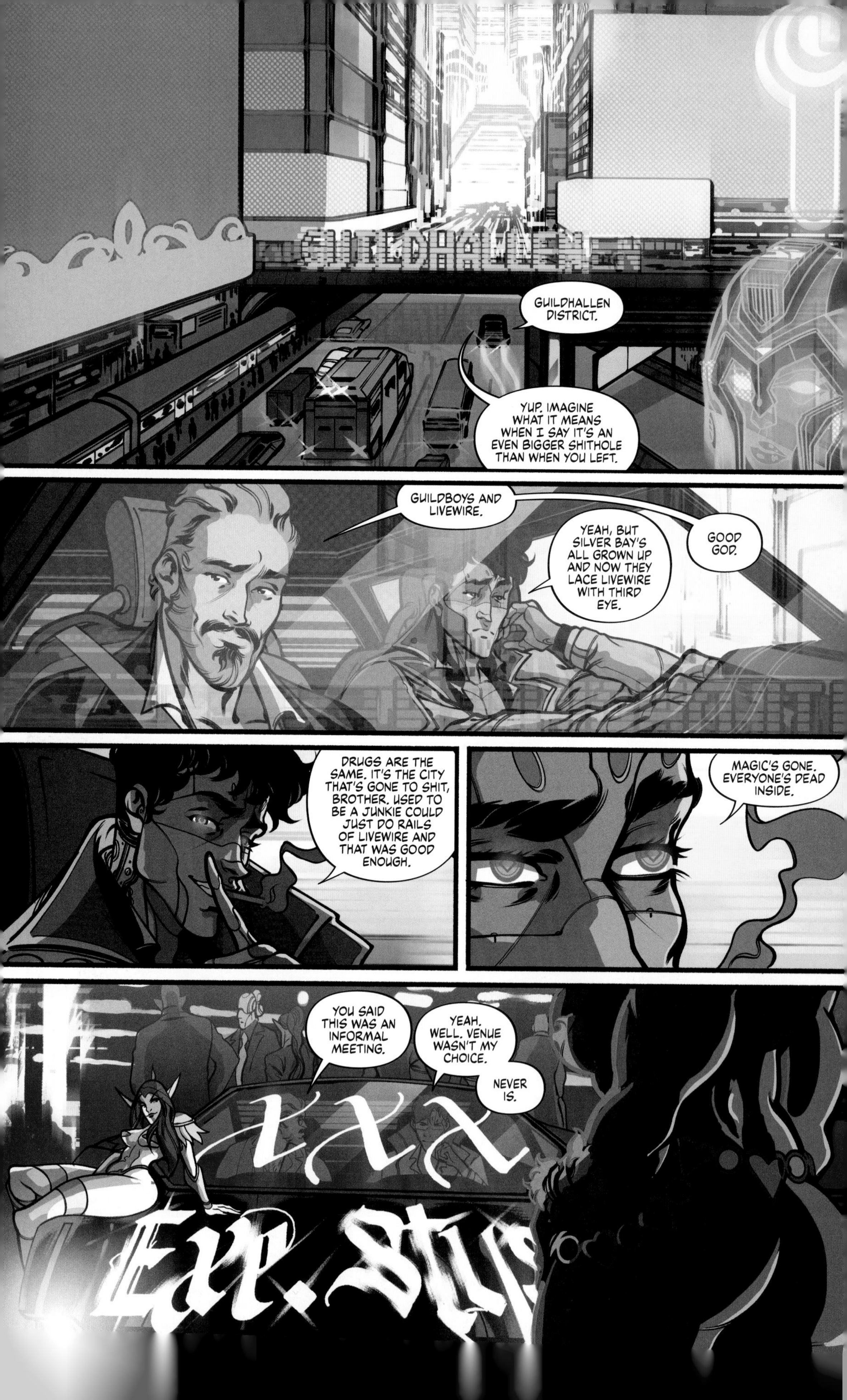
GUILDHALLEN
GUILDHALLEN DISTRICT.
YUP. IMAGINE WHAT IT MEANS WHEN I SAY IT'S AN EVEN BIGGER SHITHOLE THAN WHEN YOU LEFT.
GUILDBOYS AND LIVEWIRE.
YEAH, BUT SILVER BAY'S ALL GROWN UP AND NOW THEY LACE LIVEWIRE WITH THIRD EYE.
GOOD GOD.
DRUGS ARE THE SAME. IT'S THE CITY THAT'S GONE TO SHIT, BROTHER. USED TO BE A JUNKIE COULD JUST DO RAILS OF LIVEWIRE AND THAT WAS GOOD ENOUGH.
MAGIC'S GONE. EVERYONE'S DEAD INSIDE.
YOU SAID THIS WAS AN INFORMAL MEETING.
YEAH. WELL. VENUE WASN'T MY CHOICE.
NEVER IS.
XXX

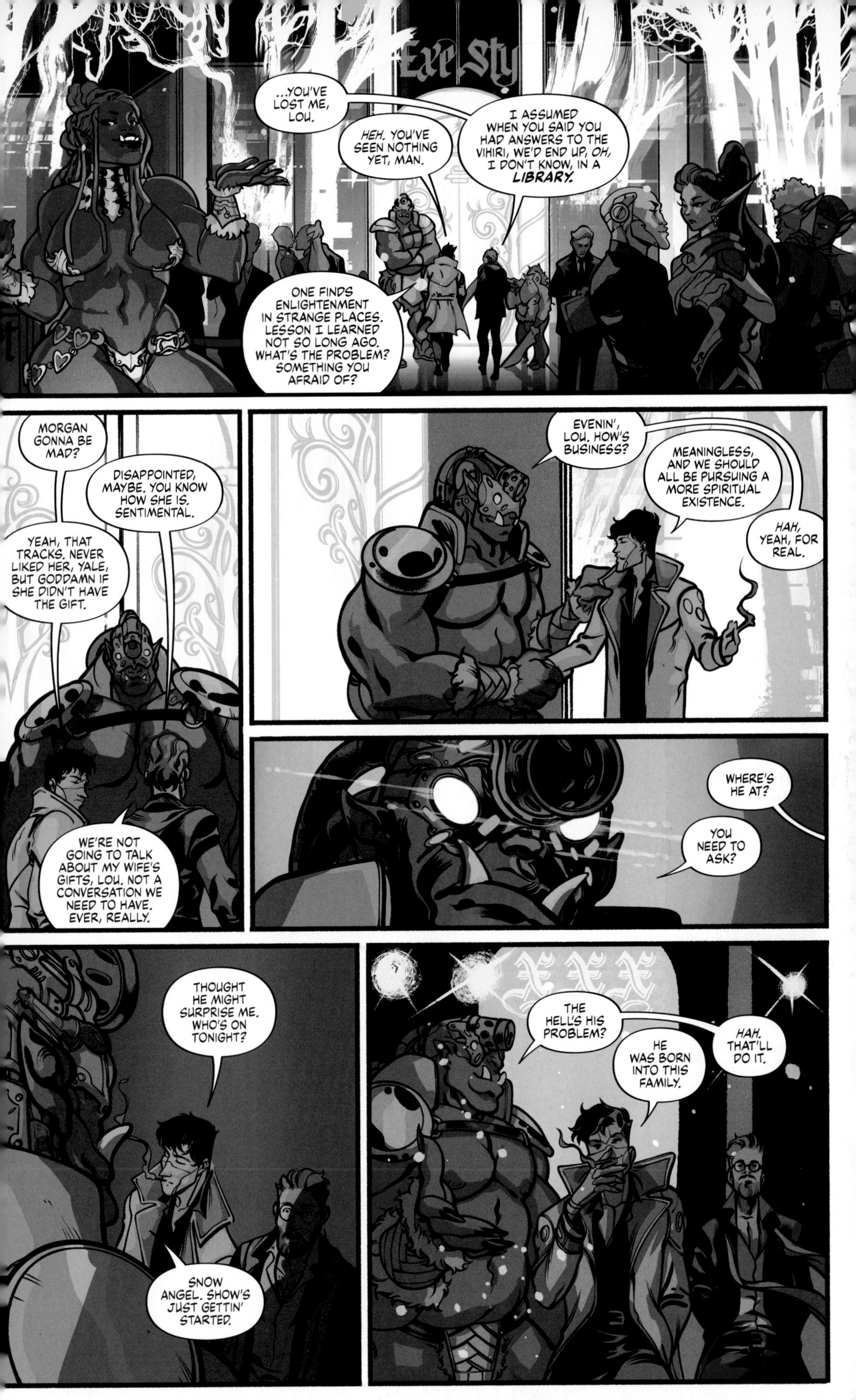
...YOU'VE LOST ME, LOU.
I ASSUMED WHEN YOU SAID YOU HAD ANSWERS TO THE VIHIRI, WE'D END UP, OH, I DON'T KNOW, IN A LIBRARY.
HEH. YOU'VE SEEN NOTHING YET, MAN.
ONE FINDS ENLIGHTENMENT IN STRANGE PLACES. LESSON I LEARNED NOT SO LONG AGO. WHAT'S THE PROBLEM? SOMETHING YOU AFRAID OF?
MORGAN GONNA BE MAD?
DISAPPOINTED, MAYBE. YOU KNOW HOW SHE IS. SENTIMENTAL.
YEAH, THAT TRACKS. NEVER LIKED HER, YALE, BUT GODDAMN IF SHE DIDN'T HAVE THE GIFT.
WE'RE NOT GOING TO TALK ABOUT MY WIFE'S GIFTS, LOU. NOT A CONVERSATION WE NEED TO HAVE. EVER, REALLY.
EVENIN', LOU. HOW'S BUSINESS?
MEANINGLESS, AND WE SHOULD ALL BE PURSUING A MORE SPIRITUAL EXISTENCE.
HAH, YEAH, FOR REAL.
WHERE'S HE AT?
YOU NEED TO ASK?
THOUGHT HE MIGHT SURPRISE ME. WHO'S ON TONIGHT?
SNOW ANGEL. SHOW'S JUST GETTIN' STARTED.
THE HELL'S HIS PROBLEM?
HE WAS BORN INTO THIS FAMILY.
HAH. THAT'LL DO IT.

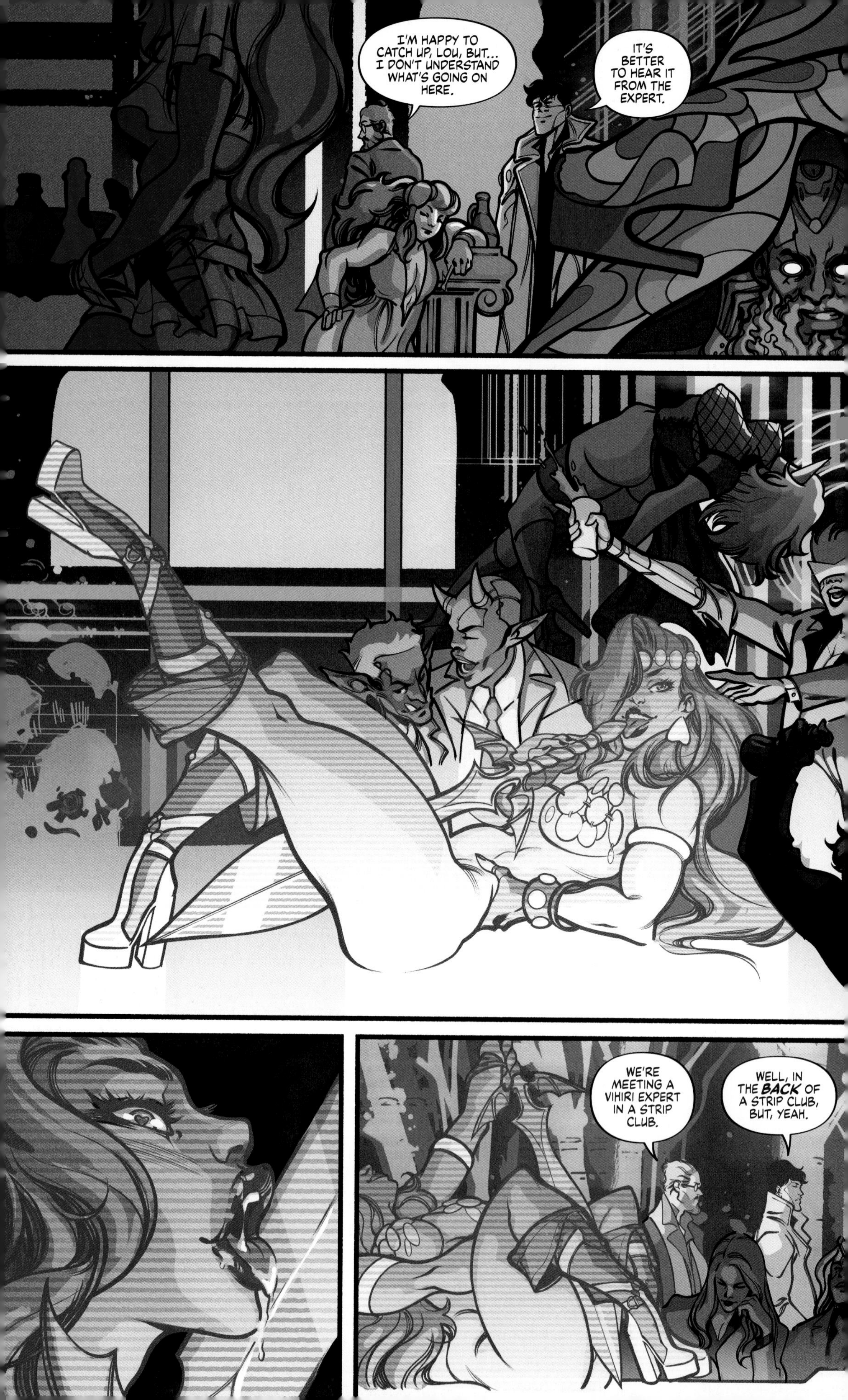
I'M HAPPY TO CATCH UP, LOU, BUT... I DON'T UNDERSTAND WHAT'S GOING ON HERE.
IT'S BETTER TO HEAR IT FROM THE EXPERT.
WE'RE MEETING A VIHIRI EXPERT IN A STRIP CLUB.
WELL, IN THE BACK OF A STRIP CLUB, BUT, YEAH.

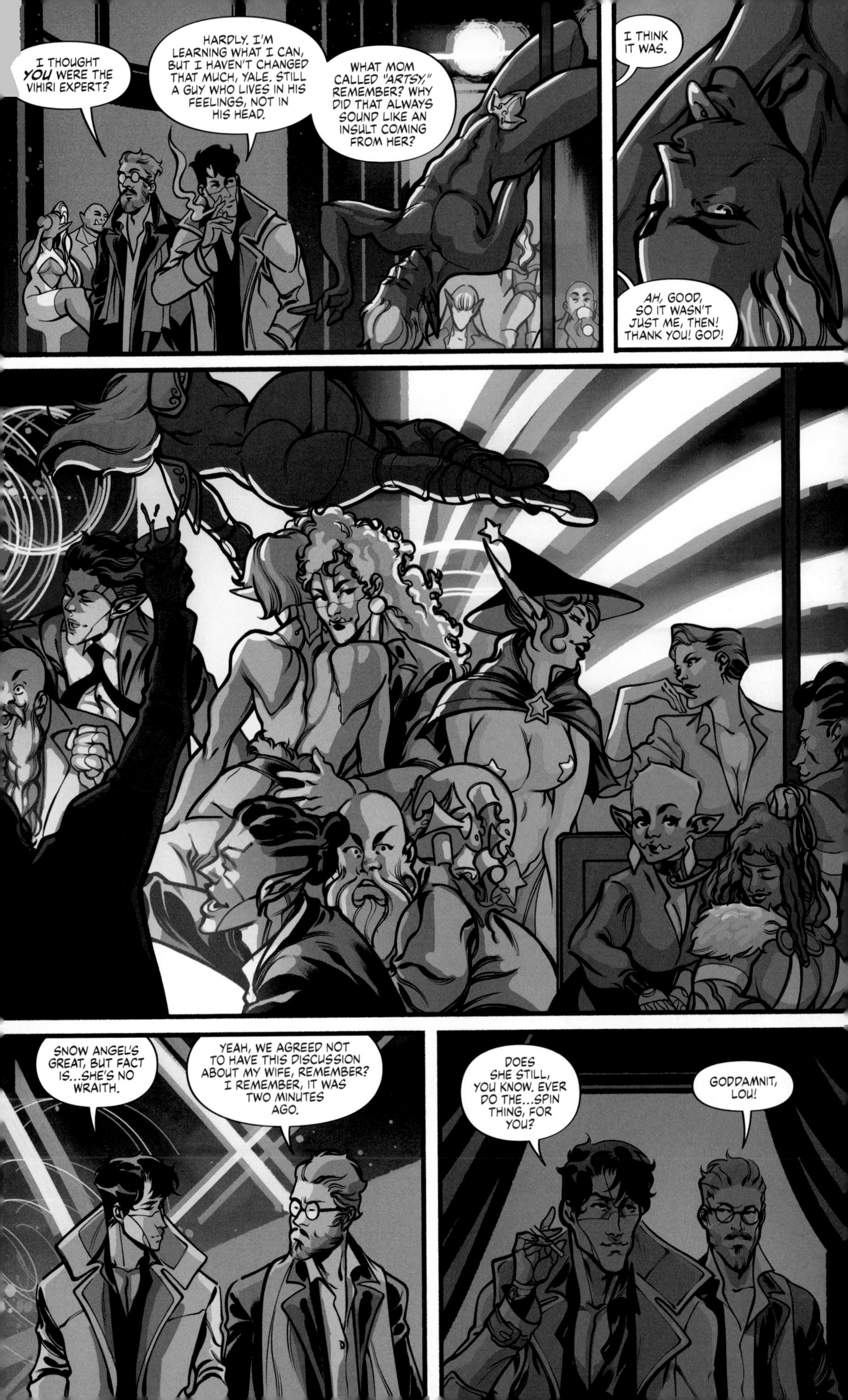

I THOUGHT YOU WERE THE VIHIRI EXPERT?
HARDLY. I'M LEARNING WHAT I CAN, BUT I HAVEN'T CHANGED THAT MUCH, YALE. STILL A GUY WHO LIVES IN HIS FEELINGS, NOT IN HIS HEAD.
WHAT MOM CALLED "ARTSY," REMEMBER? WHY DID THAT ALWAYS SOUND LIKE AN INSULT COMING FROM HER?
I THINK IT WAS.
AH, GOOD, SO IT WASN'T JUST ME, THEN! THANK YOU! GOD!
SNOW ANGEL'S GREAT, BUT FACT IS...SHE'S NO WRAITH.
YEAH, WE AGREED NOT TO HAVE THIS DISCUSSION ABOUT MY WIFE, REMEMBER? I REMEMBER, IT WAS TWO MINUTES AGO.
DOES SHE STILL, YOU KNOW. EVER DO THE...SPIN THING, FOR YOU?
GODDAMNIT, LOU!

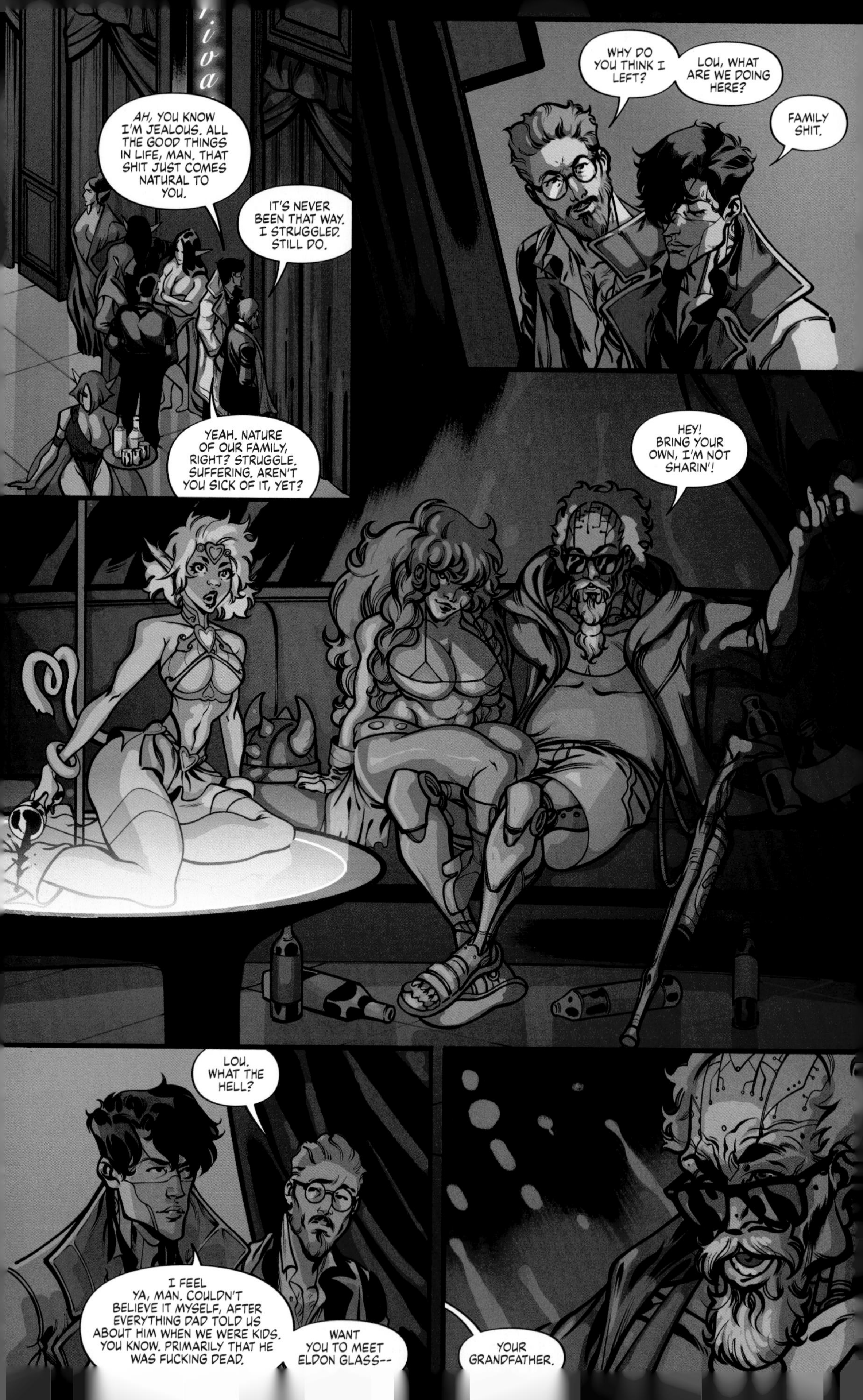
AH, YOU KNOW I'M JEALOUS. ALL THE GOOD THINGS IN LIFE, MAN. THAT SHIT JUST COMES NATURAL TO YOU.
IT'S NEVER BEEN THAT WAY. I STRUGGLED. STILL DO.
YEAH. NATURE OF OUR FAMILY, RIGHT? STRUGGLE. SUFFERING. AREN'T YOU SICK OF IT, YET?
WHY DO YOU THINK I LEFT?
LOU, WHAT ARE WE DOING HERE?
FAMILY SHIT.
HEY! BRING YOUR OWN, I'M NOT SHARIN'!
LOU. WHAT THE HELL?
I FEEL YA, MAN. COULDN'T BELIEVE IT MYSELF, AFTER EVERYTHING DAD TOLD US ABOUT HIM WHEN WE WERE KIDS. YOU KNOW. PRIMARILY THAT HE WAS FUCKING DEAD.
WANT YOU TO MEET ELDON GLASS--
YOUR GRANDFATHER.

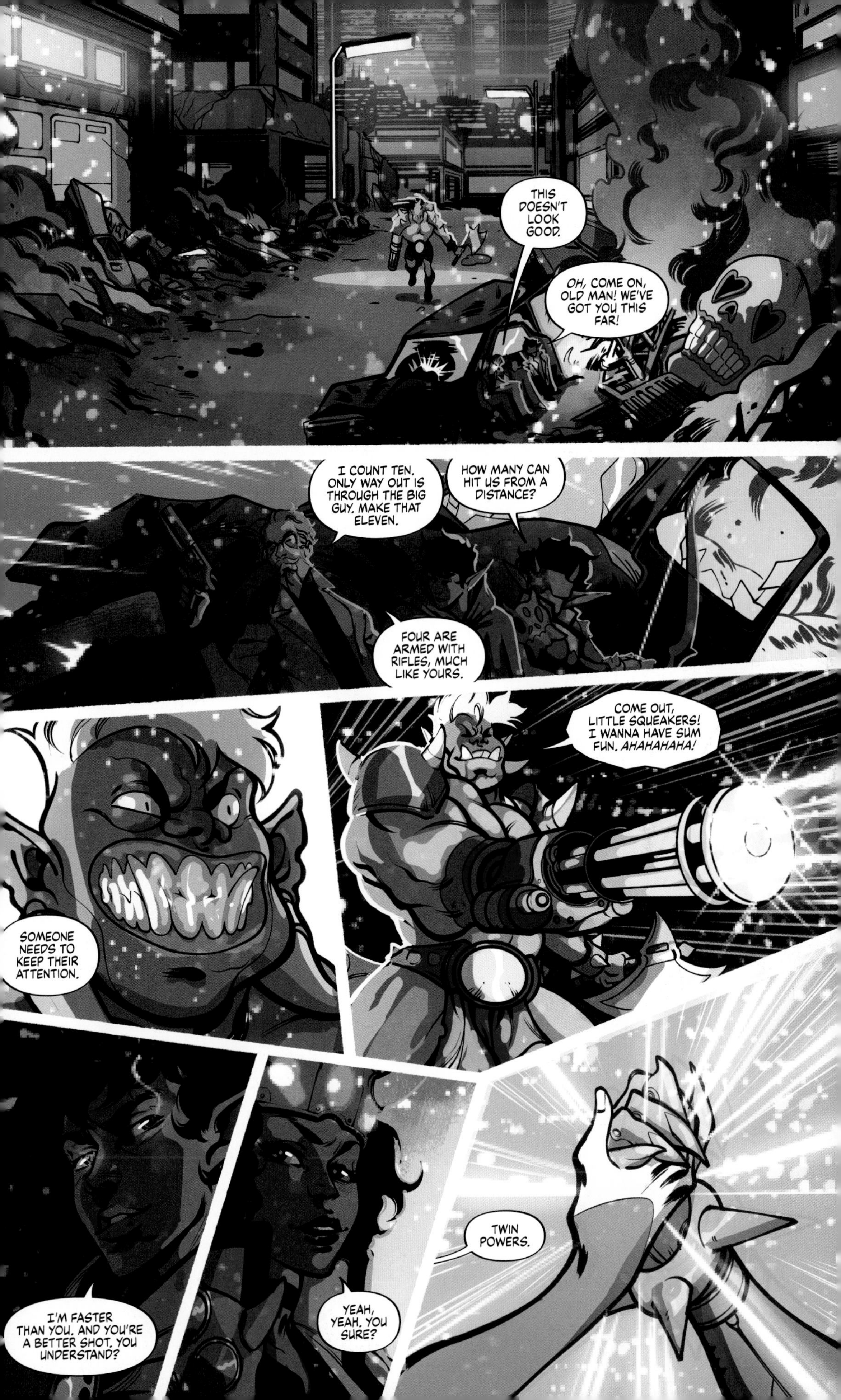

THIS DOESN'T LOOK GOOD.
OH, COME ON, OLD MAN! WE'VE GOT YOU THIS FAR!
I COUNT TEN. ONLY WAY OUT IS THROUGH THE BIG GUY. MAKE THAT ELEVEN.
HOW MANY CAN HIT US FROM A DISTANCE?
FOUR ARE ARMED WITH RIFLES, MUCH LIKE YOURS.
COME OUT, LITTLE SQUEAKERS! I WANNA HAVE SUM FUN. *AHAHAHAHA!*
SOMEONE NEEDS TO KEEP THEIR ATTENTION.
I'M FASTER THAN YOU. AND YOU'RE A BETTER SHOT. YOU UNDERSTAND?
YEAH, YEAH. YOU SURE?
TWIN POWERS.

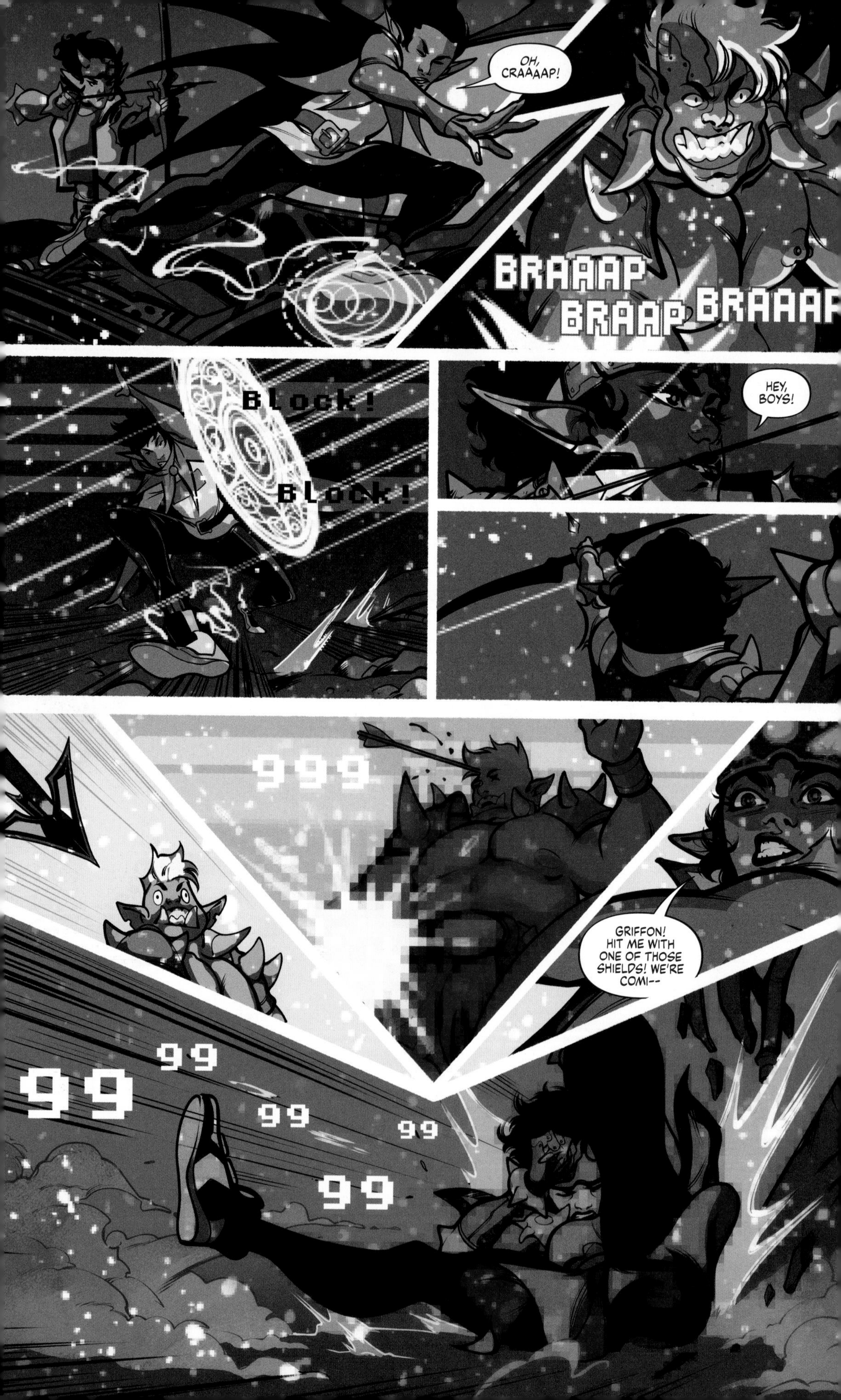
OH, CRAAAAP!
BRAAAP
BRAAP
BRAAAP
Block!
Block!
HEY, BOYS!
999
GRIFFON! HIT ME WITH ONE OF THOSE SHIELDS! WE'RE COMI--
99
99
99
99
99

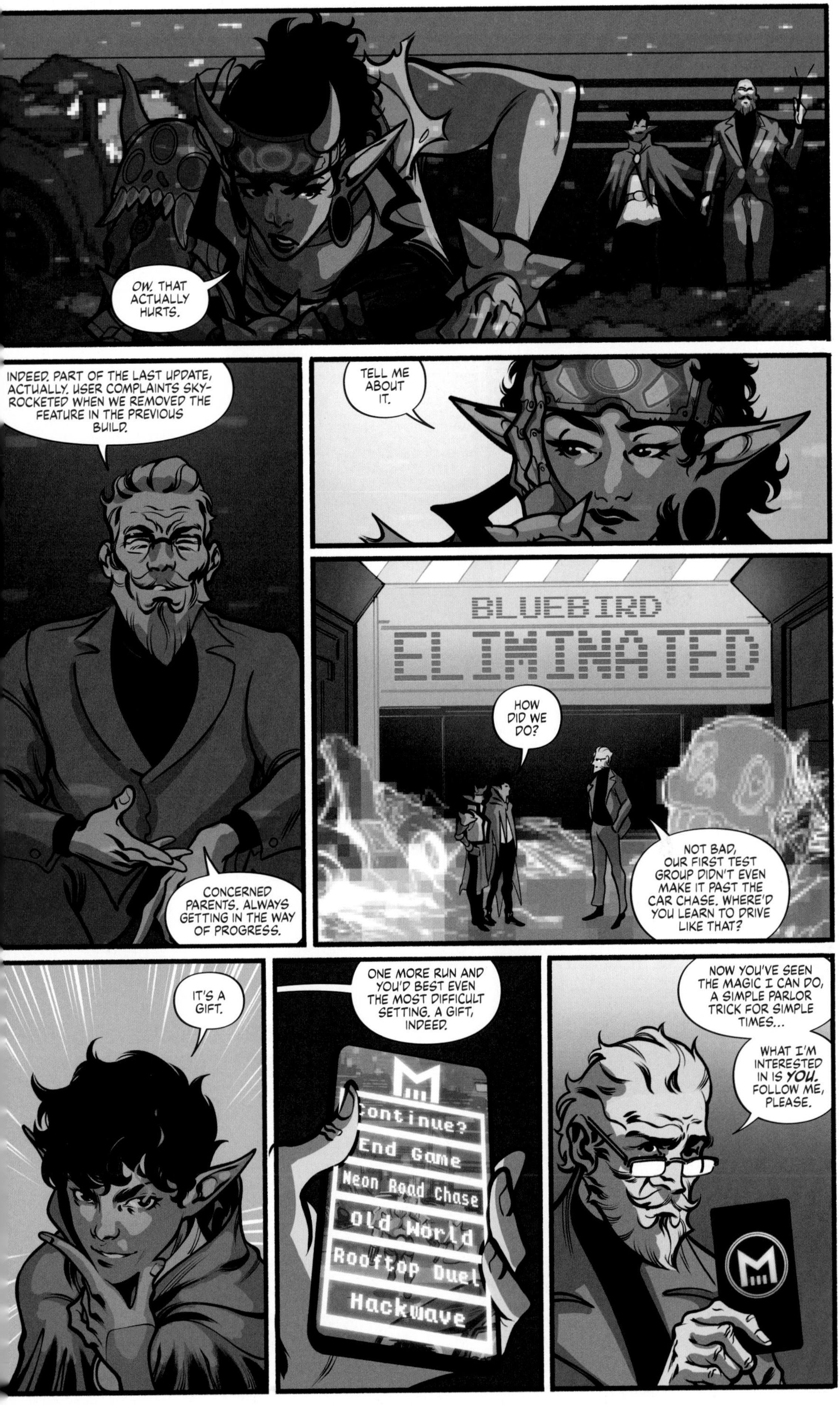
OW. THAT ACTUALLY HURTS.
INDEED. PART OF THE LAST UPDATE, ACTUALLY. USER COMPLAINTS SKY-ROCKETED WHEN WE REMOVED THE FEATURE IN THE PREVIOUS BUILD.
CONCERNED PARENTS. ALWAYS GETTING IN THE WAY OF PROGRESS.
TELL ME ABOUT IT.
BLUEBIRD
ELIMINATED
HOW DID WE DO?
NOT BAD, OUR FIRST TEST GROUP DIDN'T EVEN MAKE IT PAST THE CAR CHASE. WHERE'D YOU LEARN TO DRIVE LIKE THAT?
IT'S A GIFT.
ONE MORE RUN AND YOU'D BEST EVEN THE MOST DIFFICULT SETTING. A GIFT, INDEED.
Continue?
End Game
Neon Road Chase
old World
Rooftop Duel
Hackwave
NOW YOU'VE SEEN THE MAGIC I CAN DO, A SIMPLE PARLOR TRICK FOR SIMPLE TIMES...
WHAT I'M INTERESTED IN IS *YOU.* FOLLOW ME, PLEASE.

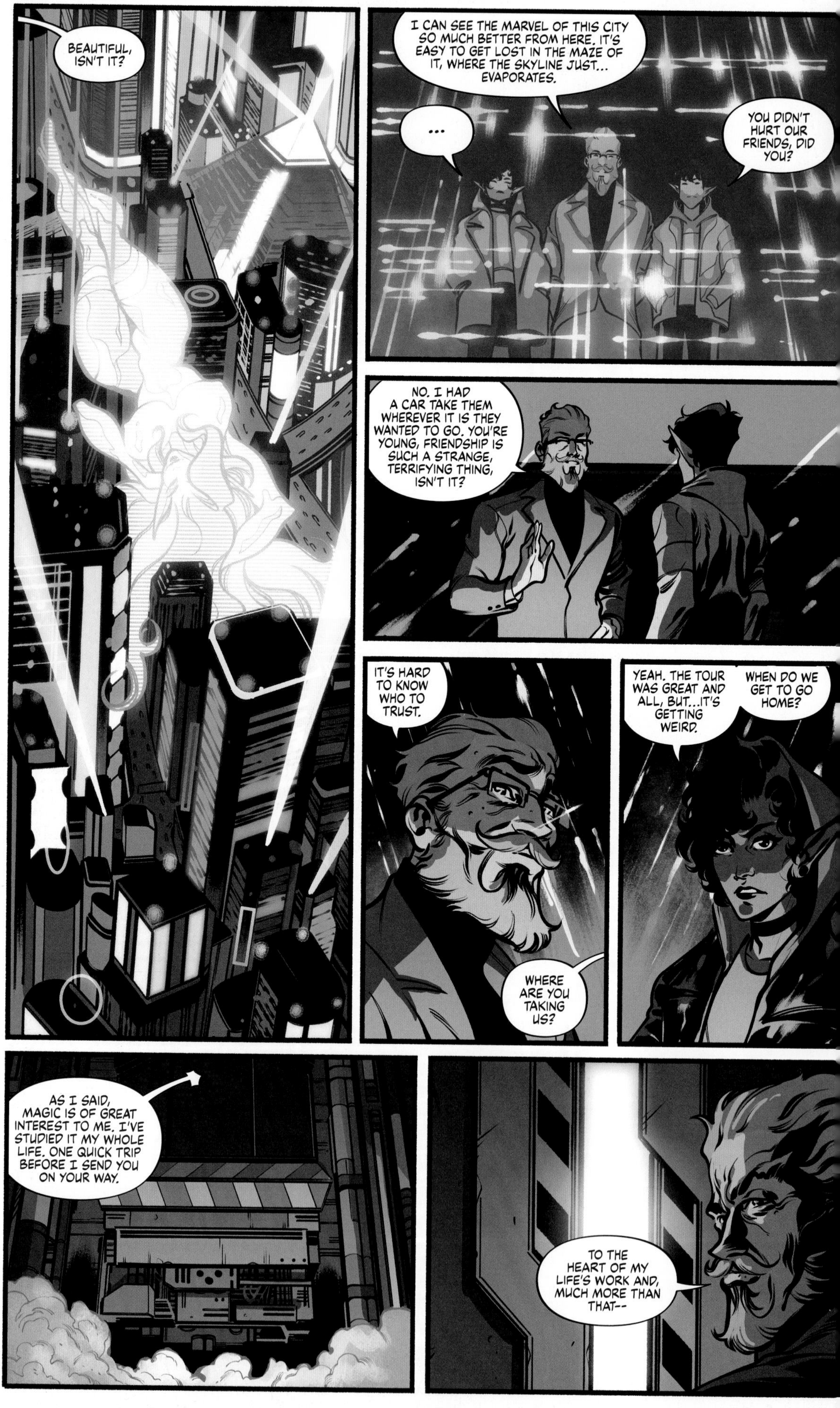
BEAUTIFUL, ISN'T IT?
I CAN SEE THE MARVEL OF THIS CITY SO MUCH BETTER FROM HERE. IT'S EASY TO GET LOST IN THE MAZE OF IT, WHERE THE SKYLINE JUST... EVAPORATES.
...
YOU DIDN'T HURT OUR FRIENDS, DID YOU?
NO. I HAD A CAR TAKE THEM WHEREVER IT IS THEY WANTED TO GO. YOU'RE YOUNG, FRIENDSHIP IS SUCH A STRANGE, TERRIFYING THING, ISN'T IT?
IT'S HARD TO KNOW WHO TO TRUST.
YEAH. THE TOUR WAS GREAT AND ALL, BUT...IT'S GETTING WEIRD.
WHEN DO WE GET TO GO HOME?
WHERE ARE YOU TAKING US?
AS I SAID, MAGIC IS OF GREAT INTEREST TO ME. I'VE STUDIED IT MY WHOLE LIFE. ONE QUICK TRIP BEFORE I SEND YOU ON YOUR WAY.
TO THE HEART OF MY LIFE'S WORK AND, MUCH MORE THAN THAT--

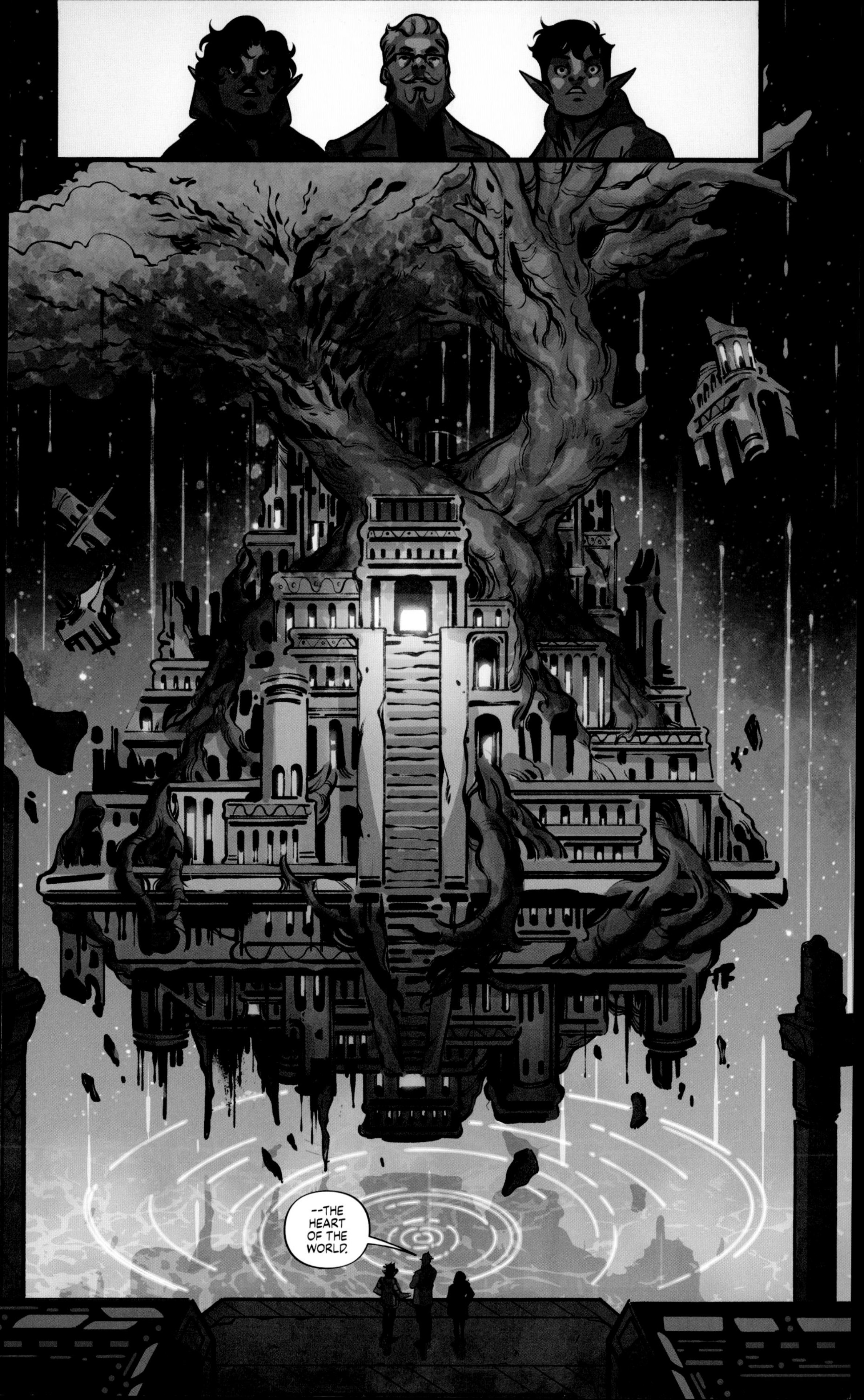
--THE HEART OF THE WORLD.

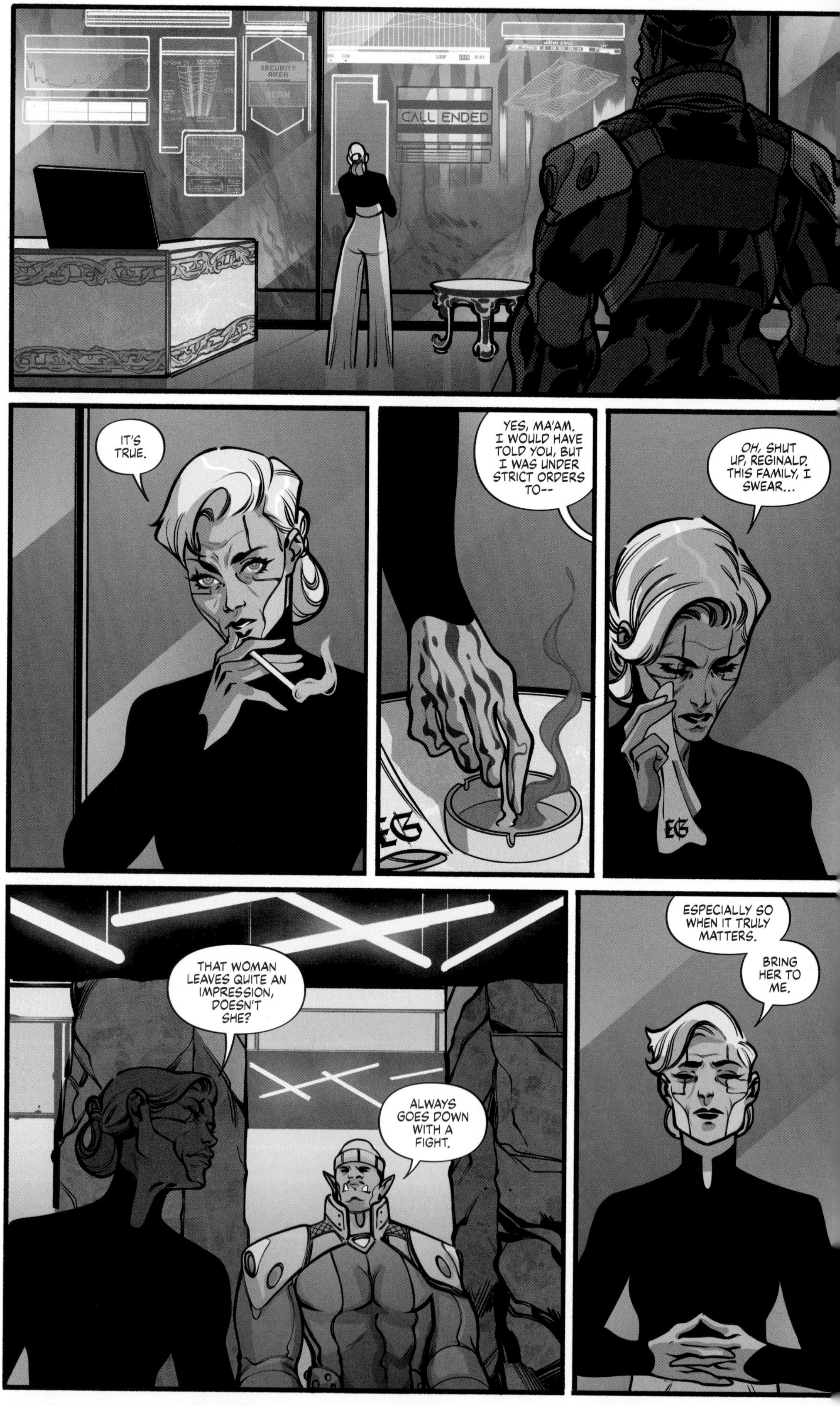
SECURITY AREA
SCAN
CALL ENDED
IT'S TRUE.
YES, MA'AM. I WOULD HAVE TOLD YOU, BUT I WAS UNDER STRICT ORDERS TO--
OH, SHUT UP, REGINALD. THIS FAMILY, I SWEAR...
EG
THAT WOMAN LEAVES QUITE AN IMPRESSION, DOESN'T SHE?
ALWAYS GOES DOWN WITH A FIGHT.
ESPECIALLY SO WHEN IT TRULY MATTERS.
BRING HER TO ME.

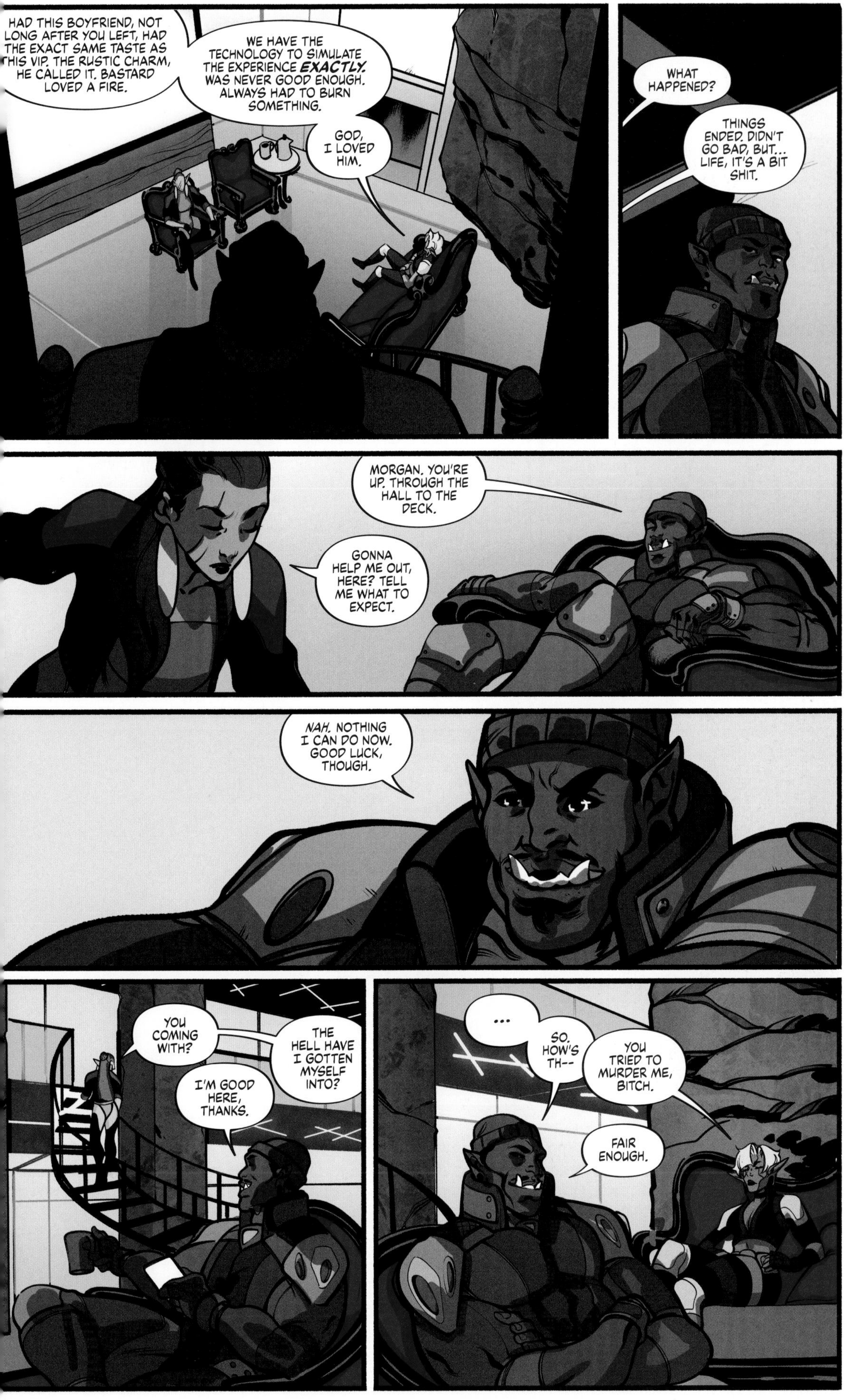
HAD THIS BOYFRIEND, NOT LONG AFTER YOU LEFT, HAD THE EXACT SAME TASTE AS THIS VIP. THE RUSTIC CHARM, HE CALLED IT. BASTARD LOVED A FIRE.
WE HAVE THE TECHNOLOGY TO SIMULATE THE EXPERIENCE EXACTLY. WAS NEVER GOOD ENOUGH. ALWAYS HAD TO BURN SOMETHING.
GOD, I LOVED HIM.
WHAT HAPPENED?
THINGS ENDED. DIDN'T GO BAD, BUT... LIFE, IT'S A BIT SHIT.
MORGAN. YOU'RE UP. THROUGH THE HALL TO THE DECK.
GONNA HELP ME OUT, HERE? TELL ME WHAT TO EXPECT.
NAH. NOTHING I CAN DO NOW. GOOD LUCK, THOUGH.
YOU COMING WITH?
THE HELL HAVE I GOTTEN MYSELF INTO?
I'M GOOD HERE, THANKS.
...
SO. HOW'S TH--
YOU TRIED TO MURDER ME, BITCH.
FAIR ENOUGH.

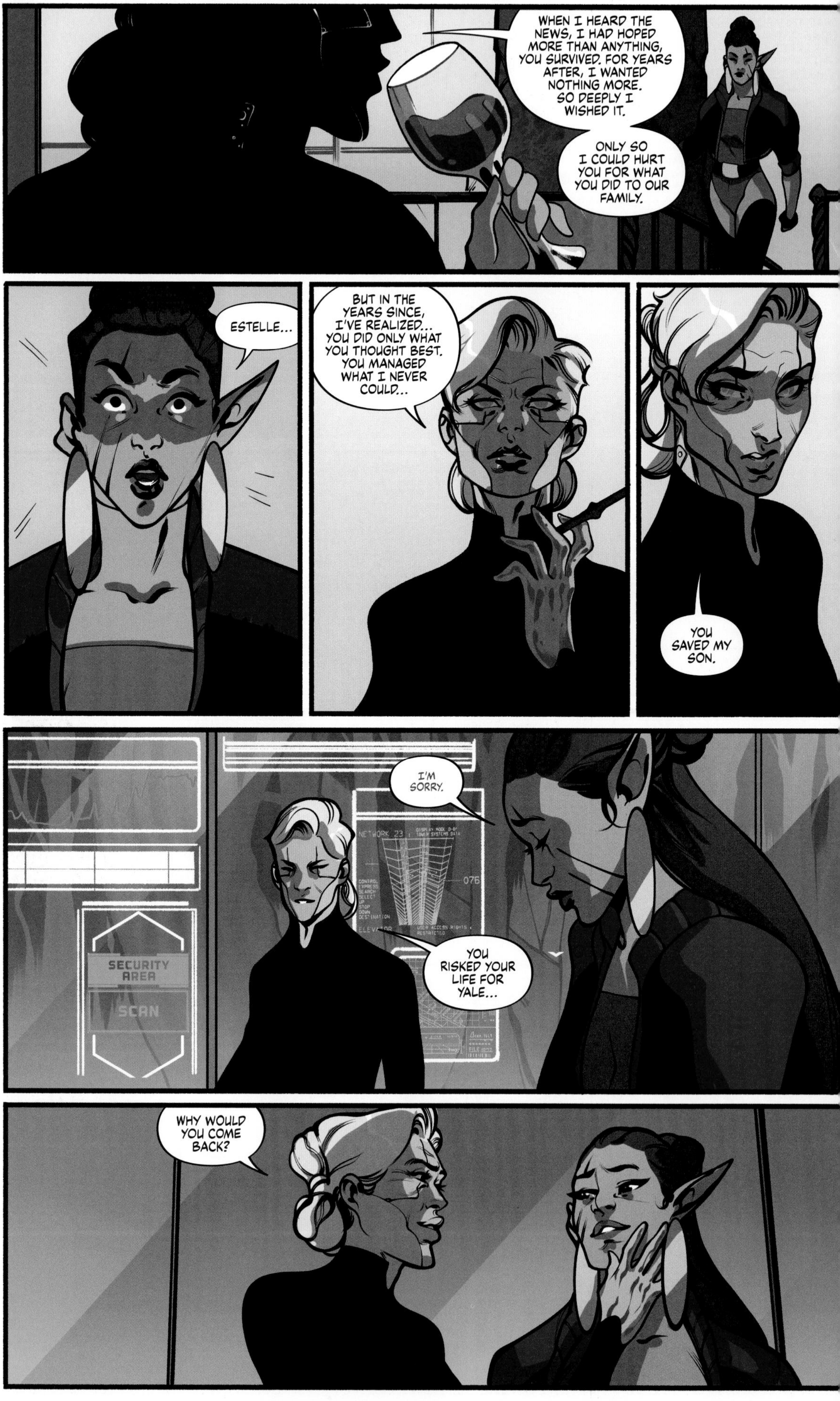
WHEN I HEARD THE NEWS, I HAD HOPED MORE THAN ANYTHING, YOU SURVIVED. FOR YEARS AFTER, I WANTED NOTHING MORE. SO DEEPLY I WISHED IT.
ONLY SO I COULD HURT YOU FOR WHAT YOU DID TO OUR FAMILY.
ESTELLE...
BUT IN THE YEARS SINCE, I'VE REALIZED... YOU DID ONLY WHAT YOU THOUGHT BEST. YOU MANAGED WHAT I NEVER COULD...
YOU SAVED MY SON.
I'M SORRY.
YOU RISKED YOUR LIFE FOR YALE...
SECURITY AREA
SCAN
WHY WOULD YOU COME BACK?

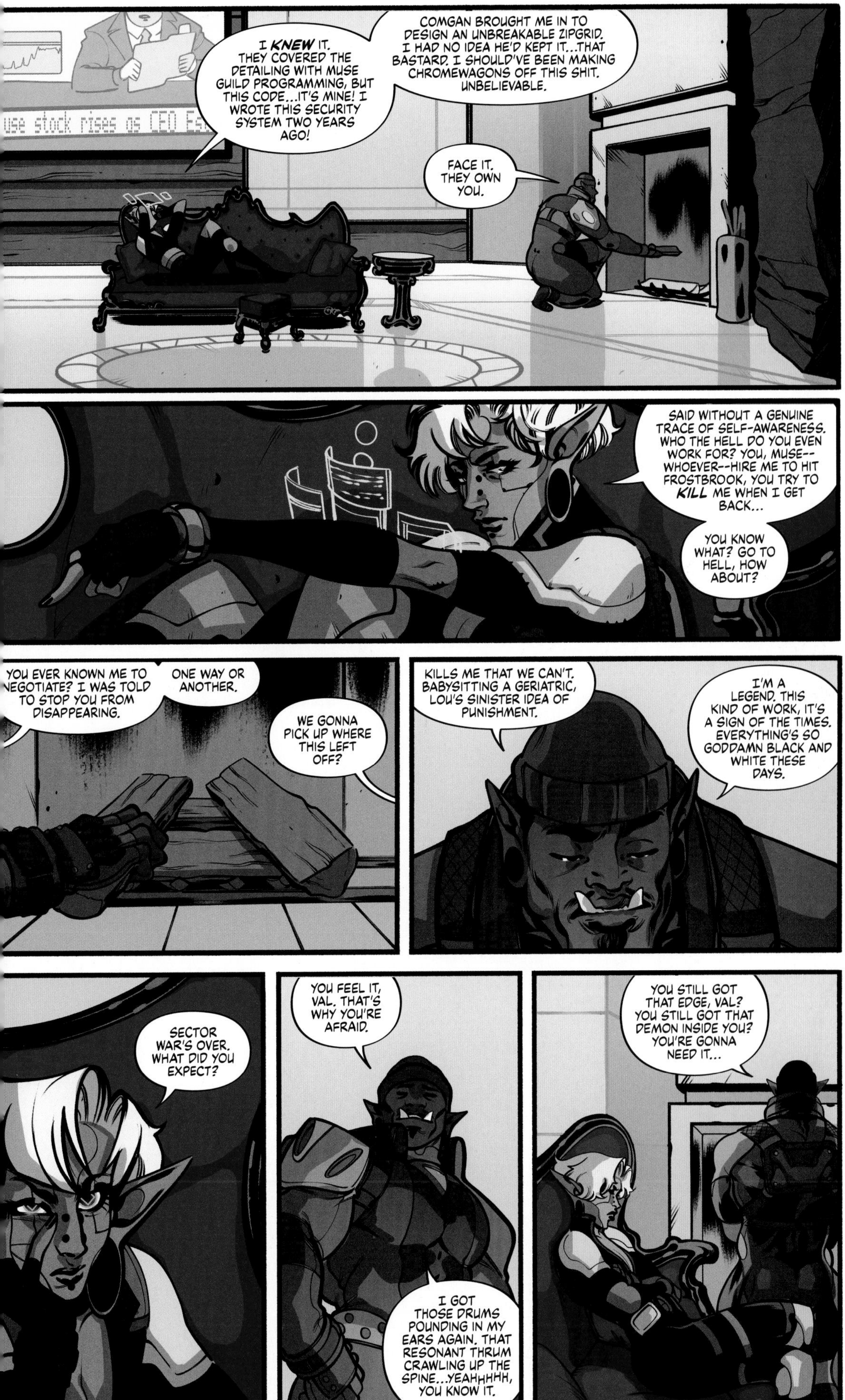
use stock rises as CEO Fsi
I KNEW IT. THEY COVERED THE DETAILING WITH MUSE GUILD PROGRAMMING, BUT THIS CODE...IT'S MINE! I WROTE THIS SECURITY SYSTEM TWO YEARS AGO!
COMGAN BROUGHT ME IN TO DESIGN AN UNBREAKABLE ZIPGRID. I HAD NO IDEA HE'D KEPT IT...THAT BASTARD. I SHOULD'VE BEEN MAKING CHROMEWAGONS OFF THIS SHIT. UNBELIEVABLE.
FACE IT. THEY OWN YOU.
SAID WITHOUT A GENUINE TRACE OF SELF-AWARENESS. WHO THE HELL DO YOU EVEN WORK FOR? YOU, MUSE--WHOEVER--HIRE ME TO HIT FROSTBROOK, YOU TRY TO KILL ME WHEN I GET BACK...
YOU KNOW WHAT? GO TO HELL, HOW ABOUT?
YOU EVER KNOWN ME TO NEGOTIATE? I WAS TOLD TO STOP YOU FROM DISAPPEARING.
ONE WAY OR ANOTHER.
WE GONNA PICK UP WHERE THIS LEFT OFF?
KILLS ME THAT WE CAN'T. BABYSITTING A GERIATRIC, LOU'S SINISTER IDEA OF PUNISHMENT.
I'M A LEGEND. THIS KIND OF WORK, IT'S A SIGN OF THE TIMES. EVERYTHING'S SO GODDAMN BLACK AND WHITE THESE DAYS.
SECTOR WAR'S OVER. WHAT DID YOU EXPECT?
YOU FEEL IT, VAL. THAT'S WHY YOU'RE AFRAID.
I GOT THOSE DRUMS POUNDING IN MY EARS AGAIN. THAT RESONANT THRUM CRAWLING UP THE SPINE...YEAHHHHHH, YOU KNOW IT.
YOU STILL GOT THAT EDGE, VAL? YOU STILL GOT THAT DEMON INSIDE YOU? YOU'RE GONNA NEED IT...

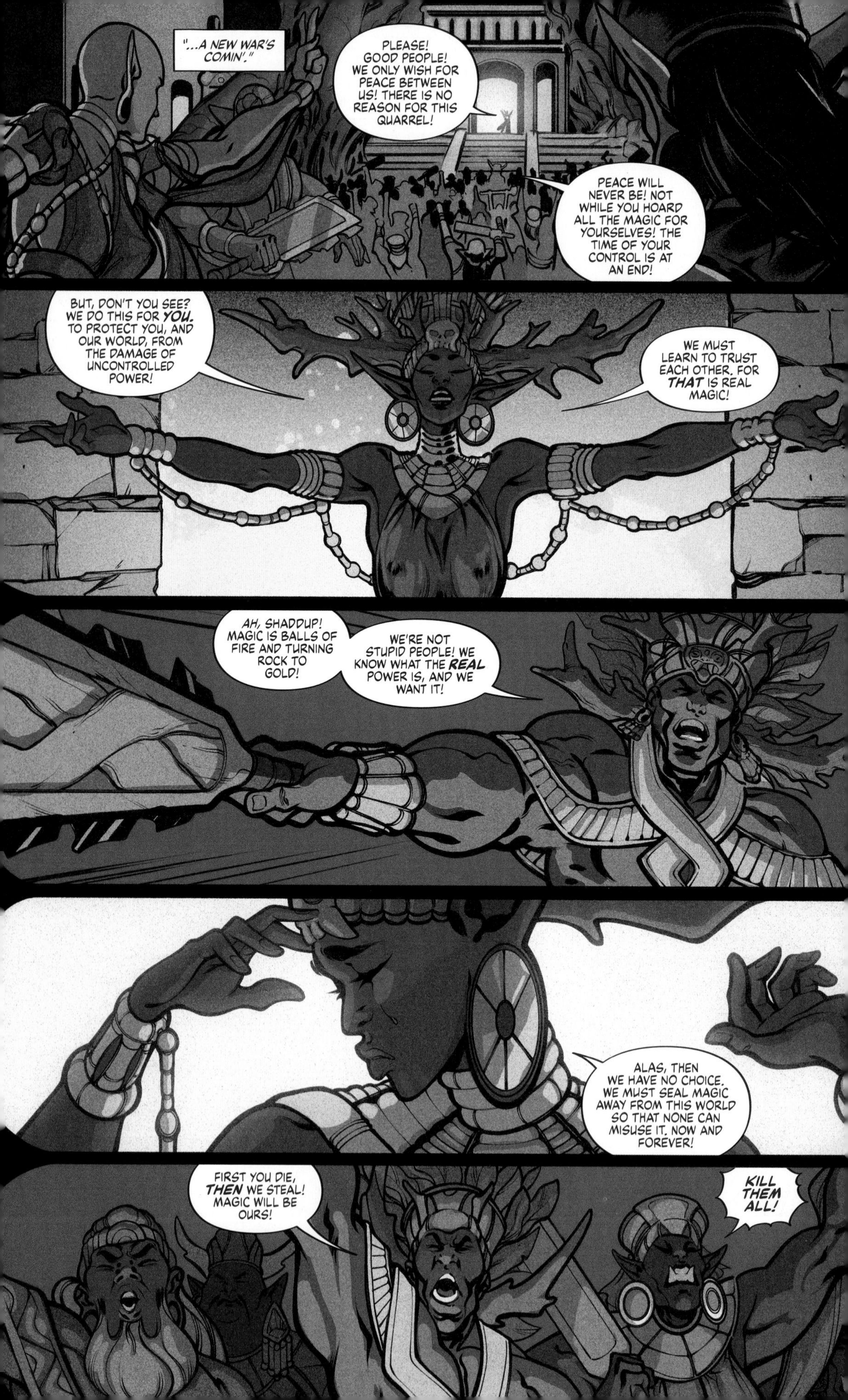
"...A NEW WAR'S COMIN'."
PLEASE! GOOD PEOPLE! WE ONLY WISH FOR PEACE BETWEEN US! THERE IS NO REASON FOR THIS QUARREL!
PEACE WILL NEVER BE! NOT WHILE YOU HOARD ALL THE MAGIC FOR YOURSELVES! THE TIME OF YOUR CONTROL IS AT AN END!
BUT, DON'T YOU SEE? WE DO THIS FOR YOU. TO PROTECT YOU, AND OUR WORLD, FROM THE DAMAGE OF UNCONTROLLED POWER!
WE MUST LEARN TO TRUST EACH OTHER. FOR THAT IS REAL MAGIC!
AH, SHADDUP! MAGIC IS BALLS OF FIRE AND TURNING ROCK TO GOLD!
WE'RE NOT STUPID PEOPLE! WE KNOW WHAT THE REAL POWER IS, AND WE WANT IT!
ALAS, THEN WE HAVE NO CHOICE. WE MUST SEAL MAGIC AWAY FROM THIS WORLD SO THAT NONE CAN MISUSE IT. NOW AND FOREVER!
FIRST YOU DIE, THEN WE STEAL! MAGIC WILL BE OURS!
KILL THEM ALL!

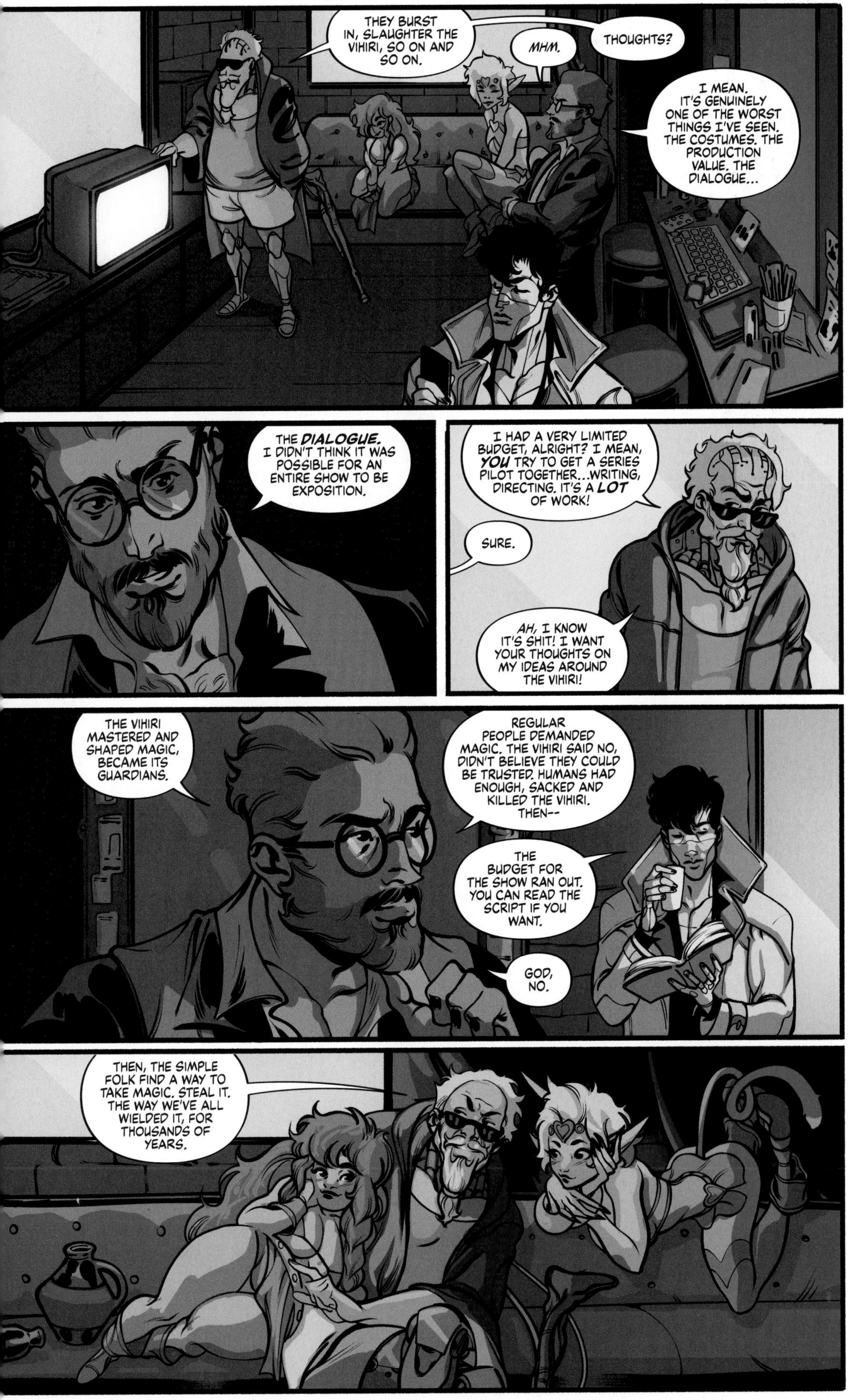
THEY BURST IN, SLAUGHTER THE VIHIRI, SO ON AND SO ON.
MHM.
THOUGHTS?
I MEAN. IT'S GENUINELY ONE OF THE WORST THINGS I'VE SEEN. THE COSTUMES. THE PRODUCTION VALUE. THE DIALOGUE...
THE DIALOGUE. I DIDN'T THINK IT WAS POSSIBLE FOR AN ENTIRE SHOW TO BE EXPOSITION.
I HAD A VERY LIMITED BUDGET, ALRIGHT? I MEAN, YOU TRY TO GET A SERIES PILOT TOGETHER...WRITING, DIRECTING. IT'S A LOT OF WORK!
SURE.
AH, I KNOW IT'S SHIT! I WANT YOUR THOUGHTS ON MY IDEAS AROUND THE VIHIRI!
THE VIHIRI MASTERED AND SHAPED MAGIC, BECAME ITS GUARDIANS.
REGULAR PEOPLE DEMANDED MAGIC. THE VIHIRI SAID NO, DIDN'T BELIEVE THEY COULD BE TRUSTED. HUMANS HAD ENOUGH, SACKED AND KILLED THE VIHIRI. THEN--
THE BUDGET FOR THE SHOW RAN OUT. YOU CAN READ THE SCRIPT IF YOU WANT.
GOD, NO.
THEN, THE SIMPLE FOLK FIND A WAY TO TAKE MAGIC. STEAL IT. THE WAY WE'VE ALL WIELDED IT, FOR THOUSANDS OF YEARS.

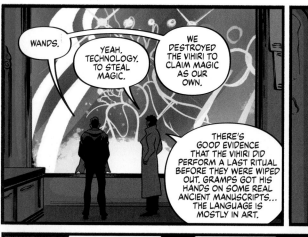

WANDS.

YEAH. TECHNOLOGY. TO STEAL MAGIC.

WE DESTROYED THE VIHIRI TO CLAIM MAGIC AS OUR OWN.

THERE'S GOOD EVIDENCE THAT THE VIHIRI DID PERFORM A LAST RITUAL BEFORE THEY WERE WIPED OUT. GRAMPS GOT HIS HANDS ON SOME REAL ANCIENT MANUSCRIPTS... THE LANGUAGE IS MOSTLY IN ART.

I FOUND THE SAME IN FROSTBROOK. STORY IN ART. MY OWN STUDIES REVEALED THAT THE VIHIRI WERE NATURALISTS THAT EITHER BELIEVED THAT NATURE ITSELF WAS GOD, OR--

NATURE WAS MAGIC.

YES. EXACTLY.

THIS ENTIRE CITY IS BUILT ON THAT VIHIRI RUIN, STRETCHES ON FOR...GOD KNOWS.

FROSTBROOK, AT LEAST. HUNDREDS OF BANDS.

YOUR FATHER BUILT MUSE ON TOP OF THE MAIN TEMPLE. IT WAS ALL PART OF HIS PLAN. THAT TOWER. THE TWINS. ALL OF IT.

WHAT WERE HIS PLANS FOR THEM?

A NEW KIND OF WAND.

A *WHAT?*

WE DON'T KNOW HOW EXACTLY, OR WHAT IT WAS HE DID TO THEM. ONLY COMGAN HAS THAT KNOWLEDGE.

BUT HE PLANS TO USE THEM TO DRAW MAGIC BACK INTO THE WORLD. YOU SAID YOURSELF, THEY'RE CONDUITS. MAGIC FLOWS OUT OF THEM WITHOUT THEIR KNOWLEDGE OF HOW OR WHY.

THEY'RE BAIT, SON. A LURE TO CALL THE VIHIRI HOME.

ALL WE CAN DO NOW IS MAKE SURE...

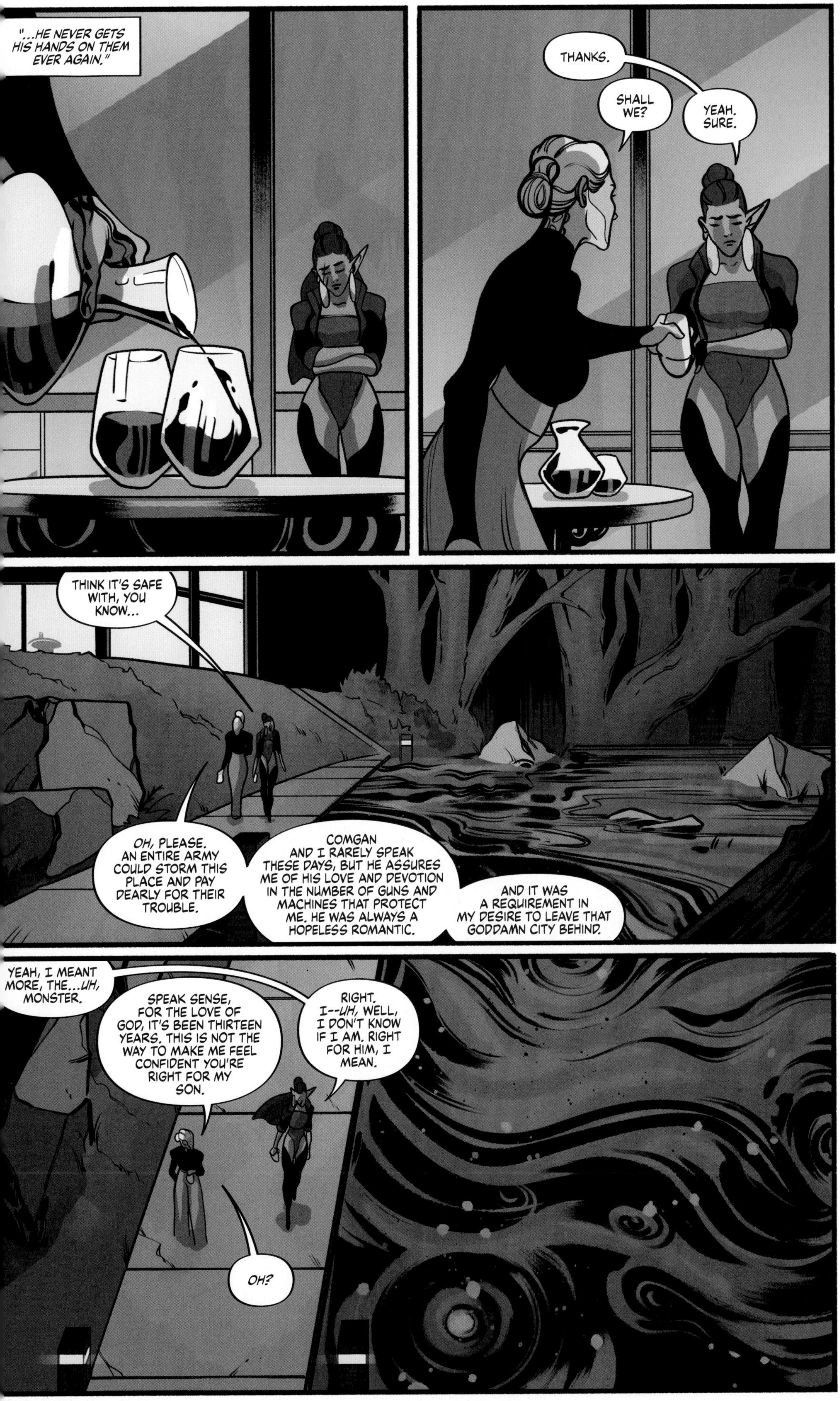
"...HE NEVER GETS HIS HANDS ON THEM EVER AGAIN."
THANKS.
SHALL WE?
YEAH. SURE.
THINK IT'S SAFE WITH, YOU KNOW...
OH, PLEASE. AN ENTIRE ARMY COULD STORM THIS PLACE AND PAY DEARLY FOR THEIR TROUBLE.
COMGAN AND I RARELY SPEAK THESE DAYS, BUT HE ASSURES ME OF HIS LOVE AND DEVOTION IN THE NUMBER OF GUNS AND MACHINES THAT PROTECT ME. HE WAS ALWAYS A HOPELESS ROMANTIC.
AND IT WAS A REQUIREMENT IN MY DESIRE TO LEAVE THAT GODDAMN CITY BEHIND.
YEAH, I MEANT MORE, THE...UH, MONSTER.
OH?
SPEAK SENSE, FOR THE LOVE OF GOD, IT'S BEEN THIRTEEN YEARS. THIS IS NOT THE WAY TO MAKE ME FEEL CONFIDENT YOU'RE RIGHT FOR MY SON.
RIGHT. I--UH, WELL, I DON'T KNOW IF I AM. RIGHT FOR HIM, I MEAN.

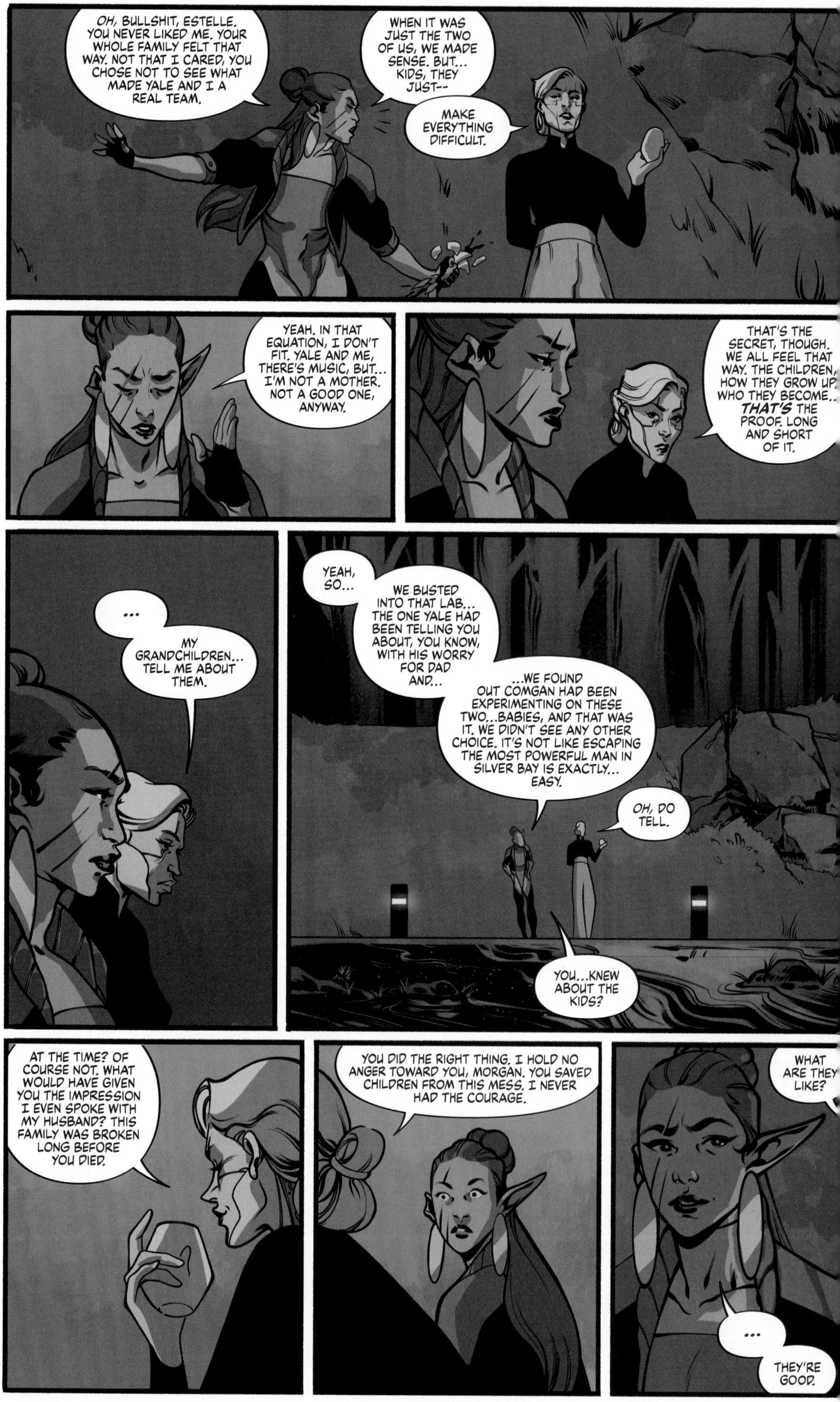
OH, BULLSHIT, ESTELLE. YOU NEVER LIKED ME. YOUR WHOLE FAMILY FELT THAT WAY. NOT THAT I CARED, YOU CHOSE NOT TO SEE WHAT MADE YALE AND I A REAL TEAM.
WHEN IT WAS JUST THE TWO OF US, WE MADE SENSE. BUT... KIDS, THEY JUST--
MAKE EVERYTHING DIFFICULT.
YEAH. IN THAT EQUATION, I DON'T FIT. YALE AND ME, THERE'S MUSIC, BUT... I'M NOT A MOTHER. NOT A GOOD ONE, ANYWAY.
THAT'S THE SECRET, THOUGH. WE ALL FEEL THAT WAY. THE CHILDREN, HOW THEY GROW UP, WHO THEY BECOME... THAT'S THE PROOF. LONG AND SHORT OF IT.
...
MY GRANDCHILDREN... TELL ME ABOUT THEM.
YEAH, SO...
WE BUSTED INTO THAT LAB... THE ONE YALE HAD BEEN TELLING YOU ABOUT, YOU KNOW, WITH HIS WORRY FOR DAD AND...
...WE FOUND OUT COMGAN HAD BEEN EXPERIMENTING ON THESE TWO...BABIES, AND THAT WAS IT. WE DIDN'T SEE ANY OTHER CHOICE. IT'S NOT LIKE ESCAPING THE MOST POWERFUL MAN IN SILVER BAY IS EXACTLY... EASY.
OH, DO TELL.
YOU...KNEW ABOUT THE KIDS?
AT THE TIME? OF COURSE NOT. WHAT WOULD HAVE GIVEN YOU THE IMPRESSION I EVEN SPOKE WITH MY HUSBAND? THIS FAMILY WAS BROKEN LONG BEFORE YOU DIED.
YOU DID THE RIGHT THING. I HOLD NO ANGER TOWARD YOU, MORGAN. YOU SAVED CHILDREN FROM THIS MESS. I NEVER HAD THE COURAGE.
WHAT ARE THEY LIKE?
...
THEY'RE GOOD.

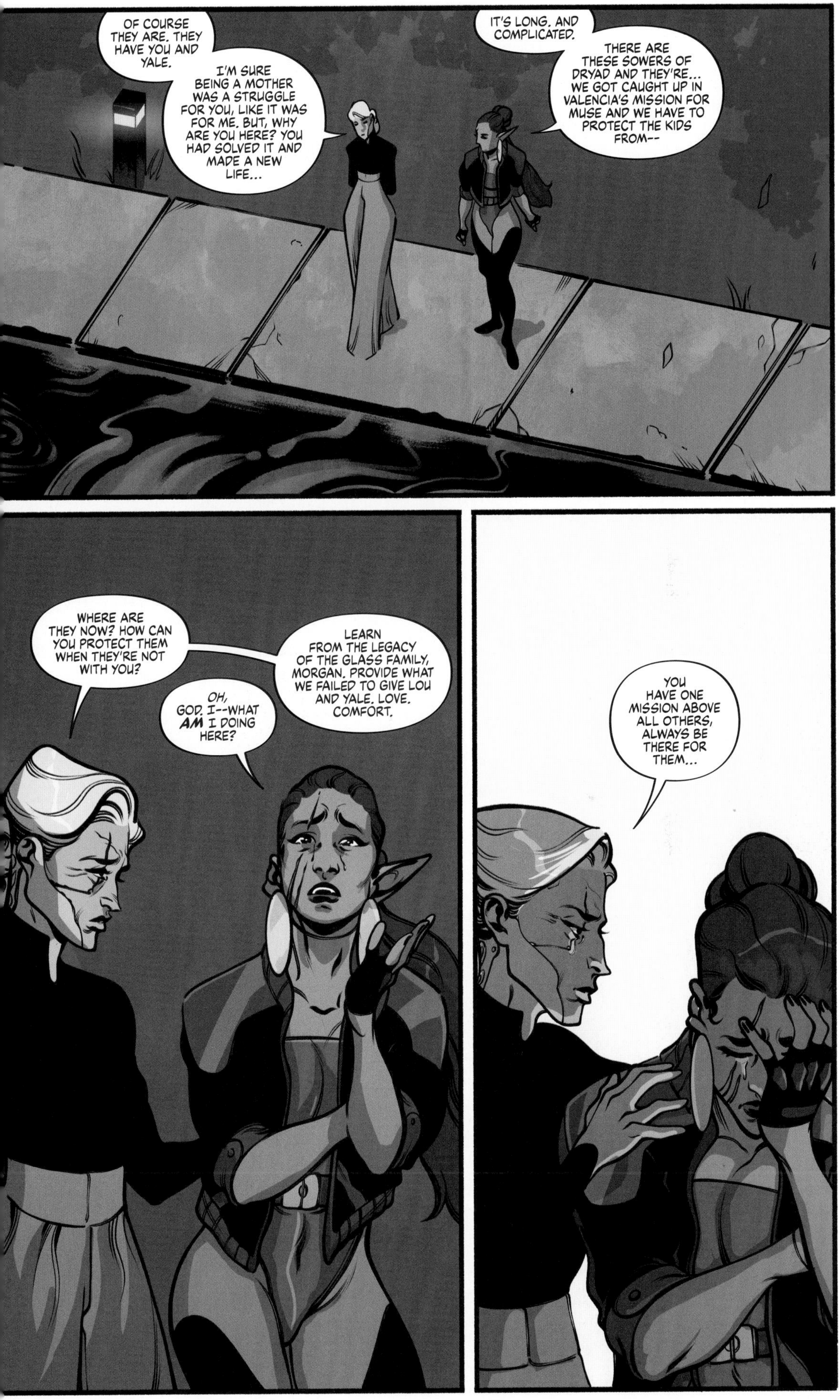
OF COURSE THEY ARE. THEY HAVE YOU AND YALE.
I'M SURE BEING A MOTHER WAS A STRUGGLE FOR YOU, LIKE IT WAS FOR ME. BUT, WHY ARE YOU HERE? YOU HAD SOLVED IT AND MADE A NEW LIFE...
IT'S LONG. AND COMPLICATED.
THERE ARE THESE SOWERS OF DRYAD AND THEY'RE... WE GOT CAUGHT UP IN VALENCIA'S MISSION FOR MUSE AND WE HAVE TO PROTECT THE KIDS FROM--
WHERE ARE THEY NOW? HOW CAN YOU PROTECT THEM WHEN THEY'RE NOT WITH YOU?
LEARN FROM THE LEGACY OF THE GLASS FAMILY, MORGAN. PROVIDE WHAT WE FAILED TO GIVE LOU AND YALE. LOVE. COMFORT.
OH, GOD. I--WHAT ***AM*** I DOING HERE?
YOU HAVE ONE MISSION ABOVE ALL OTHERS, ALWAYS BE THERE FOR THEM...

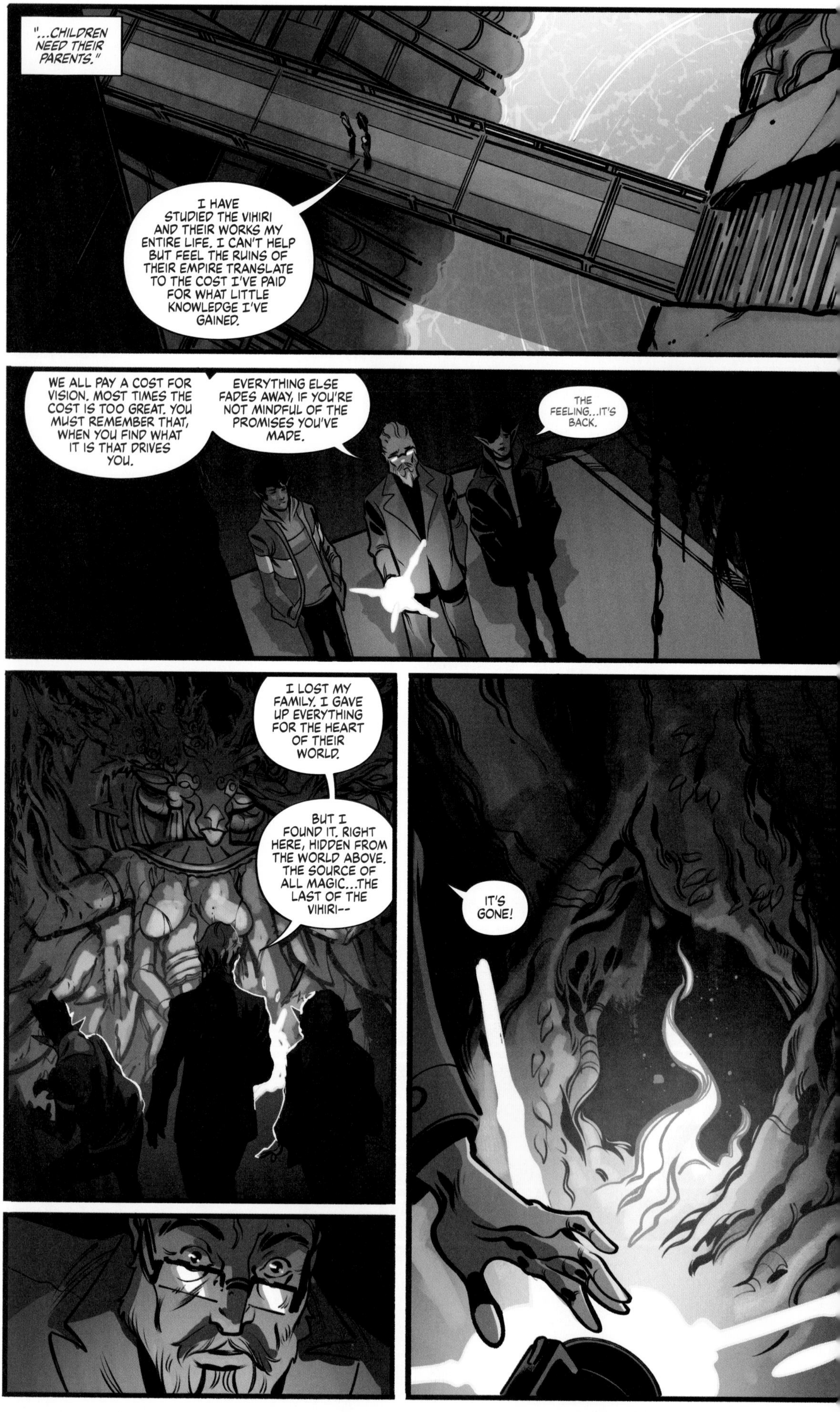
"...CHILDREN NEED THEIR PARENTS."
I HAVE STUDIED THE VIHIRI AND THEIR WORKS MY ENTIRE LIFE. I CAN'T HELP BUT FEEL THE RUINS OF THEIR EMPIRE TRANSLATE TO THE COST I'VE PAID FOR WHAT LITTLE KNOWLEDGE I'VE GAINED.
WE ALL PAY A COST FOR VISION. MOST TIMES THE COST IS TOO GREAT. YOU MUST REMEMBER THAT, WHEN YOU FIND WHAT IT IS THAT DRIVES YOU.
EVERYTHING ELSE FADES AWAY, IF YOU'RE NOT MINDFUL OF THE PROMISES YOU'VE MADE.
THE FEELING...IT'S BACK.
I LOST MY FAMILY. I GAVE UP EVERYTHING FOR THE HEART OF THEIR WORLD.
BUT I FOUND IT. RIGHT HERE, HIDDEN FROM THE WORLD ABOVE. THE SOURCE OF ALL MAGIC...THE LAST OF THE VIHIRI--
IT'S GONE!

CHAPTER TEN

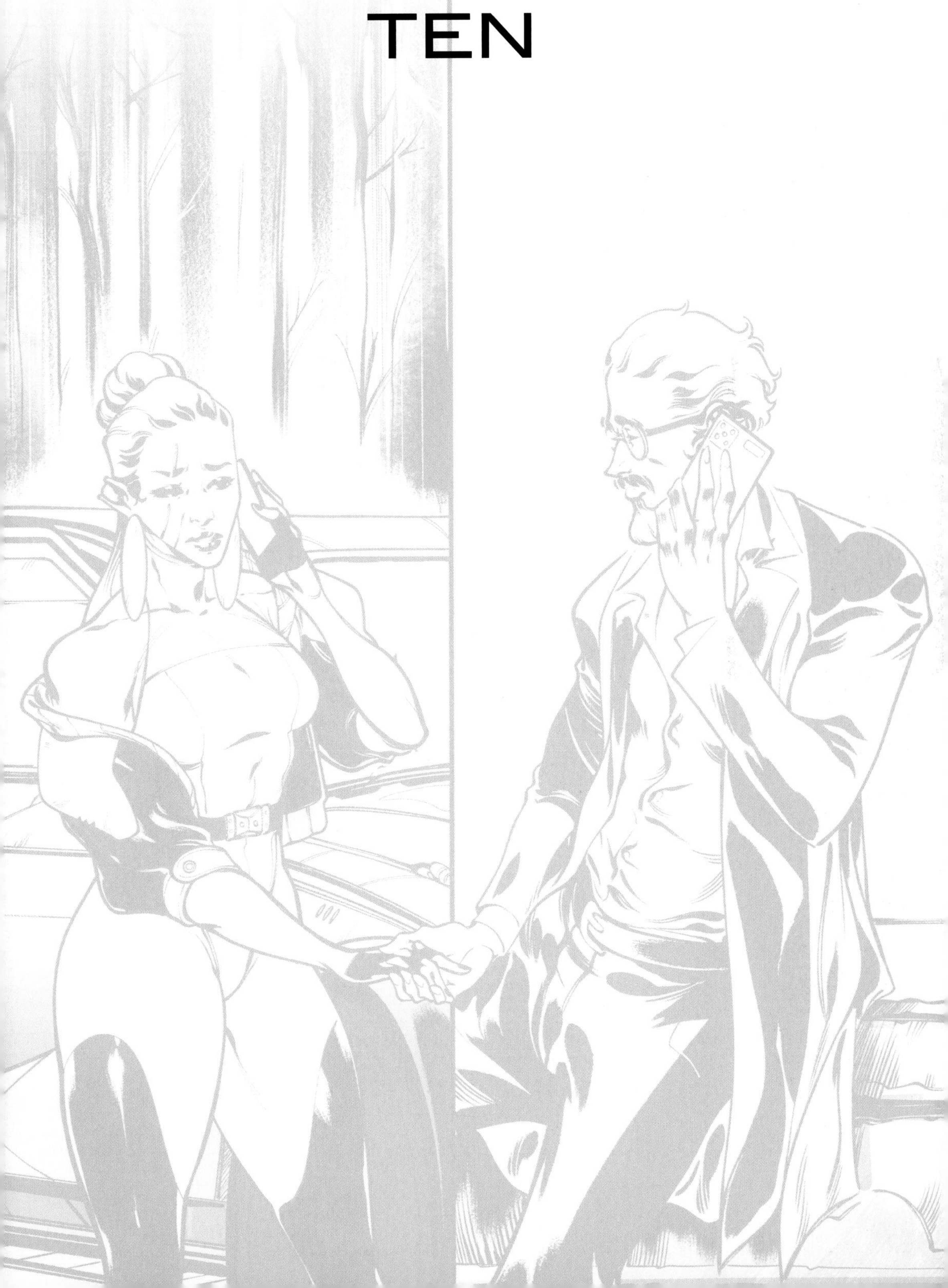

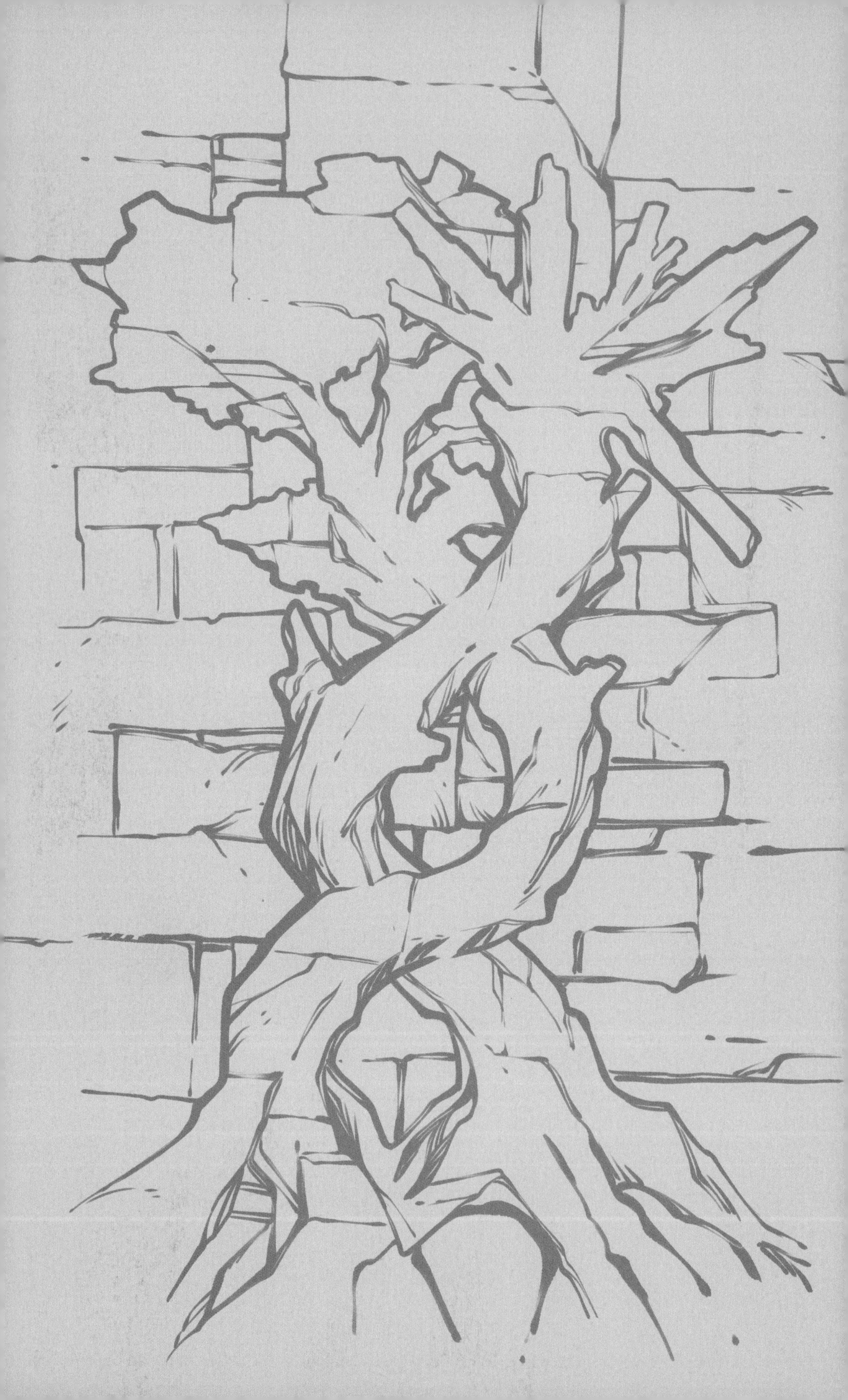

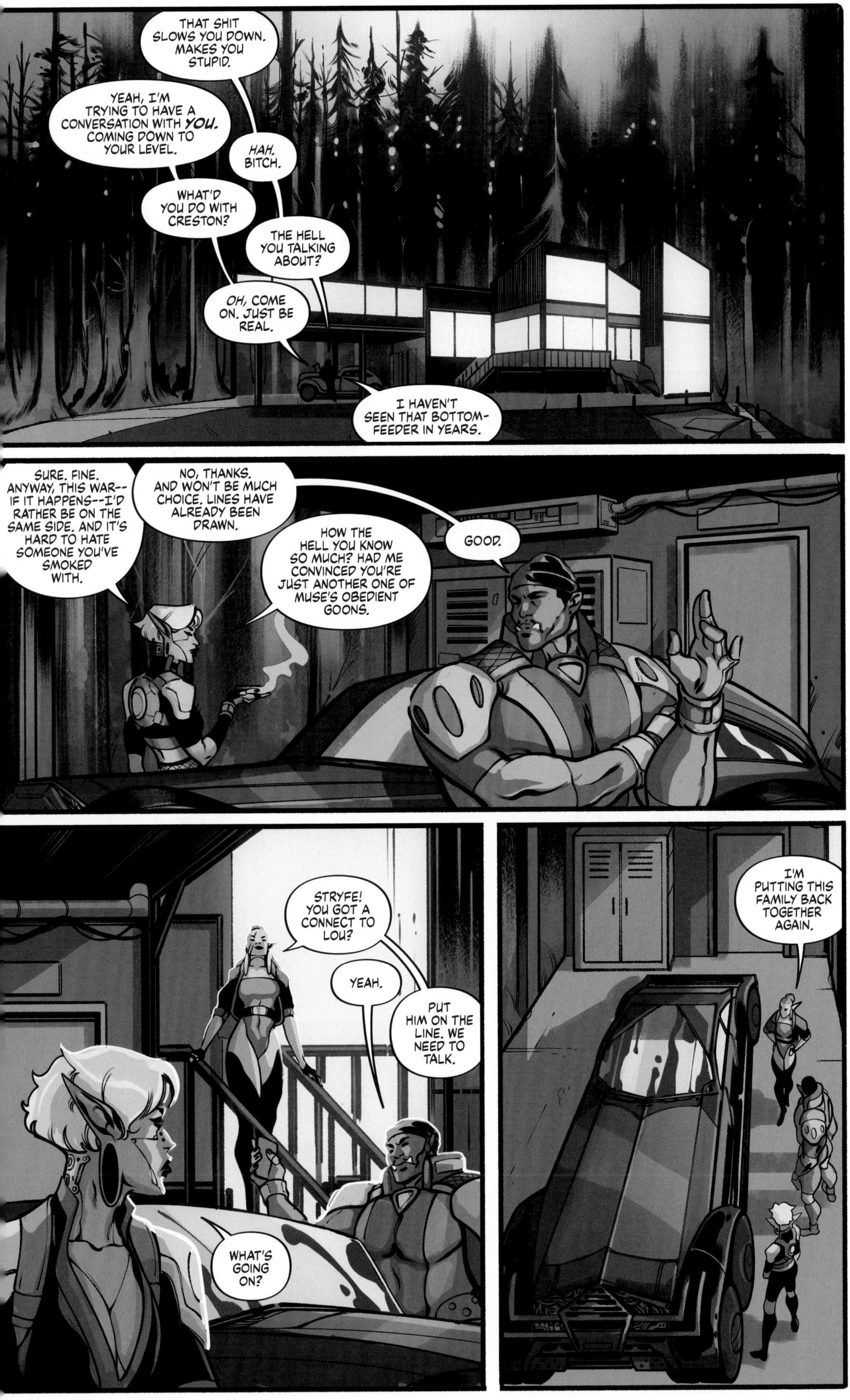
THAT SHIT SLOWS YOU DOWN. MAKES YOU STUPID.
YEAH, I'M TRYING TO HAVE A CONVERSATION WITH *YOU.* COMING DOWN TO YOUR LEVEL.
HAH. BITCH.
WHAT'D YOU DO WITH CRESTON?
THE HELL YOU TALKING ABOUT?
OH, COME ON. JUST BE REAL.
I HAVEN'T SEEN THAT BOTTOM-FEEDER IN YEARS.
SURE. FINE. ANYWAY, THIS WAR--IF IT HAPPENS--I'D RATHER BE ON THE SAME SIDE. AND IT'S HARD TO HATE SOMEONE YOU'VE SMOKED WITH.
NO, THANKS. AND WON'T BE MUCH CHOICE. LINES HAVE ALREADY BEEN DRAWN.
HOW THE HELL YOU KNOW SO MUCH? HAD ME CONVINCED YOU'RE JUST ANOTHER ONE OF MUSE'S OBEDIENT GOONS.
GOOD.
STRYFE! YOU GOT A CONNECT TO LOU?
YEAH.
PUT HIM ON THE LINE. WE NEED TO TALK.
WHAT'S GOING ON?
I'M PUTTING THIS FAMILY BACK TOGETHER AGAIN.

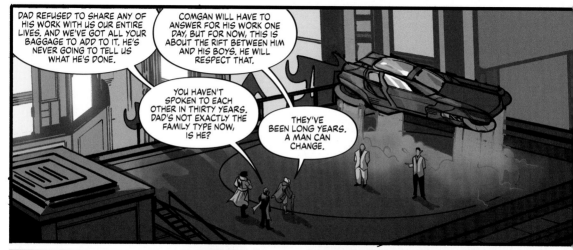

DAD REFUSED TO SHARE ANY OF HIS WORK WITH US OUR ENTIRE LIVES. AND WE'VE GOT ALL YOUR BAGGAGE TO ADD TO IT. HE'S NEVER GOING TO TELL US WHAT HE'S DONE.

COMGAN WILL HAVE TO ANSWER FOR HIS WORK ONE DAY, BUT FOR NOW, THIS IS ABOUT THE RIFT BETWEEN HIM AND HIS BOYS. HE WILL RESPECT THAT.

YOU HAVEN'T SPOKEN TO EACH OTHER IN THIRTY YEARS. DAD'S NOT EXACTLY THE FAMILY TYPE NOW, IS HE?

THEY'VE BEEN LONG YEARS. A MAN CAN CHANGE.

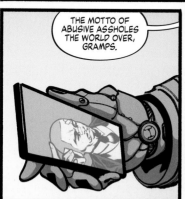

THE MOTTO OF ABUSIVE ASSHOLES THE WORLD OVER, GRAMPS.

STRYFE. EVERYTHING GOOD?

LOU. NO TIME. WE CAN CATCH UP SOON. LONG OVERDUE. YOU WITH YALE?

YEAH.

THE WIFE.

HEY, HUN. EVERYTHING OK?

NO. NOTHING REALLY IS ANYMORE, IS IT?

WHEN YOU THINK ABOUT ME, WHAT...WHAT DO SEE?

MY PARTNER. MY BEST FRIEND, MY--

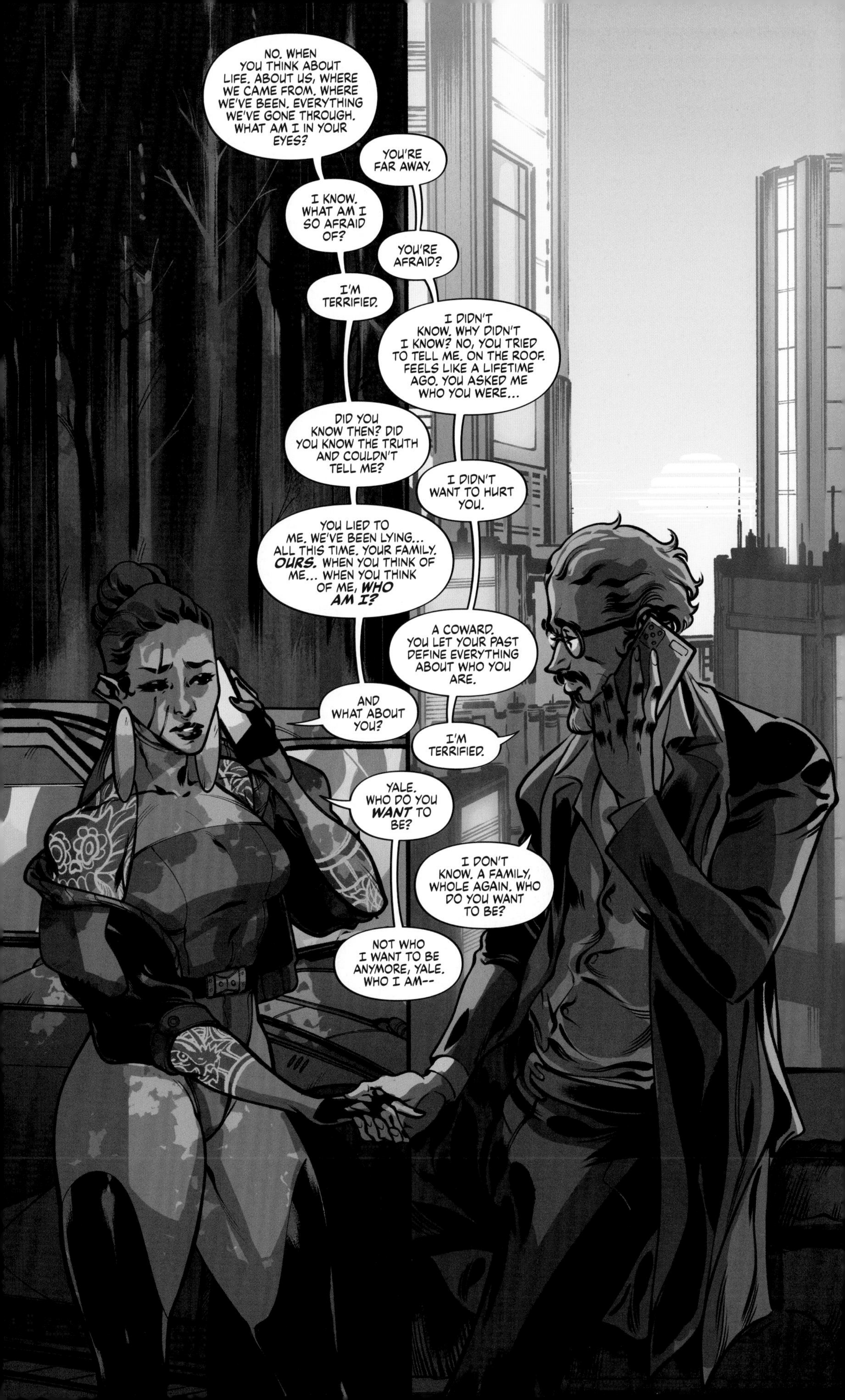
NO. WHEN YOU THINK ABOUT LIFE. ABOUT US, WHERE WE CAME FROM. WHERE WE'VE BEEN. EVERYTHING WE'VE GONE THROUGH. WHAT AM I IN YOUR EYES?
YOU'RE FAR AWAY.
I KNOW. WHAT AM I SO AFRAID OF?
YOU'RE AFRAID?
I'M TERRIFIED.
I DIDN'T KNOW. WHY DIDN'T I KNOW? NO, YOU TRIED TO TELL ME. ON THE ROOF. FEELS LIKE A LIFETIME AGO. YOU ASKED ME WHO YOU WERE...
DID YOU KNOW THEN? DID YOU KNOW THE TRUTH AND COULDN'T TELL ME?
I DIDN'T WANT TO HURT YOU.
YOU LIED TO ME. WE'VE BEEN LYING... ALL THIS TIME. YOUR FAMILY. ***OURS.*** WHEN YOU THINK OF ME... WHEN YOU THINK OF ME, ***WHO AM I?***
A COWARD. YOU LET YOUR PAST DEFINE EVERYTHING ABOUT WHO YOU ARE.
AND WHAT ABOUT YOU?
I'M TERRIFIED.
YALE. WHO DO YOU ***WANT*** TO BE?
I DON'T KNOW. A FAMILY, WHOLE AGAIN. WHO DO YOU WANT TO BE?
NOT WHO I WANT TO BE ANYMORE, YALE. WHO I AM--

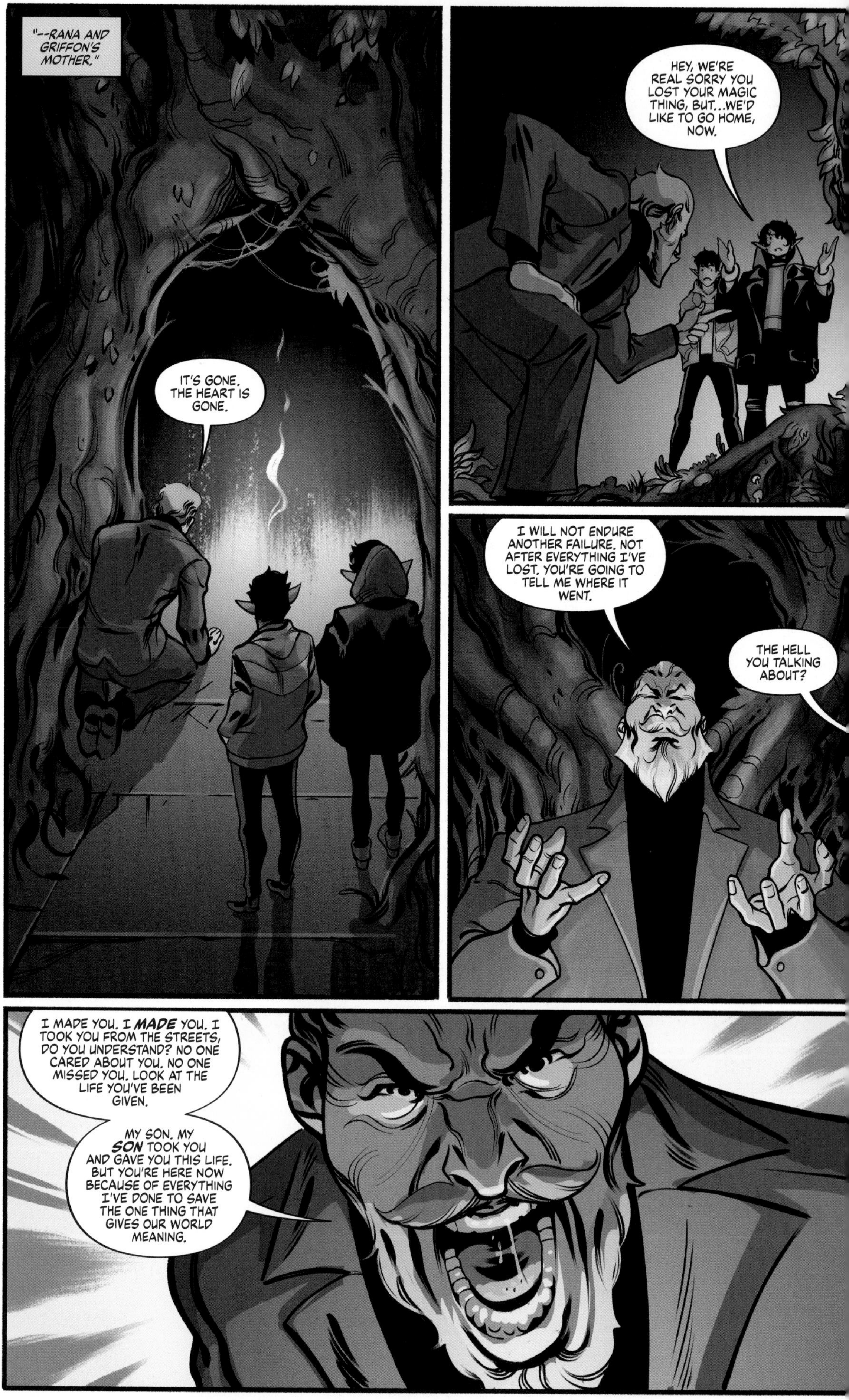
"--RANA AND GRIFFON'S MOTHER."
IT'S GONE. THE HEART IS GONE.
HEY, WE'RE REAL SORRY YOU LOST YOUR MAGIC THING, BUT...WE'D LIKE TO GO HOME, NOW.
I WILL NOT ENDURE ANOTHER FAILURE. NOT AFTER EVERYTHING I'VE LOST. YOU'RE GOING TO TELL ME WHERE IT WENT.
THE HELL YOU TALKING ABOUT?
I MADE YOU. I **MADE** YOU. I TOOK YOU FROM THE STREETS, DO YOU UNDERSTAND? NO ONE CARED ABOUT YOU. NO ONE MISSED YOU. LOOK AT THE LIFE YOU'VE BEEN GIVEN.
MY SON. MY **SON** TOOK YOU AND GAVE YOU THIS LIFE. BUT YOU'RE HERE NOW BECAUSE OF EVERYTHING I'VE DONE TO SAVE THE ONE THING THAT GIVES OUR WORLD MEANING.

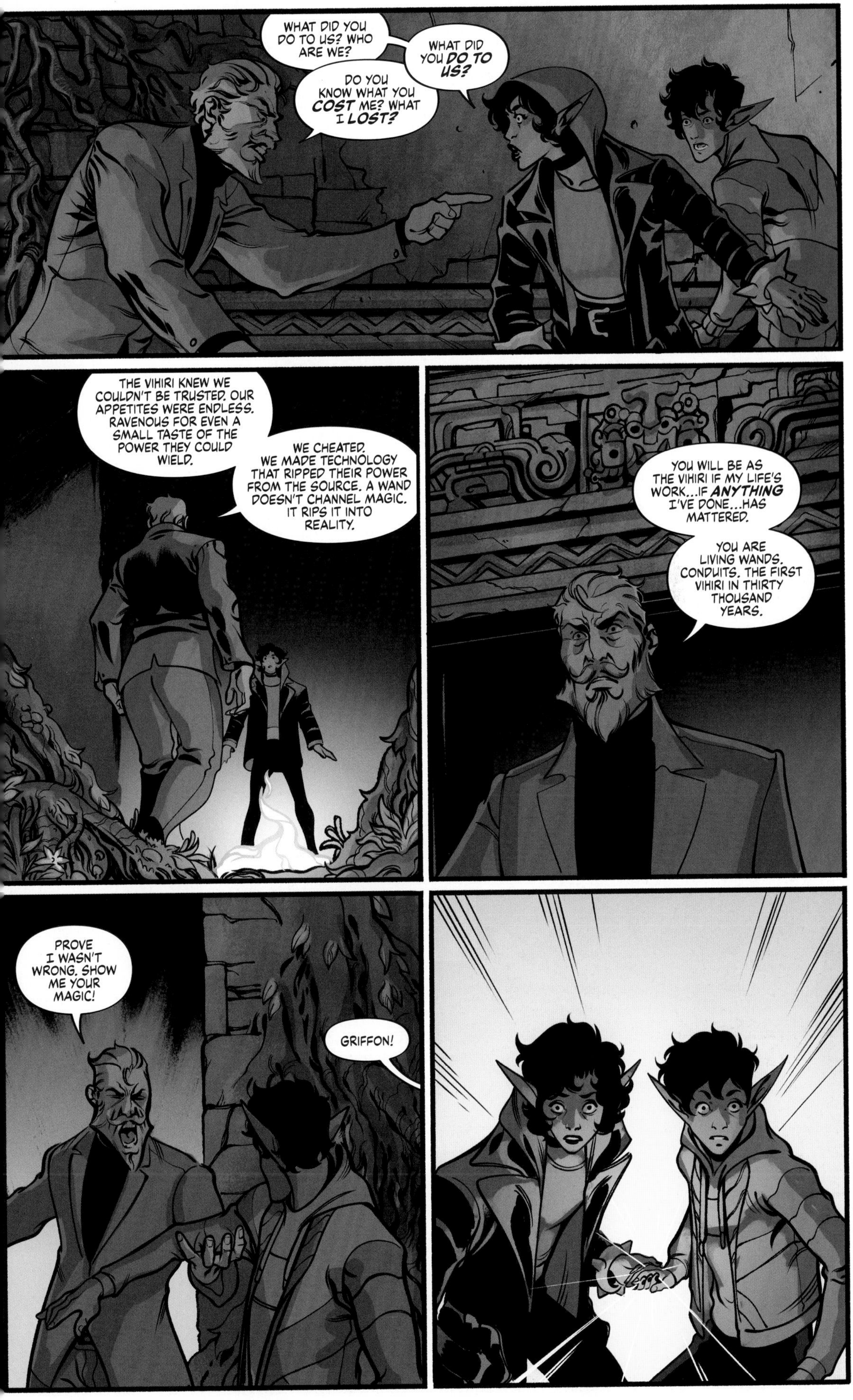
WHAT DID YOU DO TO US? WHO ARE WE?
WHAT DID YOU DO TO US?
DO YOU KNOW WHAT YOU COST ME? WHAT I LOST?
THE VIHIRI KNEW WE COULDN'T BE TRUSTED. OUR APPETITES WERE ENDLESS. RAVENOUS FOR EVEN A SMALL TASTE OF THE POWER THEY COULD WIELD.
WE CHEATED. WE MADE TECHNOLOGY THAT RIPPED THEIR POWER FROM THE SOURCE. A WAND DOESN'T CHANNEL MAGIC. IT RIPS IT INTO REALITY.
YOU WILL BE AS THE VIHIRI IF MY LIFE'S WORK...IF ANYTHING I'VE DONE...HAS MATTERED.
YOU ARE LIVING WANDS. CONDUITS. THE FIRST VIHIRI IN THIRTY THOUSAND YEARS.
PROVE I WASN'T WRONG. SHOW ME YOUR MAGIC!
GRIFFON!

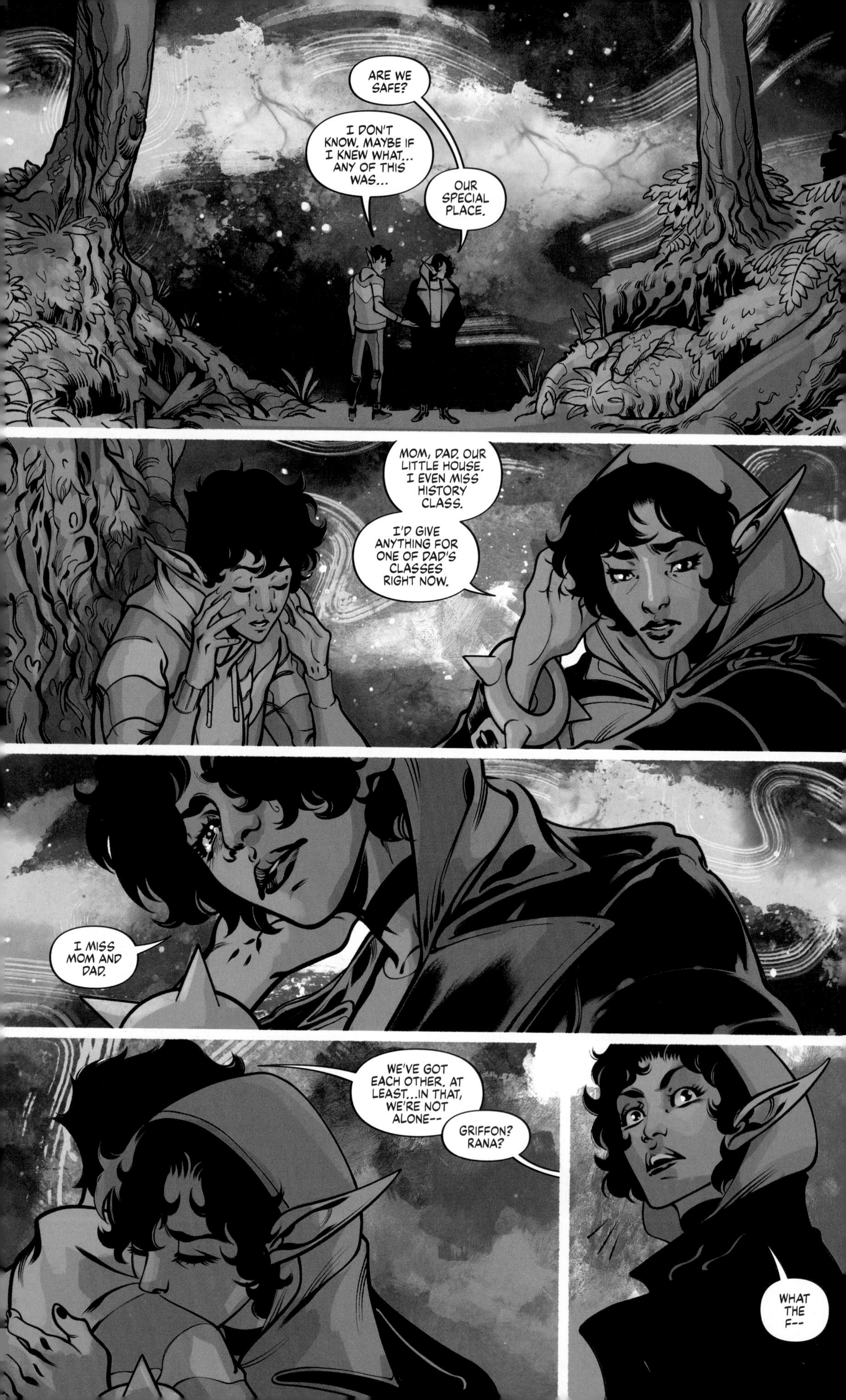
ARE WE SAFE?
I DON'T KNOW. MAYBE IF I KNEW WHAT... ANY OF THIS WAS...
OUR SPECIAL PLACE.
MOM, DAD. OUR LITTLE HOUSE. I EVEN MISS HISTORY CLASS.
I'D GIVE ANYTHING FOR ONE OF DAD'S CLASSES RIGHT NOW.
I MISS MOM AND DAD.
WE'VE GOT EACH OTHER. AT LEAST...IN THAT, WE'RE NOT ALONE--
GRIFFON? RANA?
WHAT THE F--

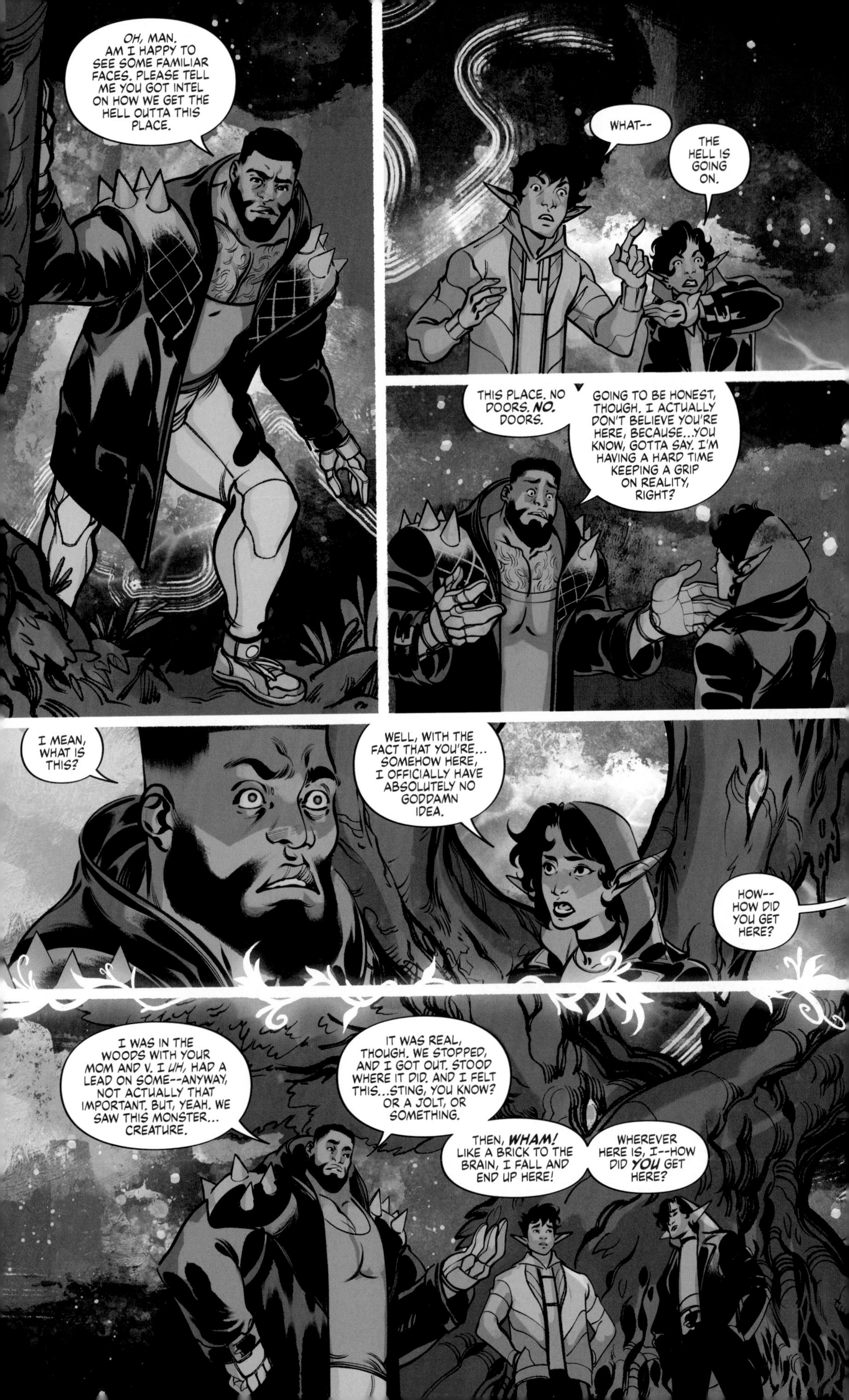
OH, MAN. AM I HAPPY TO SEE SOME FAMILIAR FACES. PLEASE TELL ME YOU GOT INTEL ON HOW WE GET THE HELL OUTTA THIS PLACE.
WHAT--
THE HELL IS GOING ON.
THIS PLACE. NO DOORS. NO. DOORS.
GOING TO BE HONEST, THOUGH. I ACTUALLY DON'T BELIEVE YOU'RE HERE, BECAUSE...YOU KNOW, GOTTA SAY. I'M HAVING A HARD TIME KEEPING A GRIP ON REALITY, RIGHT?
I MEAN, WHAT IS THIS?
WELL, WITH THE FACT THAT YOU'RE... SOMEHOW HERE, I OFFICIALLY HAVE ABSOLUTELY NO GODDAMN IDEA.
HOW-- HOW DID YOU GET HERE?
I WAS IN THE WOODS WITH YOUR MOM AND V. I UH, HAD A LEAD ON SOME--ANYWAY, NOT ACTUALLY THAT IMPORTANT. BUT, YEAH. WE SAW THIS MONSTER... CREATURE.
IT WAS REAL, THOUGH. WE STOPPED, AND I GOT OUT. STOOD WHERE IT DID. AND I FELT THIS...STING, YOU KNOW? OR A JOLT, OR SOMETHING.
THEN, WHAM! LIKE A BRICK TO THE BRAIN, I FALL AND END UP HERE!
WHEREVER HERE IS, I--HOW DID YOU GET HERE?

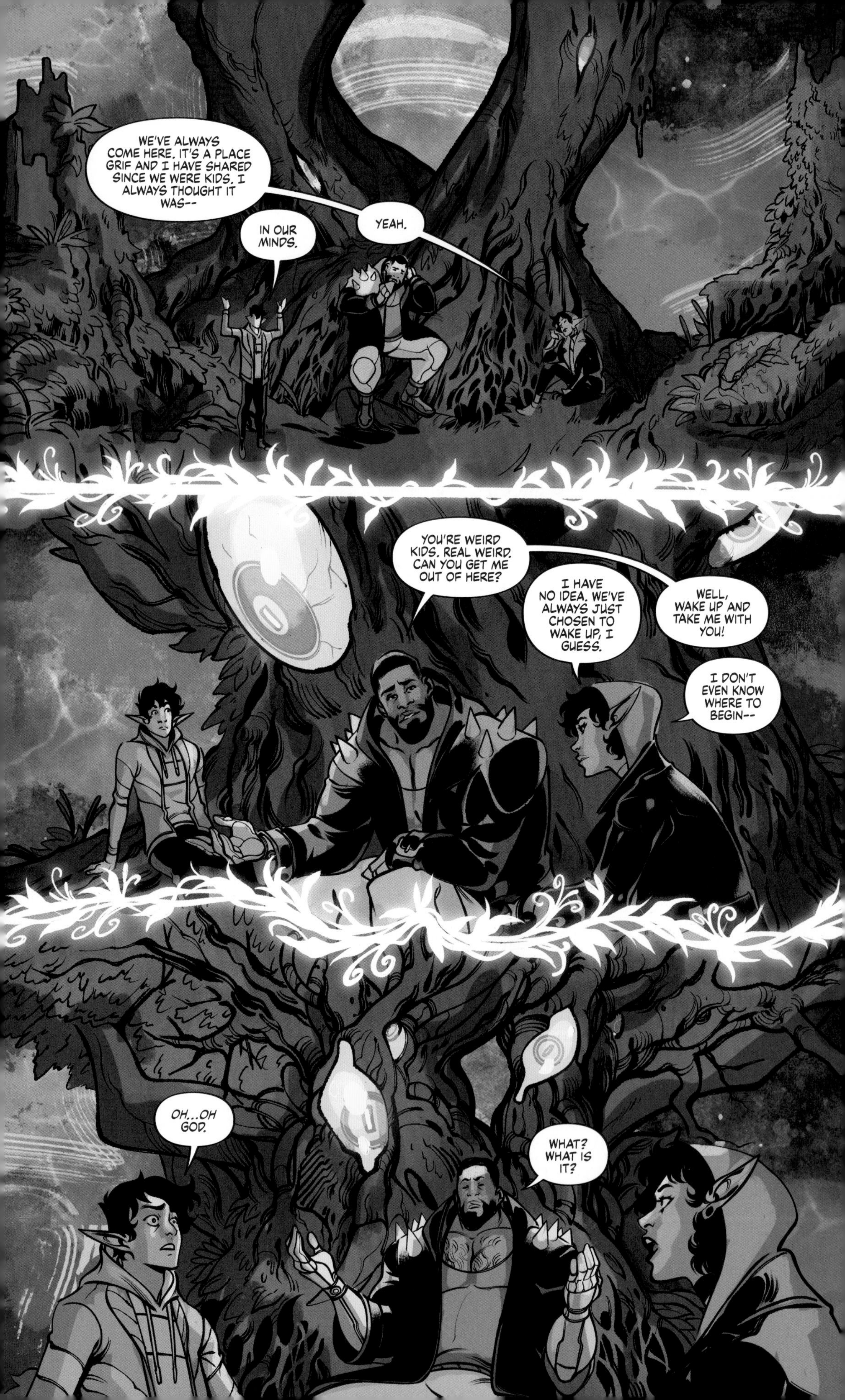
WE'VE ALWAYS COME HERE. IT'S A PLACE GRIF AND I HAVE SHARED SINCE WE WERE KIDS. I ALWAYS THOUGHT IT WAS--
IN OUR MINDS.
YEAH.
YOU'RE WEIRD KIDS. REAL WEIRD. CAN YOU GET ME OUT OF HERE?
I HAVE NO IDEA. WE'VE ALWAYS JUST CHOSEN TO WAKE UP, I GUESS.
WELL, WAKE UP AND TAKE ME WITH YOU!
I DON'T EVEN KNOW WHERE TO BEGIN--
OH...OH GOD.
WHAT? WHAT IS IT?

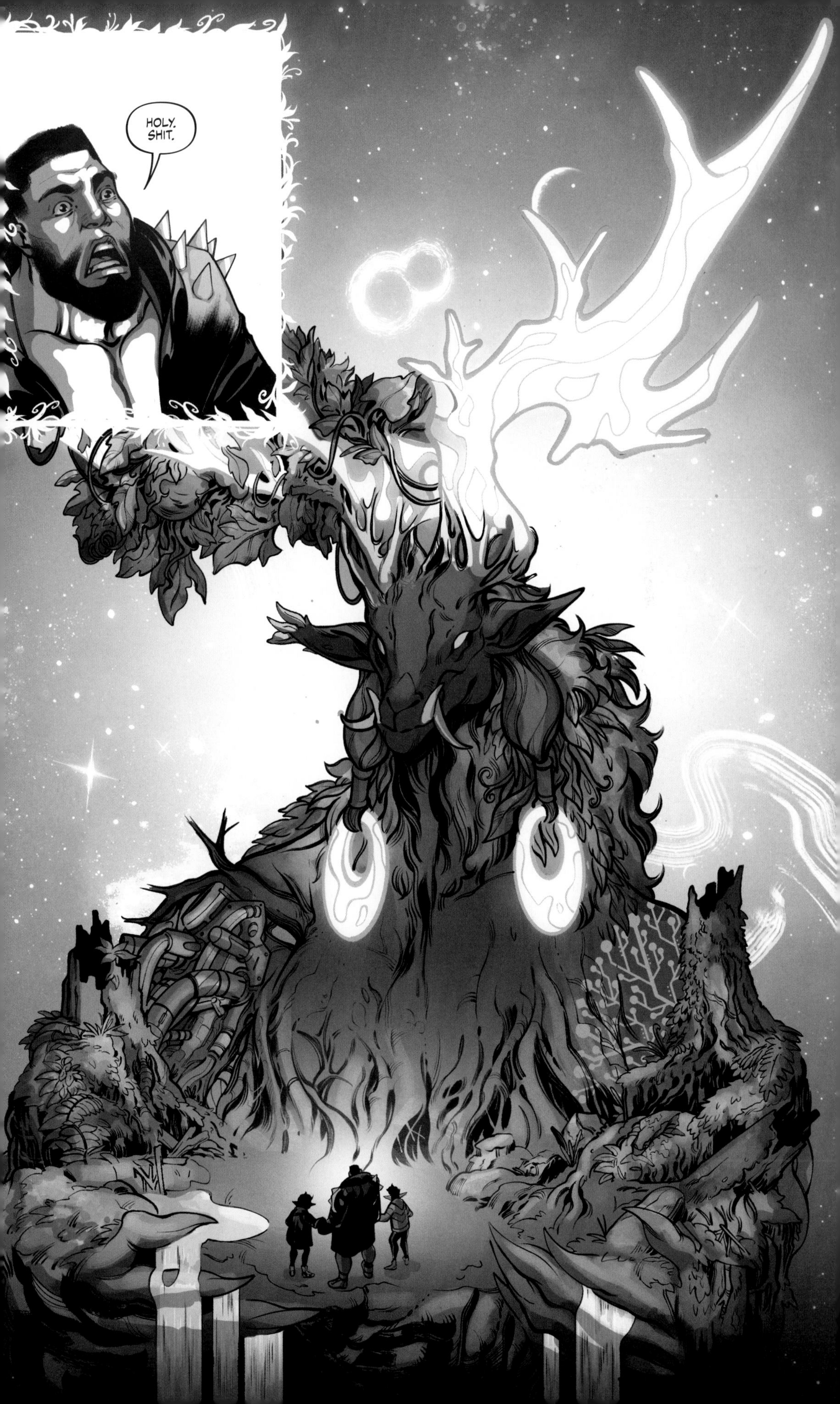
HOLY. SHIT.

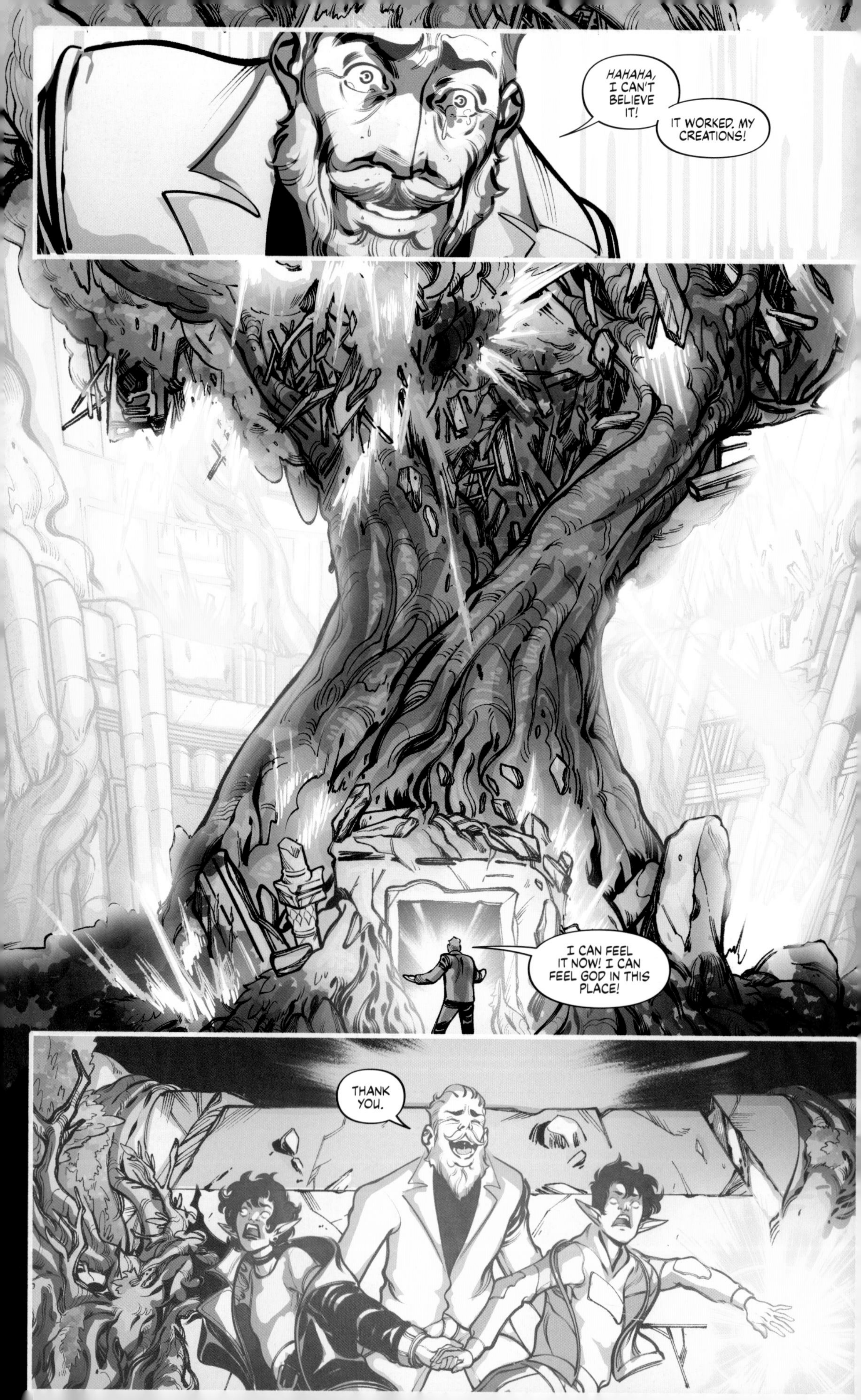
HAHAHA, I CAN'T BELIEVE IT!
IT WORKED, MY CREATIONS!
I CAN FEEL IT NOW! I CAN FEEL GOD IN THIS PLACE!
THANK YOU.

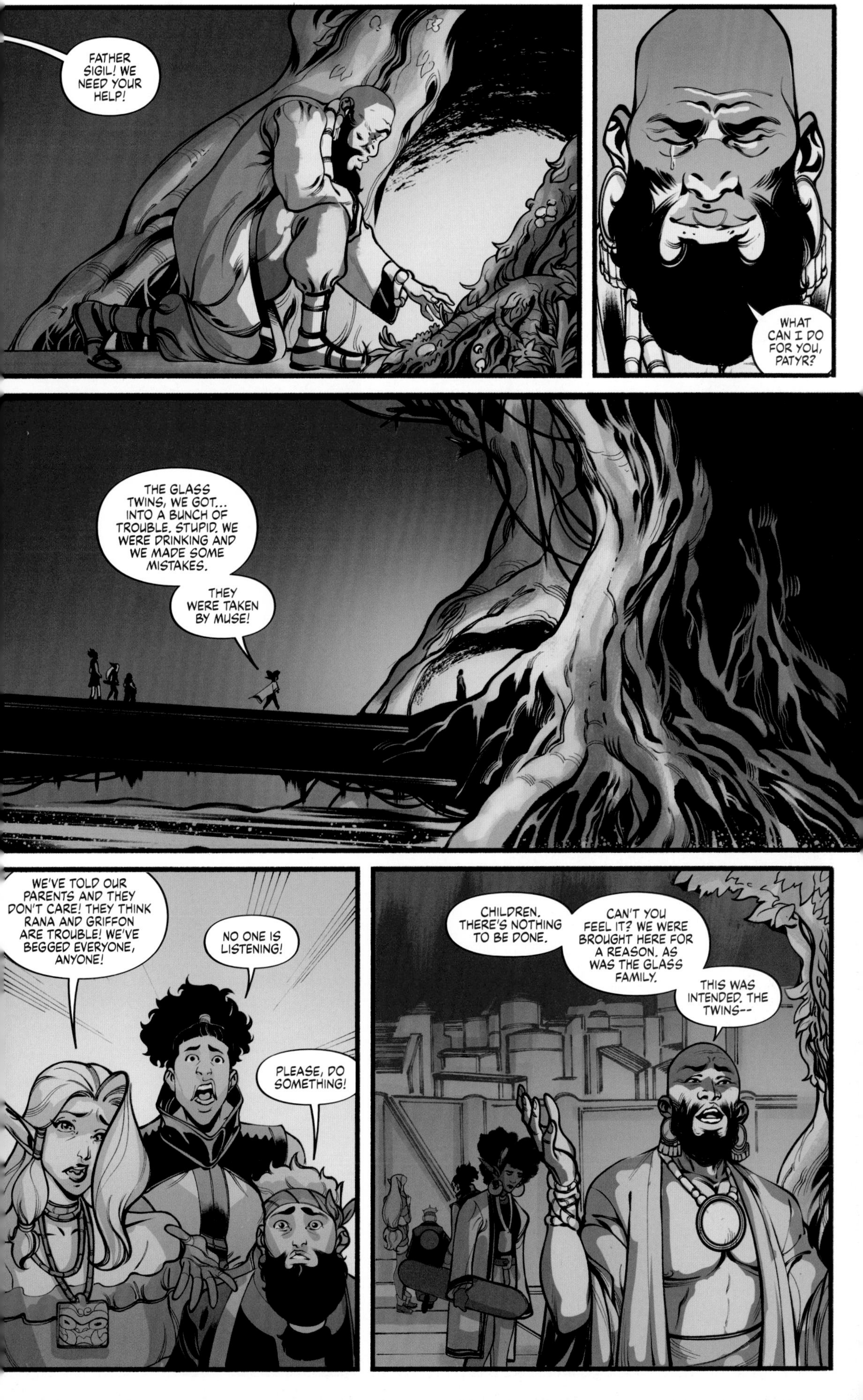
FATHER SIGIL! WE NEED YOUR HELP!
WHAT CAN I DO FOR YOU, PATYR?
THE GLASS TWINS, WE GOT... INTO A BUNCH OF TROUBLE. STUPID. WE WERE DRINKING AND WE MADE SOME MISTAKES.
THEY WERE TAKEN BY MUSE!
WE'VE TOLD OUR PARENTS AND THEY DON'T CARE! THEY THINK RANA AND GRIFFON ARE TROUBLE! WE'VE BEGGED EVERYONE, ANYONE!
NO ONE IS LISTENING!
PLEASE, DO SOMETHING!
CHILDREN. THERE'S NOTHING TO BE DONE.
CAN'T YOU FEEL IT? WE WERE BROUGHT HERE FOR A REASON. AS WAS THE GLASS FAMILY.
THIS WAS INTENDED. THE TWINS--

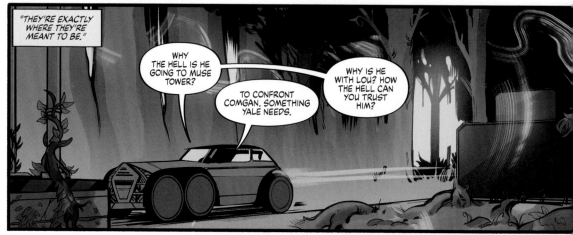

"THEY'RE EXACTLY WHERE THEY'RE MEANT TO BE."

WHY THE HELL IS HE GOING TO MUSE TOWER?

TO CONFRONT COMGAN. SOMETHING YALE NEEDS.

WHY IS HE WITH LOU? HOW THE HELL CAN YOU TRUST HIM?

I DON'T. BUT LOU ISN'T MY CONCERN. NOT FOR NOW, ANYWAY. I JUST WANT TO GET BACK. I WANT TO HOLD MY BABIES.

NEVER SEEN YOU LIKE THIS.

LIKE WHAT?

VULNERABLE.

SHUT UP.

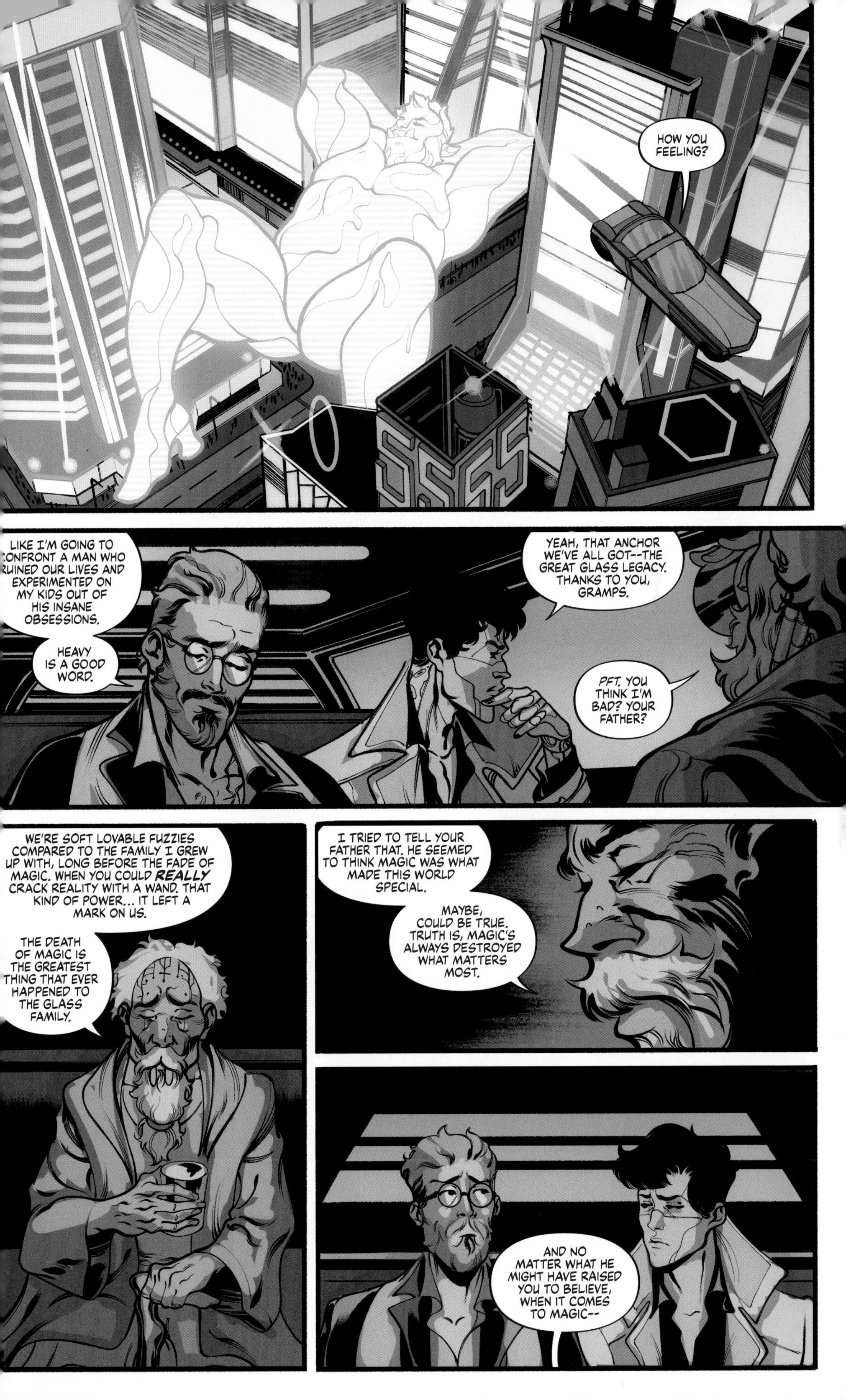

HOW YOU FEELING?
LIKE I'M GOING TO CONFRONT A MAN WHO RUINED OUR LIVES AND EXPERIMENTED ON MY KIDS OUT OF HIS INSANE OBSESSIONS.
HEAVY IS A GOOD WORD.
YEAH, THAT ANCHOR WE'VE ALL GOT--THE GREAT GLASS LEGACY. THANKS TO YOU, GRAMPS.
PFT. YOU THINK I'M BAD? YOUR FATHER?
WE'RE SOFT LOVABLE FUZZIES COMPARED TO THE FAMILY I GREW UP WITH, LONG BEFORE THE FADE OF MAGIC. WHEN YOU COULD REALLY CRACK REALITY WITH A WAND. THAT KIND OF POWER... IT LEFT A MARK ON US.
THE DEATH OF MAGIC IS THE GREATEST THING THAT EVER HAPPENED TO THE GLASS FAMILY.
I TRIED TO TELL YOUR FATHER THAT. HE SEEMED TO THINK MAGIC WAS WHAT MADE THIS WORLD SPECIAL.
MAYBE, COULD BE TRUE. TRUTH IS, MAGIC'S ALWAYS DESTROYED WHAT MATTERS MOST.
AND NO MATTER WHAT HE MIGHT HAVE RAISED YOU TO BELIEVE, WHEN IT COMES TO MAGIC--

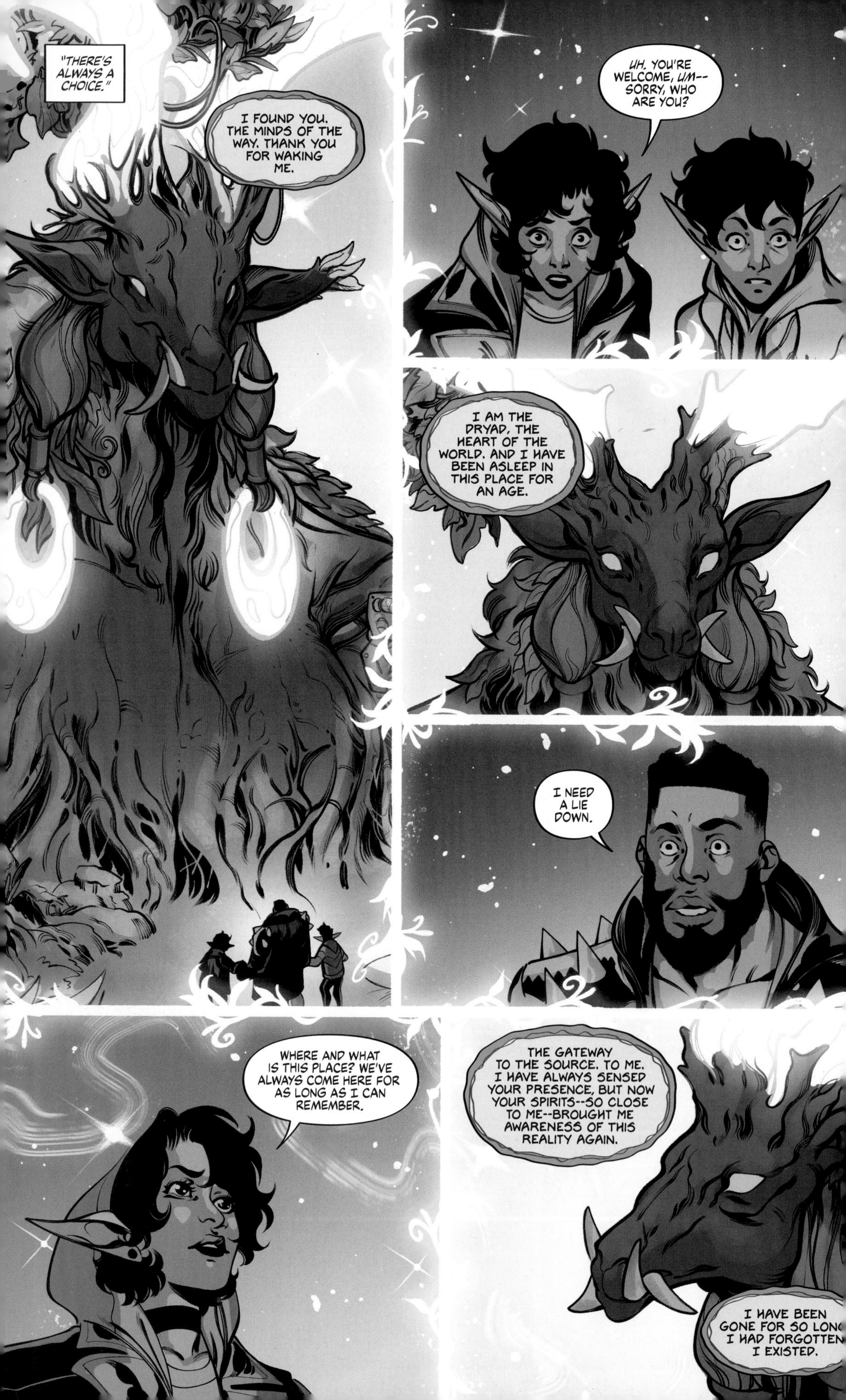
"THERE'S ALWAYS A CHOICE."
I FOUND YOU. THE MINDS OF THE WAY. THANK YOU FOR WAKING ME.
UH. YOU'RE WELCOME, UM-- SORRY, WHO ARE YOU?
I AM THE DRYAD, THE HEART OF THE WORLD. AND I HAVE BEEN ASLEEP IN THIS PLACE FOR AN AGE.
I NEED A LIE DOWN.
WHERE AND WHAT IS THIS PLACE? WE'VE ALWAYS COME HERE FOR AS LONG AS I CAN REMEMBER.
THE GATEWAY TO THE SOURCE. TO ME. I HAVE ALWAYS SENSED YOUR PRESENCE, BUT NOW YOUR SPIRITS--SO CLOSE TO ME--BROUGHT ME AWARENESS OF THIS REALITY AGAIN.
I HAVE BEEN GONE FOR SO LONG I HAD FORGOTTEN I EXISTED.

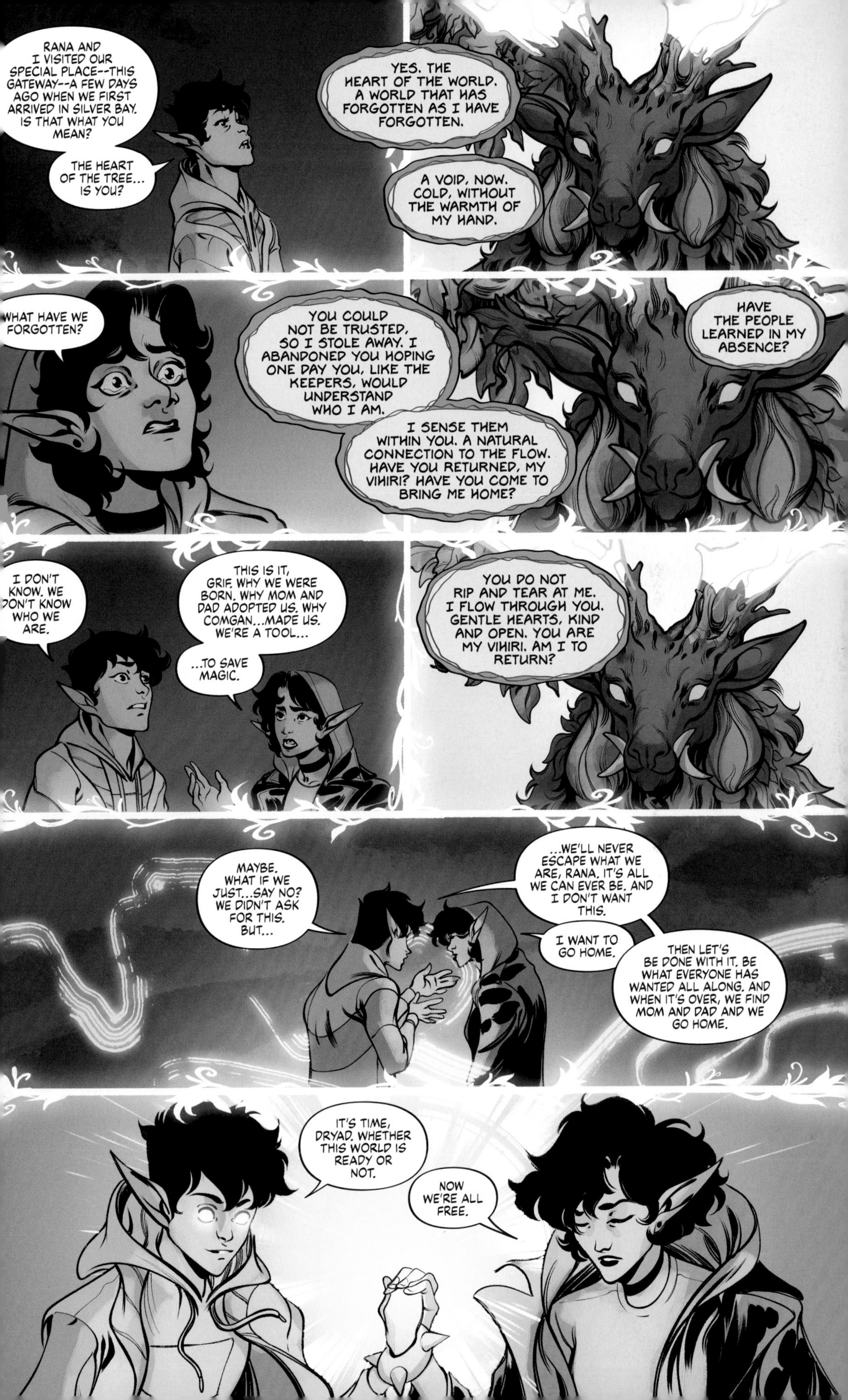

RANA AND I VISITED OUR SPECIAL PLACE--THIS GATEWAY--A FEW DAYS AGO WHEN WE FIRST ARRIVED IN SILVER BAY. IS THAT WHAT YOU MEAN?
THE HEART OF THE TREE... IS YOU?
YES. THE HEART OF THE WORLD. A WORLD THAT HAS FORGOTTEN AS I HAVE FORGOTTEN.
A VOID, NOW. COLD, WITHOUT THE WARMTH OF MY HAND.
WHAT HAVE WE FORGOTTEN?
YOU COULD NOT BE TRUSTED, SO I STOLE AWAY. I ABANDONED YOU HOPING ONE DAY YOU, LIKE THE KEEPERS, WOULD UNDERSTAND WHO I AM.
HAVE THE PEOPLE LEARNED IN MY ABSENCE?
I SENSE THEM WITHIN YOU. A NATURAL CONNECTION TO THE FLOW. HAVE YOU RETURNED, MY VIHIRI? HAVE YOU COME TO BRING ME HOME?
I DON'T KNOW. WE DON'T KNOW WHO WE ARE.
THIS IS IT, GRIF. WHY WE WERE BORN. WHY MOM AND DAD ADOPTED US. WHY COMGAN...MADE US. WE'RE A TOOL...
...TO SAVE MAGIC.
YOU DO NOT RIP AND TEAR AT ME. I FLOW THROUGH YOU. GENTLE HEARTS, KIND AND OPEN. YOU ARE MY VIHIRI. AM I TO RETURN?
MAYBE. WHAT IF WE JUST...SAY NO? WE DIDN'T ASK FOR THIS. BUT...
...WE'LL NEVER ESCAPE WHAT WE ARE, RANA. IT'S ALL WE CAN EVER BE. AND I DON'T WANT THIS.
I WANT TO GO HOME.
THEN LET'S BE DONE WITH IT. BE WHAT EVERYONE HAS WANTED ALL ALONG. AND WHEN IT'S OVER, WE FIND MOM AND DAD AND WE GO HOME.
IT'S TIME, DRYAD. WHETHER THIS WORLD IS READY OR NOT.
NOW WE'RE ALL FREE.

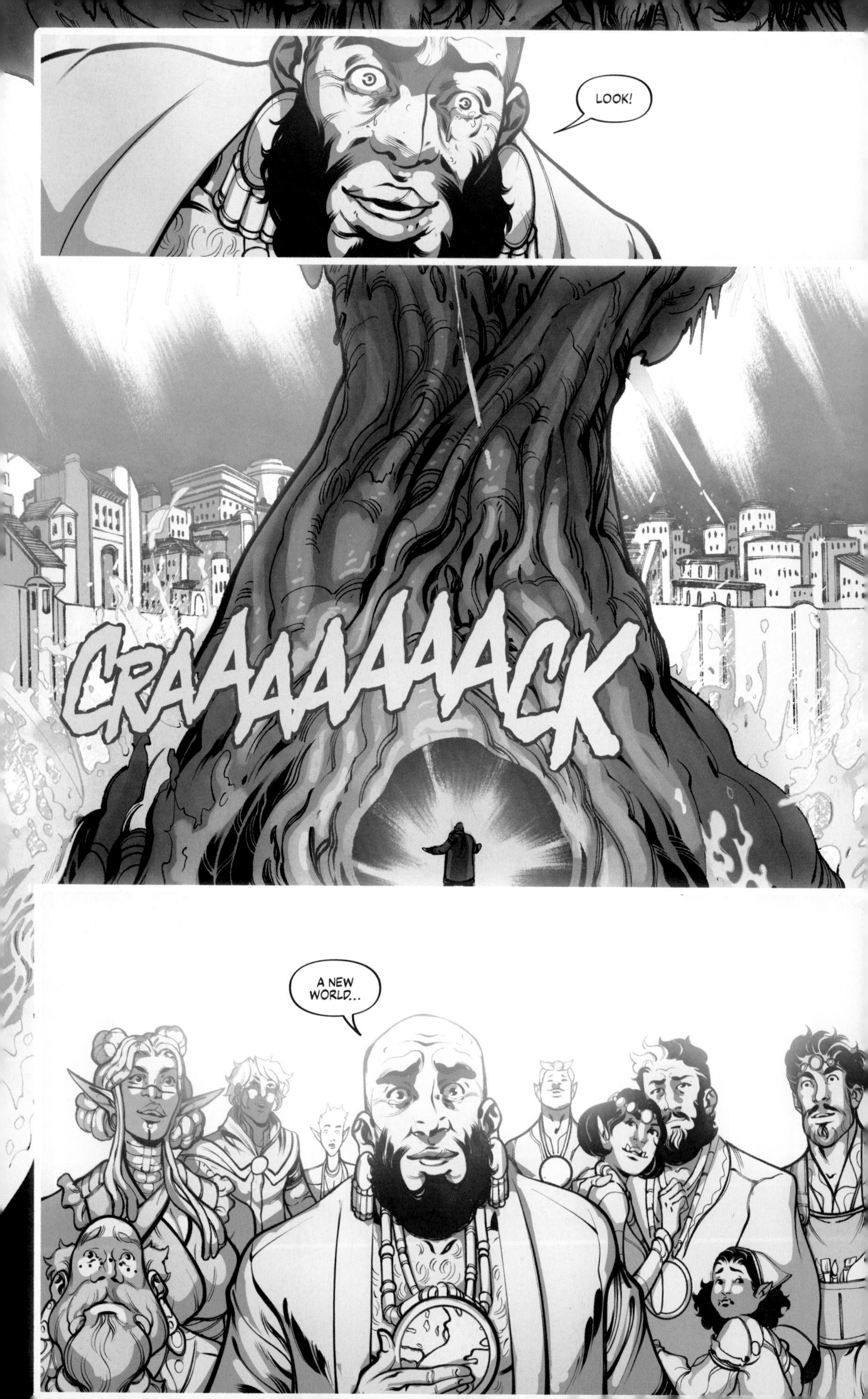
LOOK!
CRAAAAAACK
A NEW WORLD...

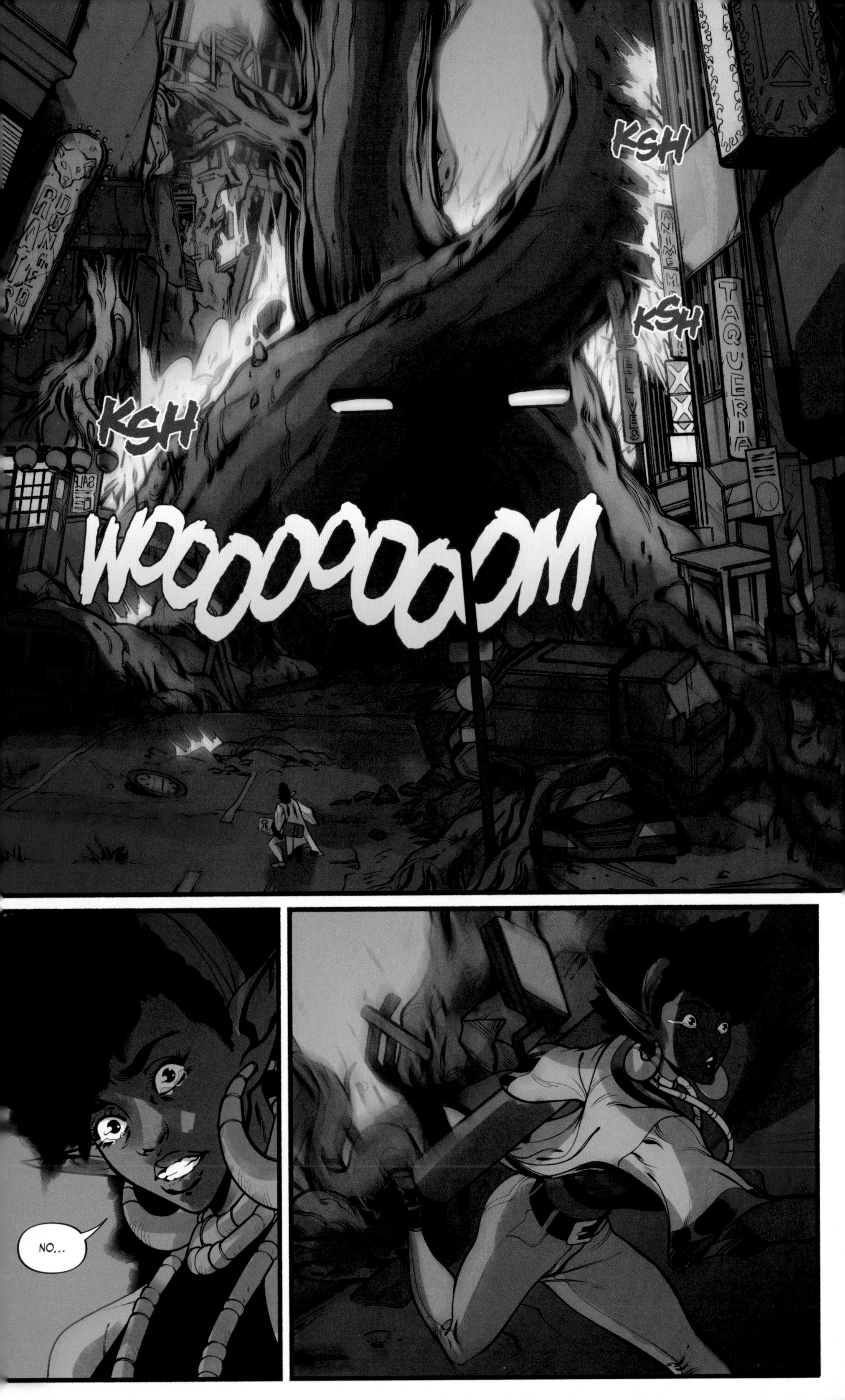
KSH
KSH
KSH
WOOOOOOOOM
TAQUERIA
ELVES
SALE
NO...

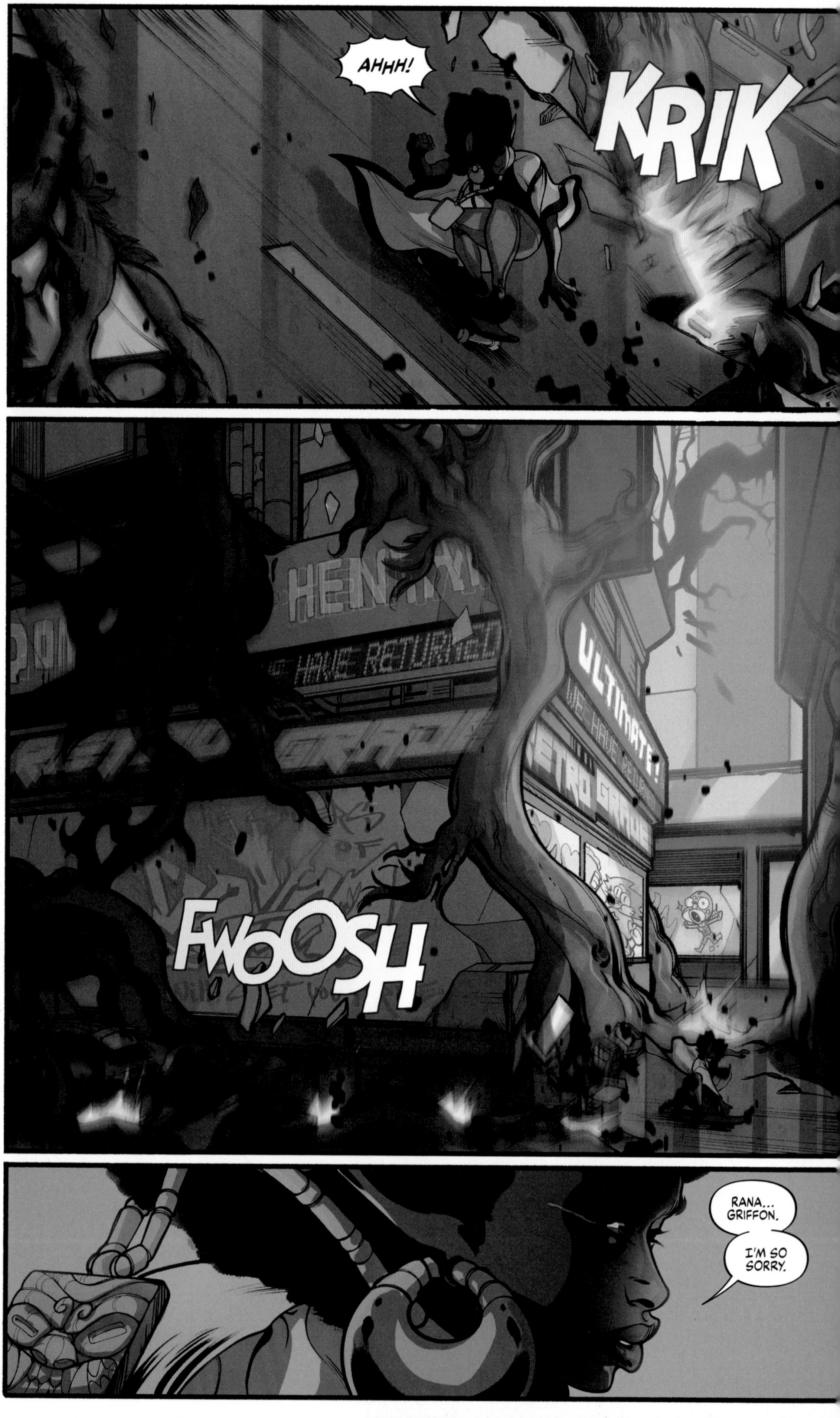
AHHH!
KRIK
ULTIMATE!
FWOOSH
RANA... GRIFFON.
I'M SO SORRY.

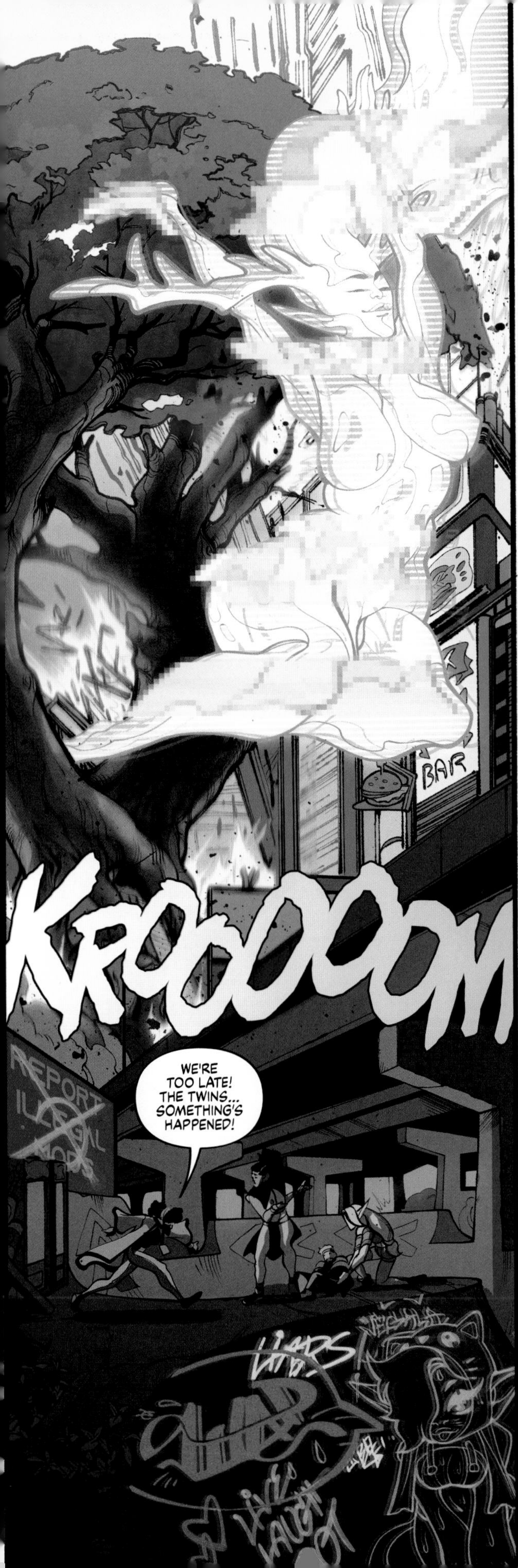
BAR
KROOOOOM
REPORT
WE'RE TOO LATE! THE TWINS... SOMETHING'S HAPPENED!

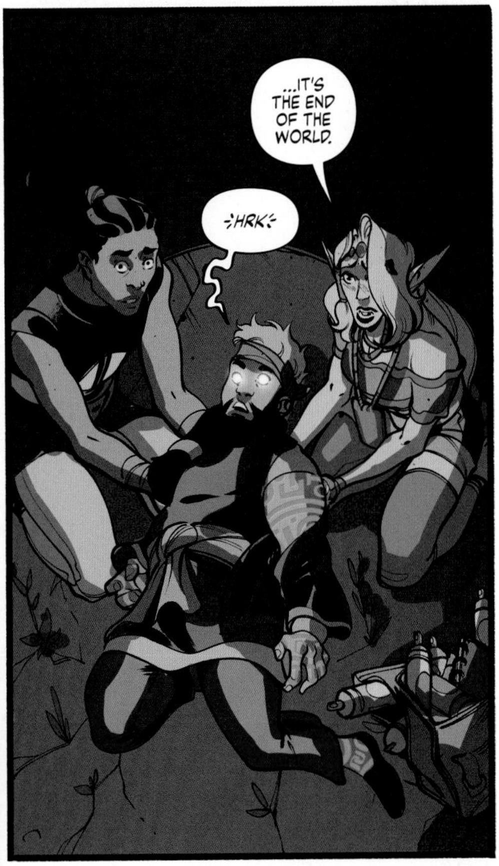
...IT'S THE END OF THE WORLD.
HRK

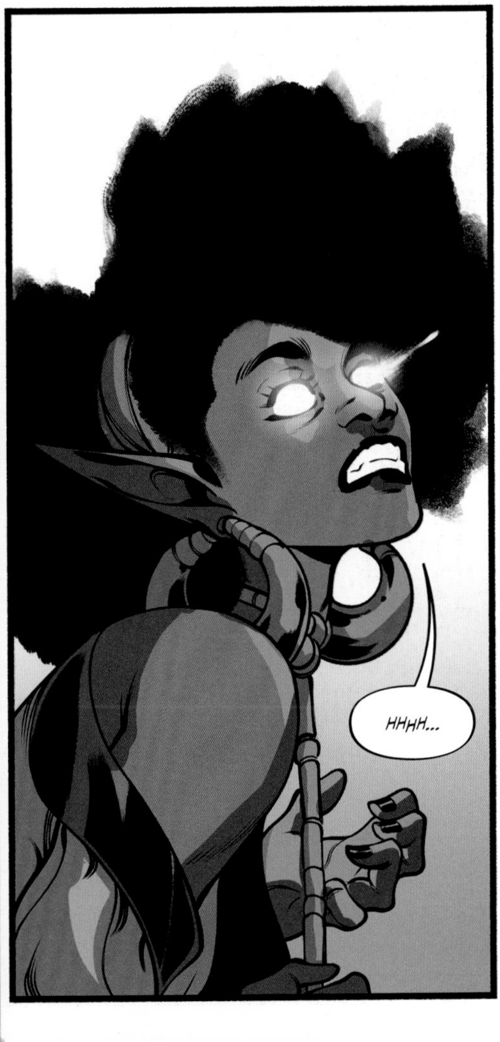
HHHH...

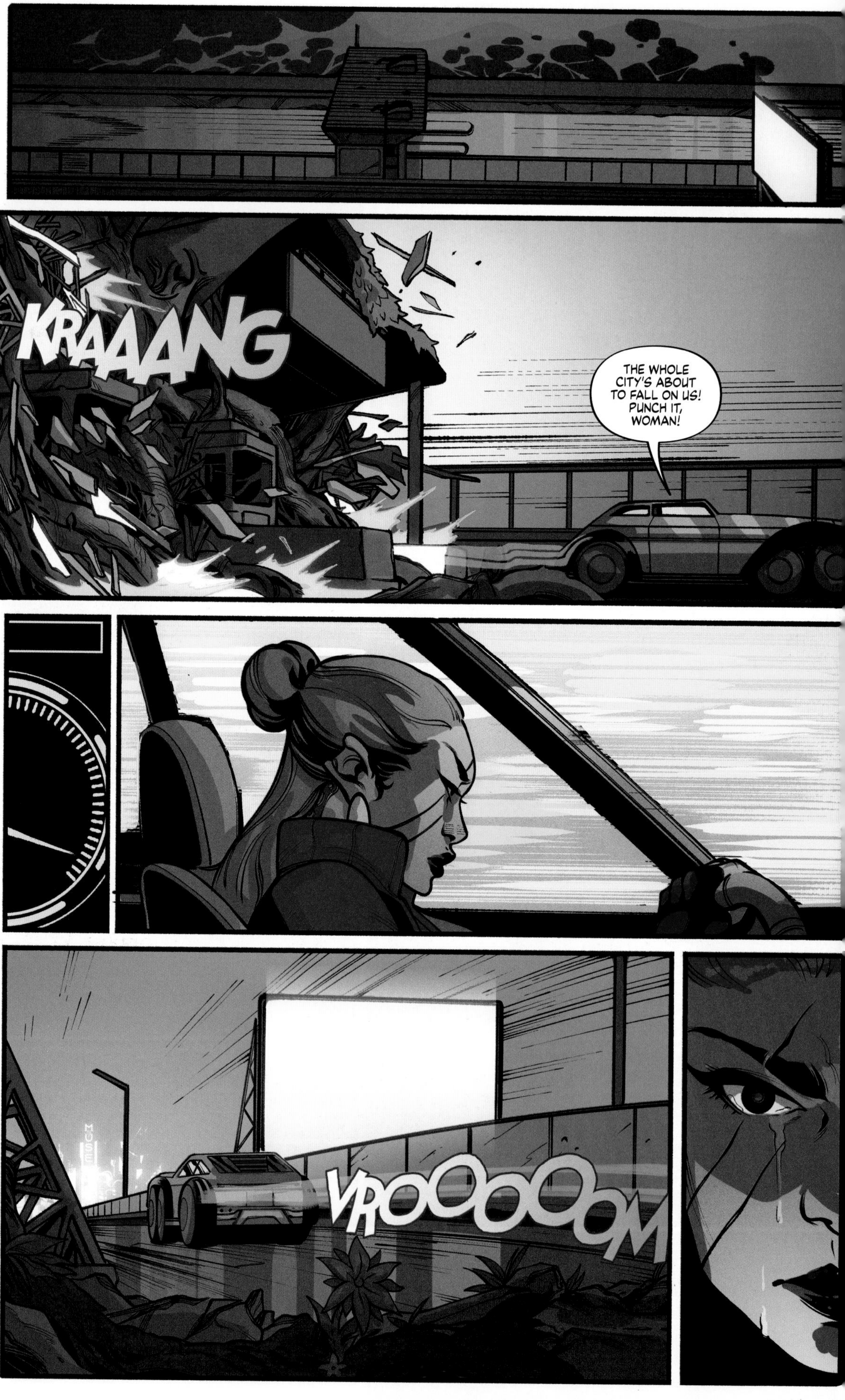
KRAAANG
THE WHOLE CITY'S ABOUT TO FALL ON US! PUNCH IT, WOMAN!
VROOOOOM

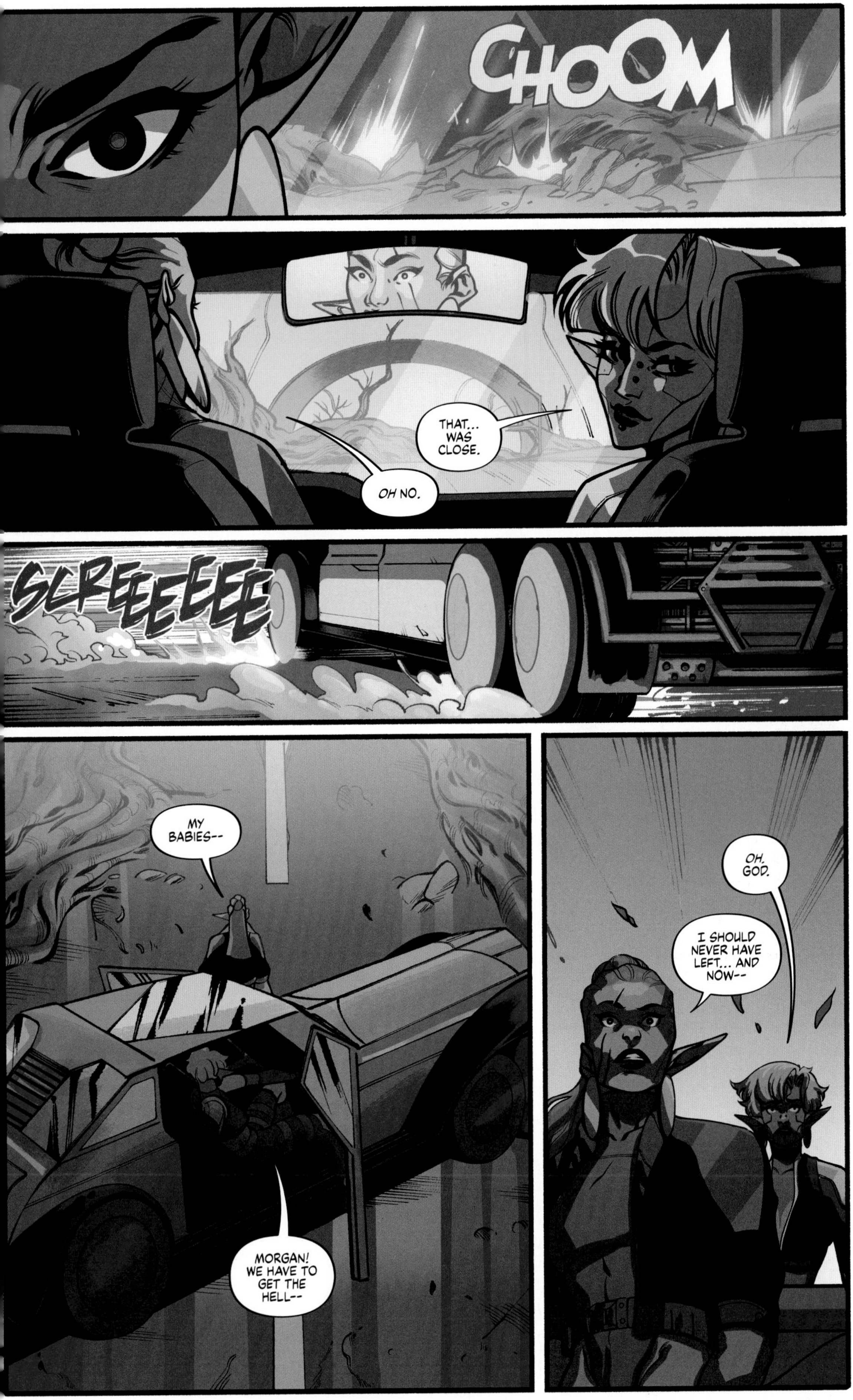
CHOOM
THAT... WAS CLOSE.
OH NO.
SCREEEEEEE
MY BABIES--
MORGAN! WE HAVE TO GET THE HELL--
OH. GOD.
I SHOULD NEVER HAVE LEFT... AND NOW--

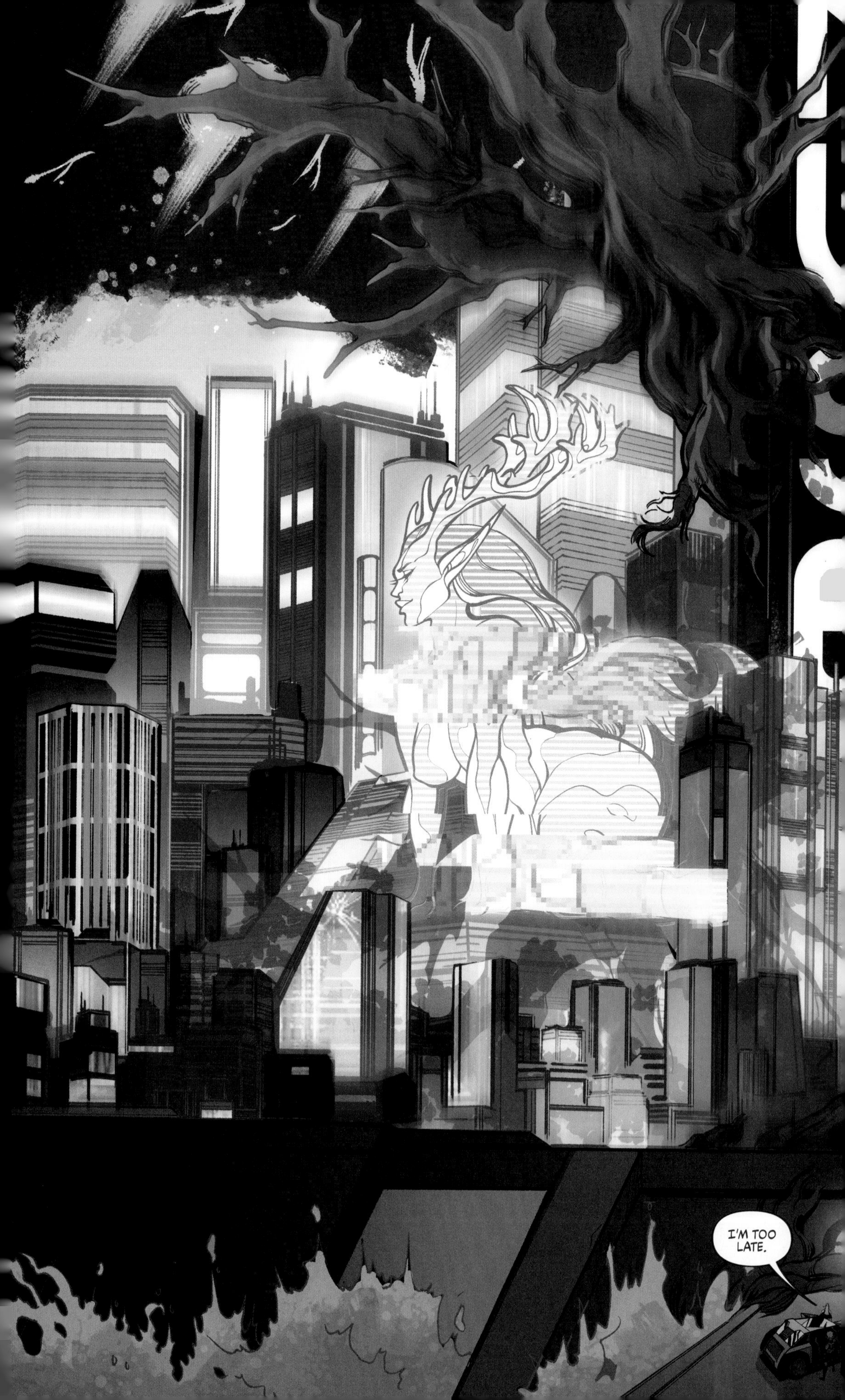
I'M TOO
LATE.

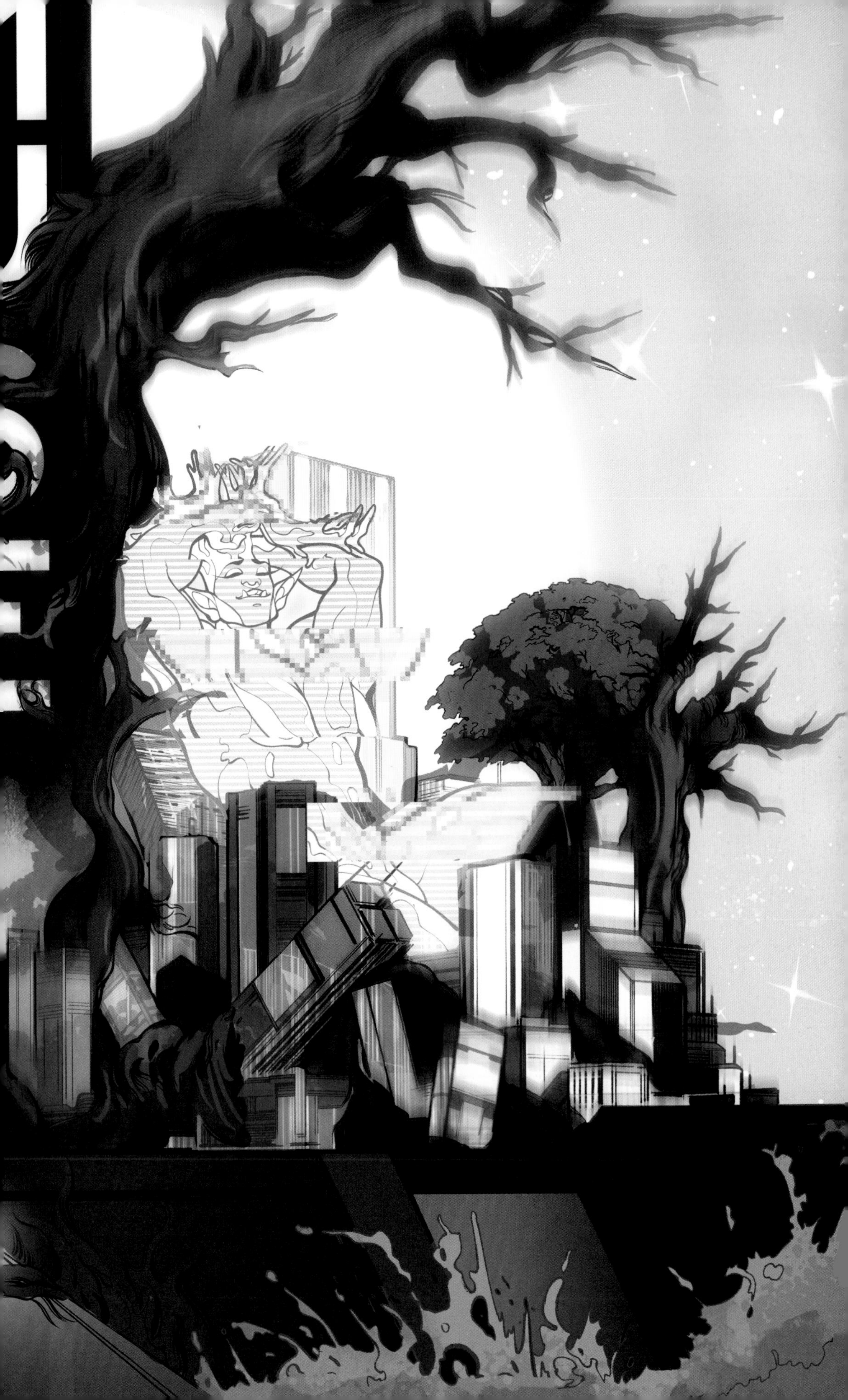

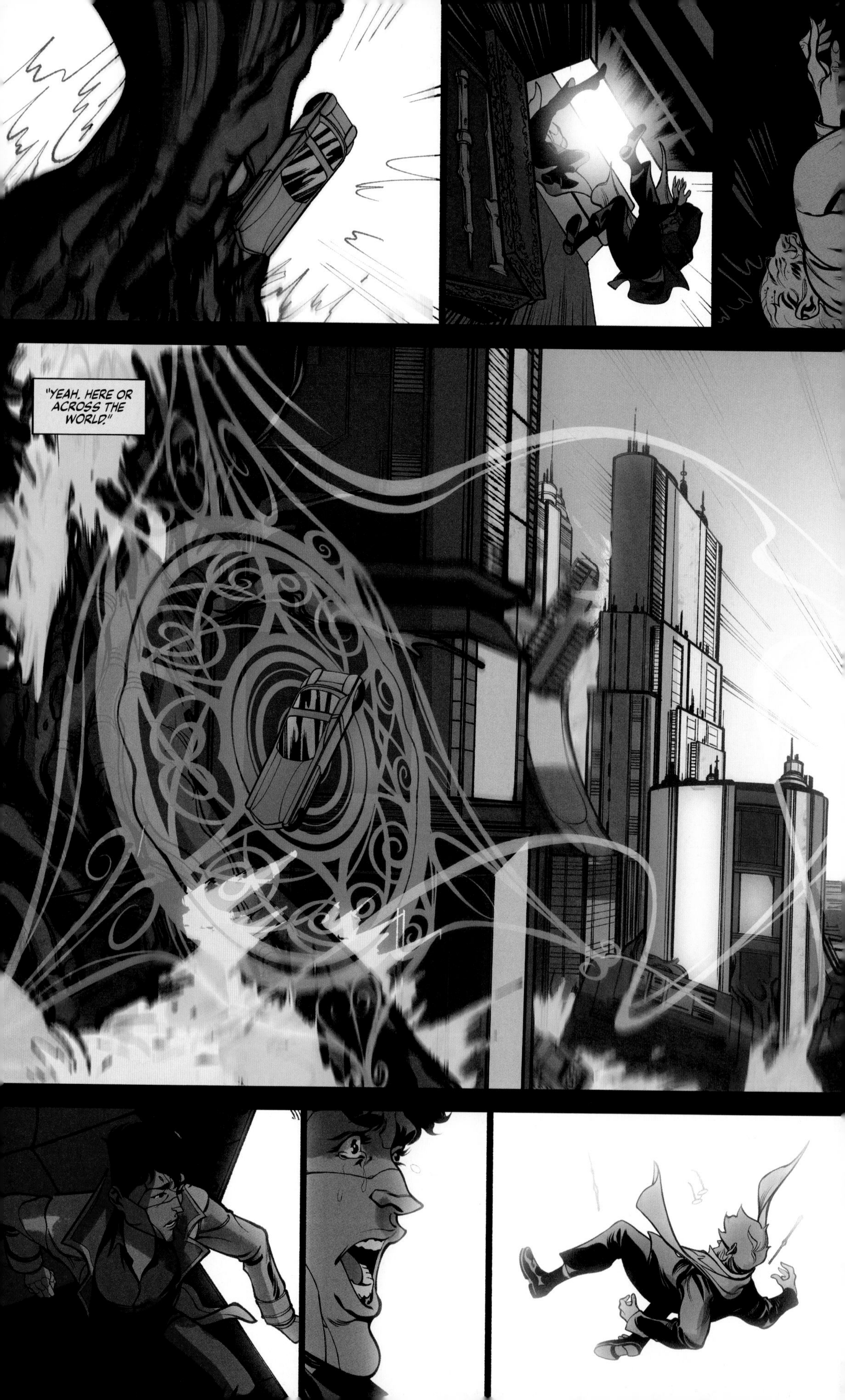
"YEAH. HERE OR ACROSS THE WORLD."

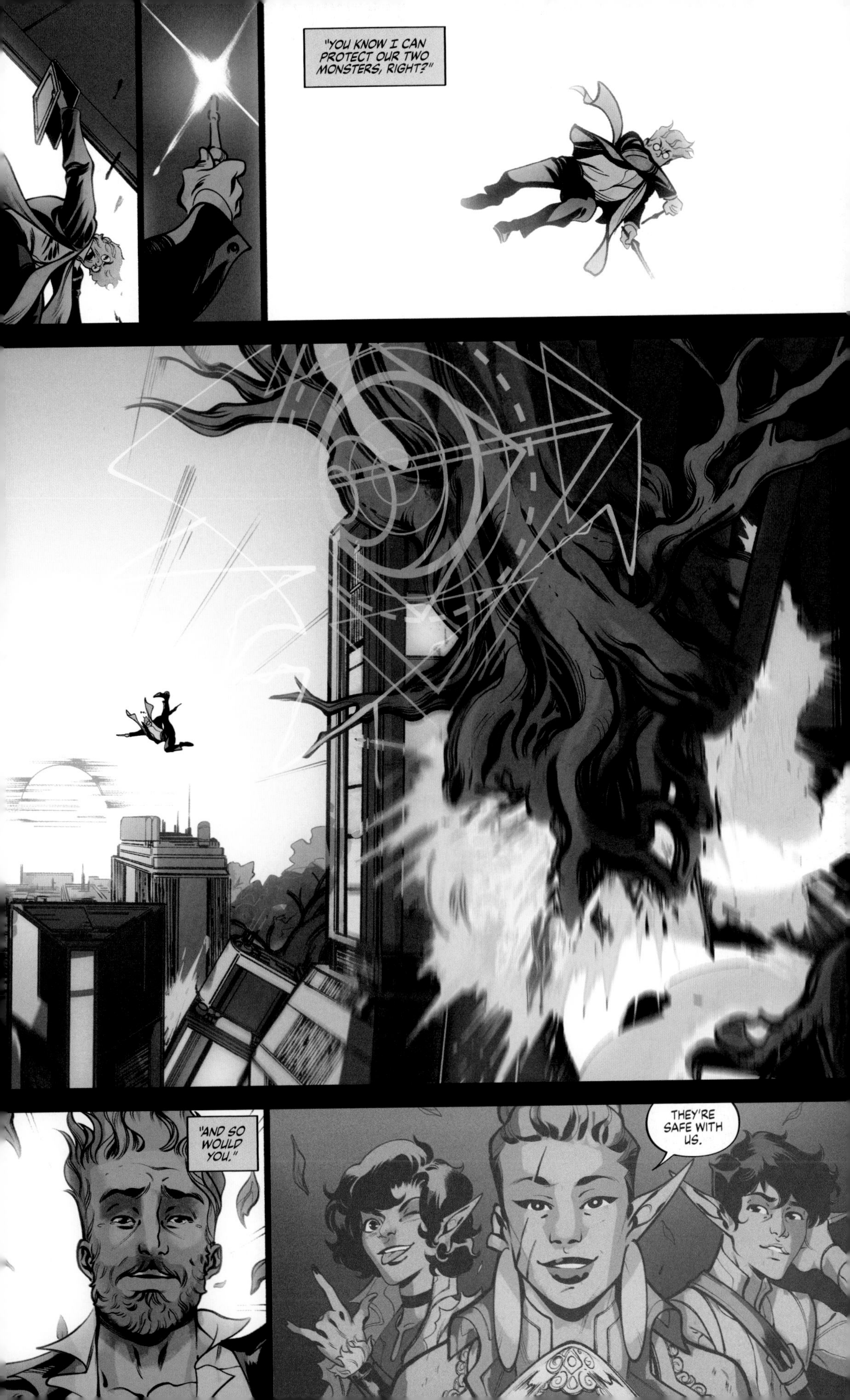
"YOU KNOW I CAN PROTECT OUR TWO MONSTERS, RIGHT?"
"AND SO WOULD YOU."
THEY'RE SAFE WITH US.

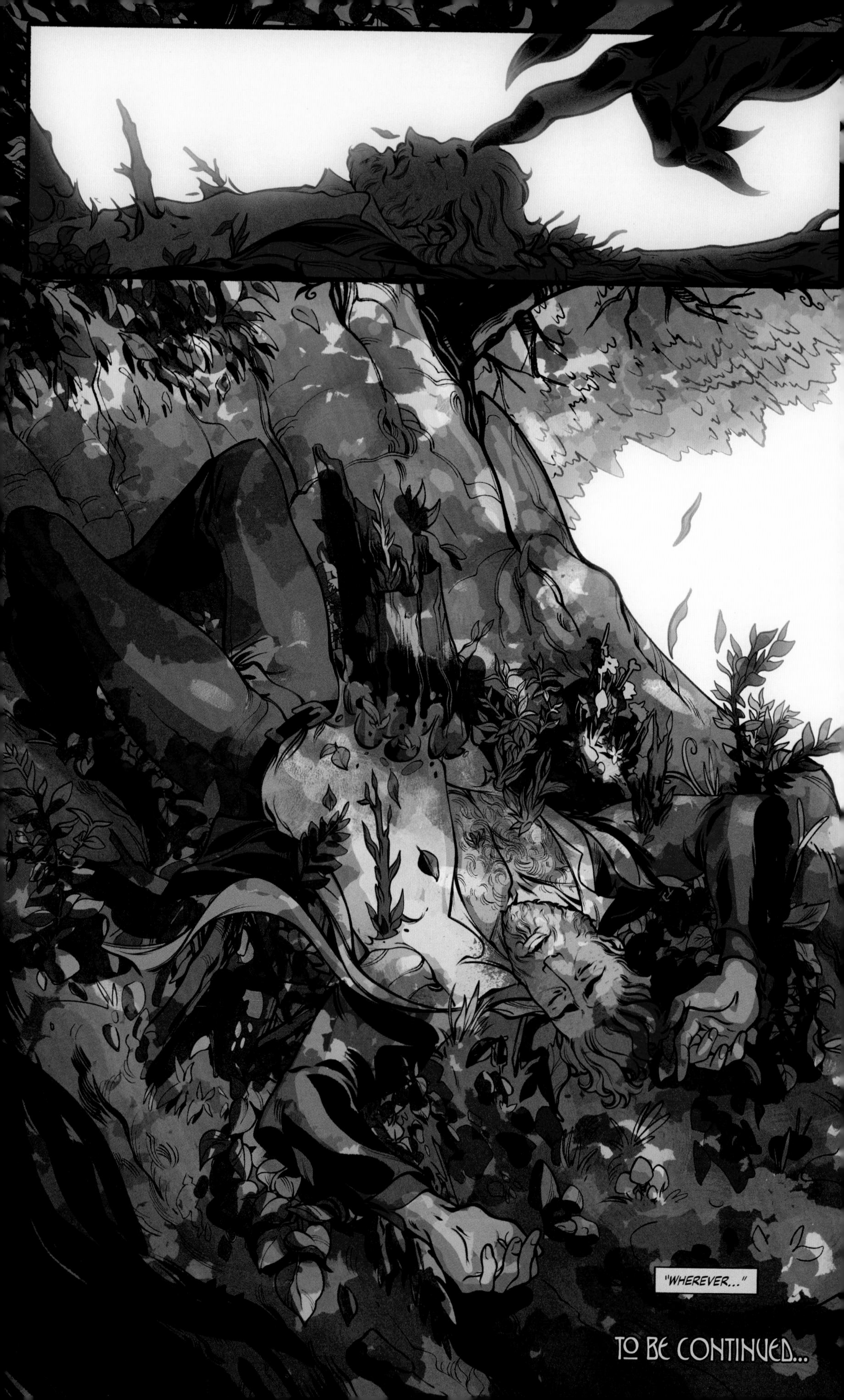
"WHEREVER..."
TO BE CONTINUED...

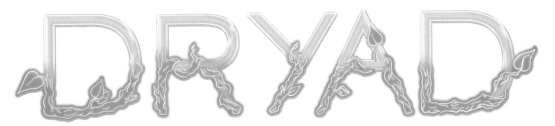

DRYAD

SKETCHES & COVER GALLERY

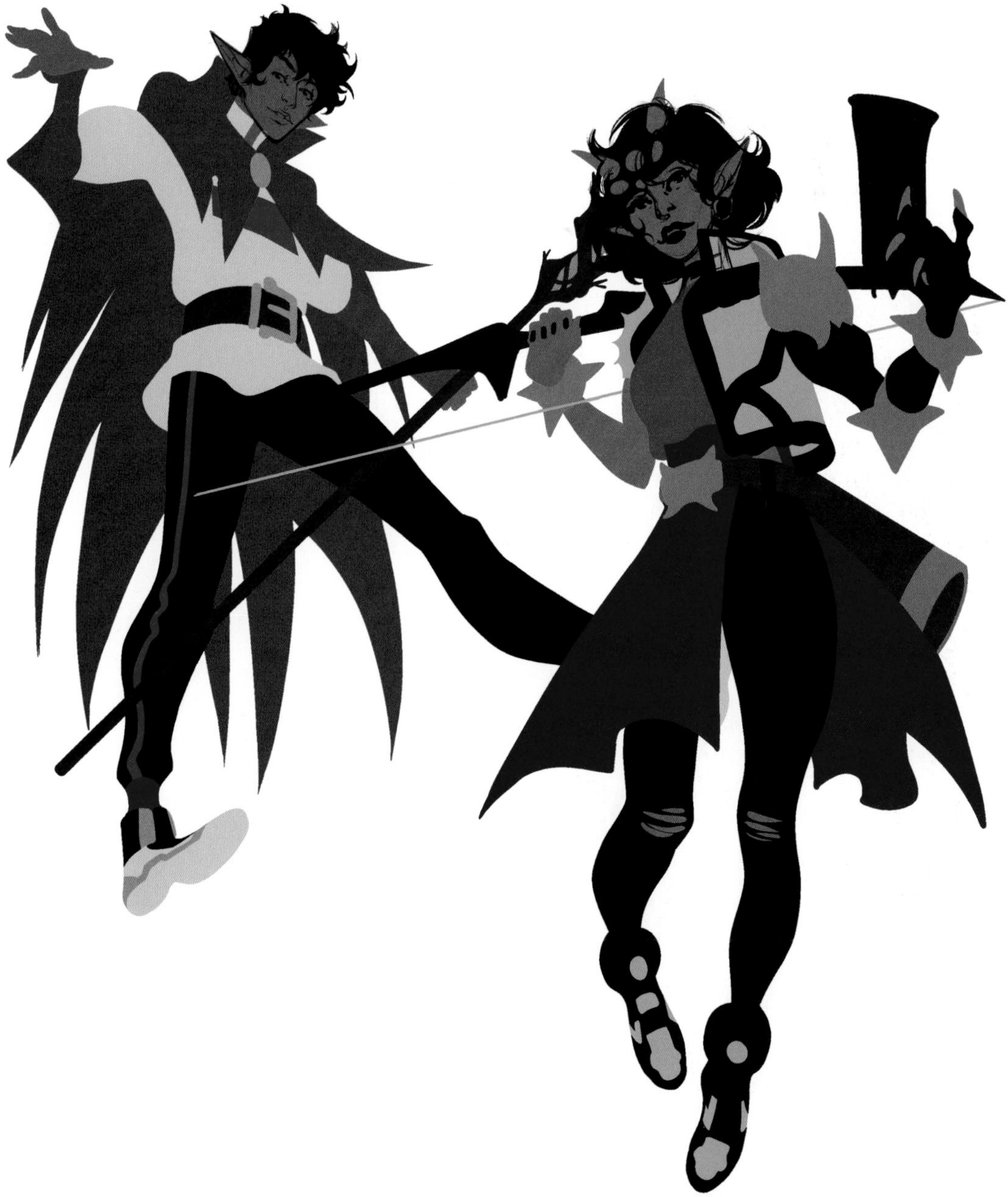

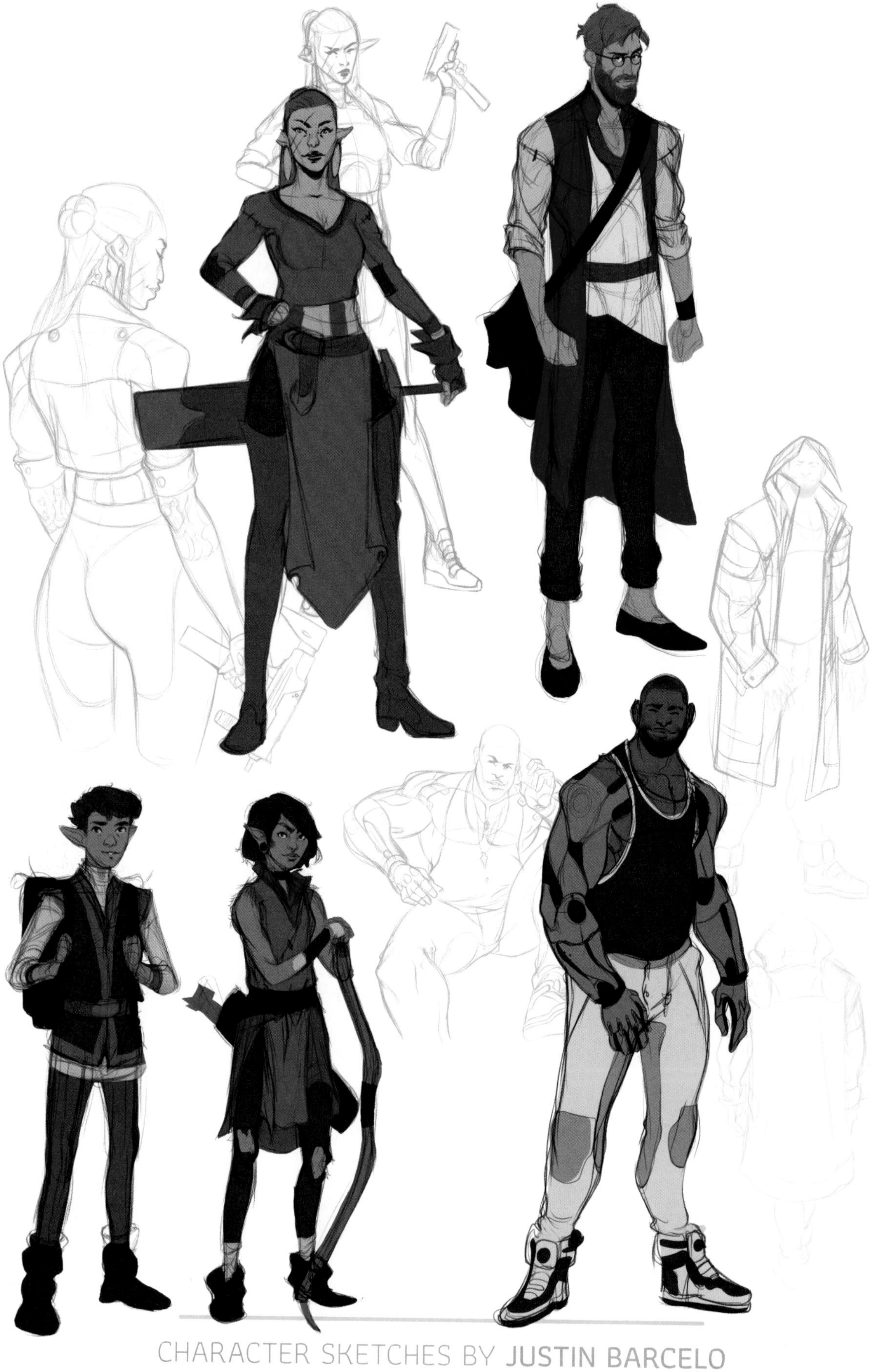

CHARACTER SKETCHES BY **JUSTIN BARCELO**

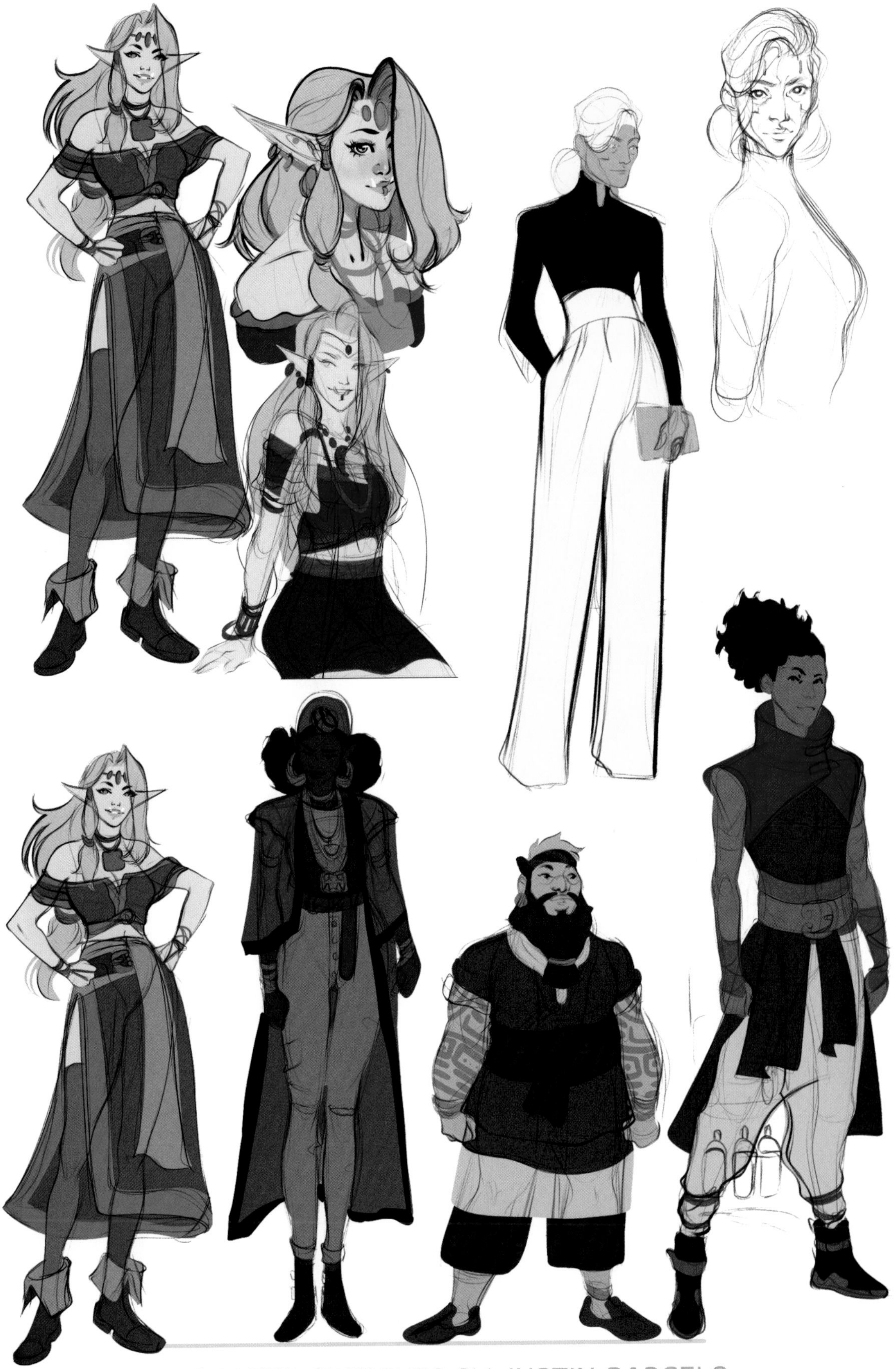

CHARACTER SKETCHES BY **JUSTIN BARCELO**

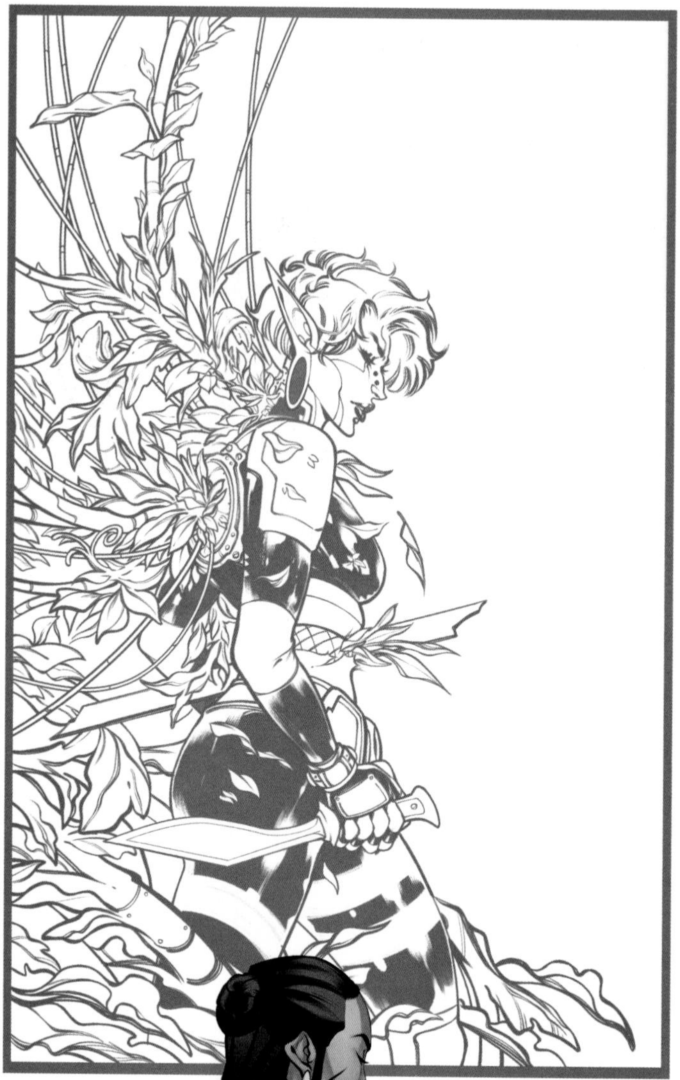

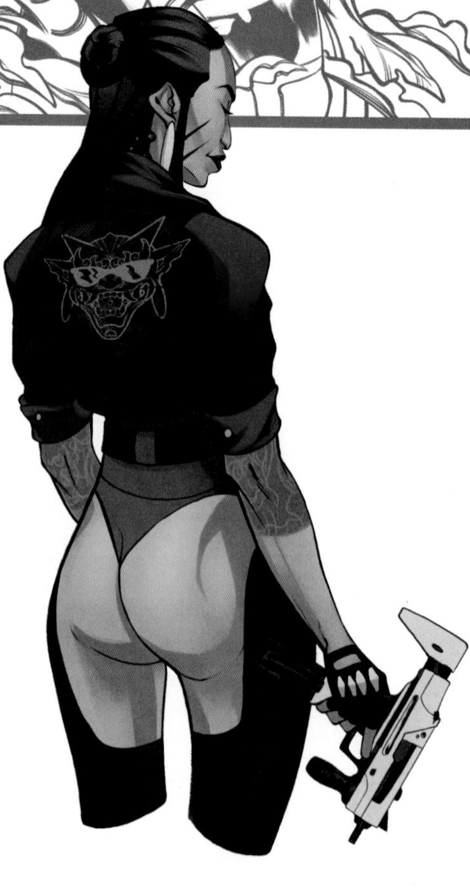

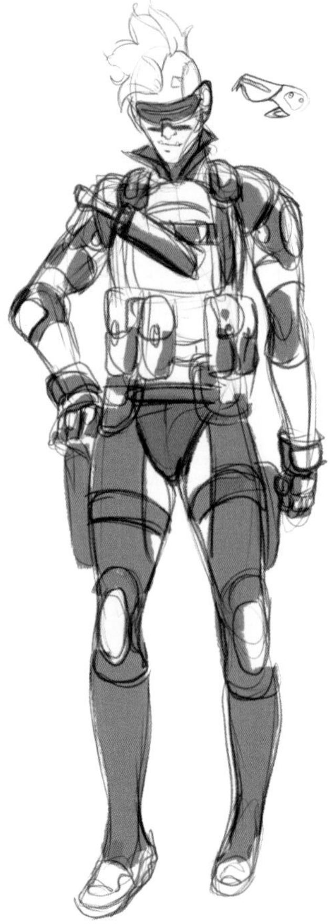

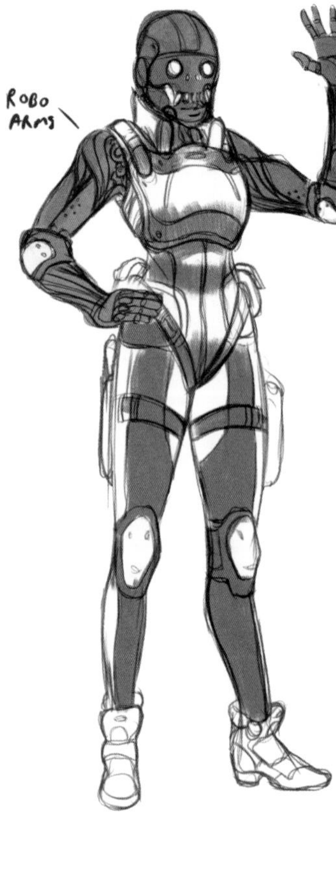
ROBO ARMS

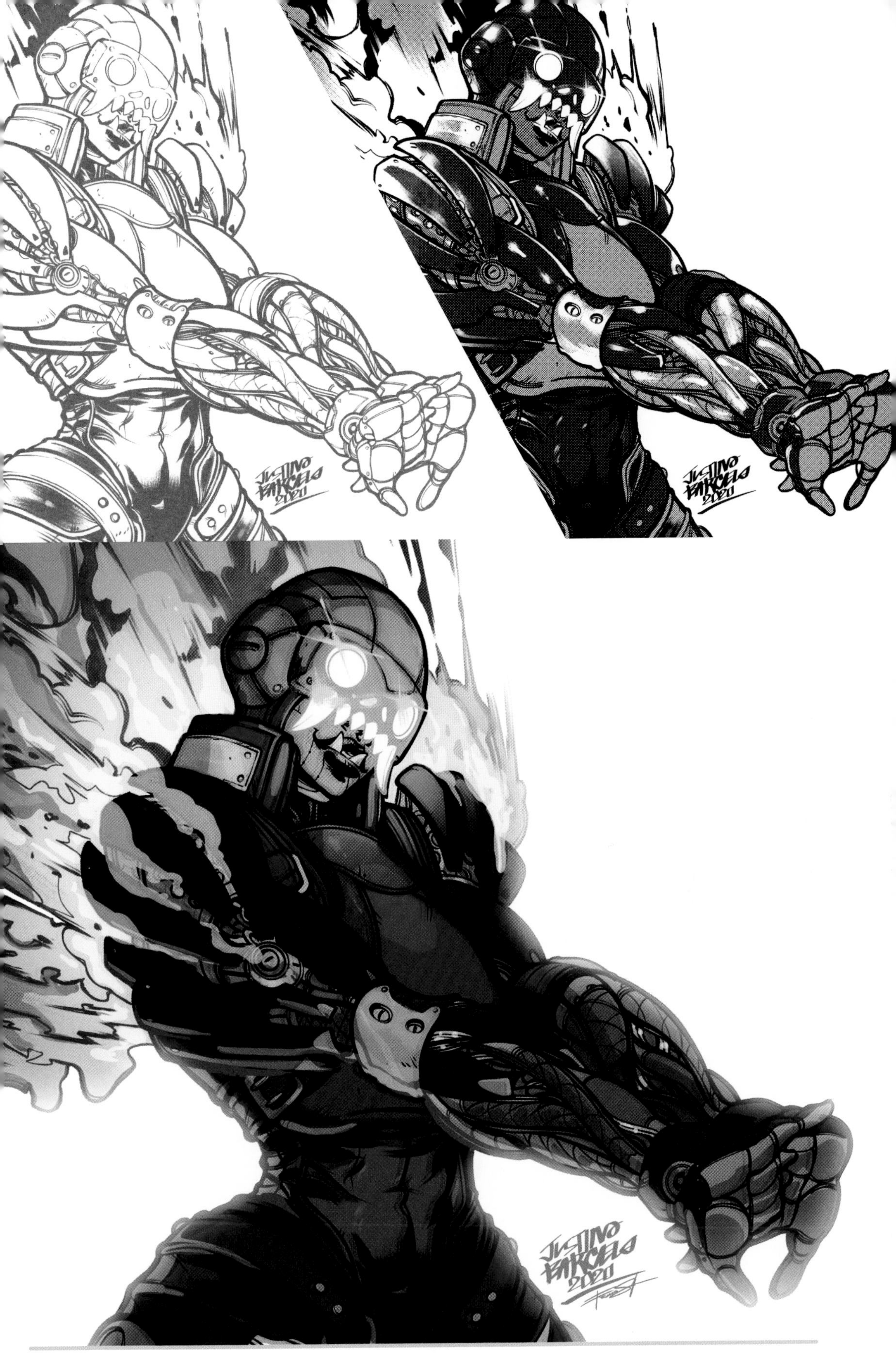

PENCILS / INKS / COLOR BY BY **JUSTIN BARCELO**

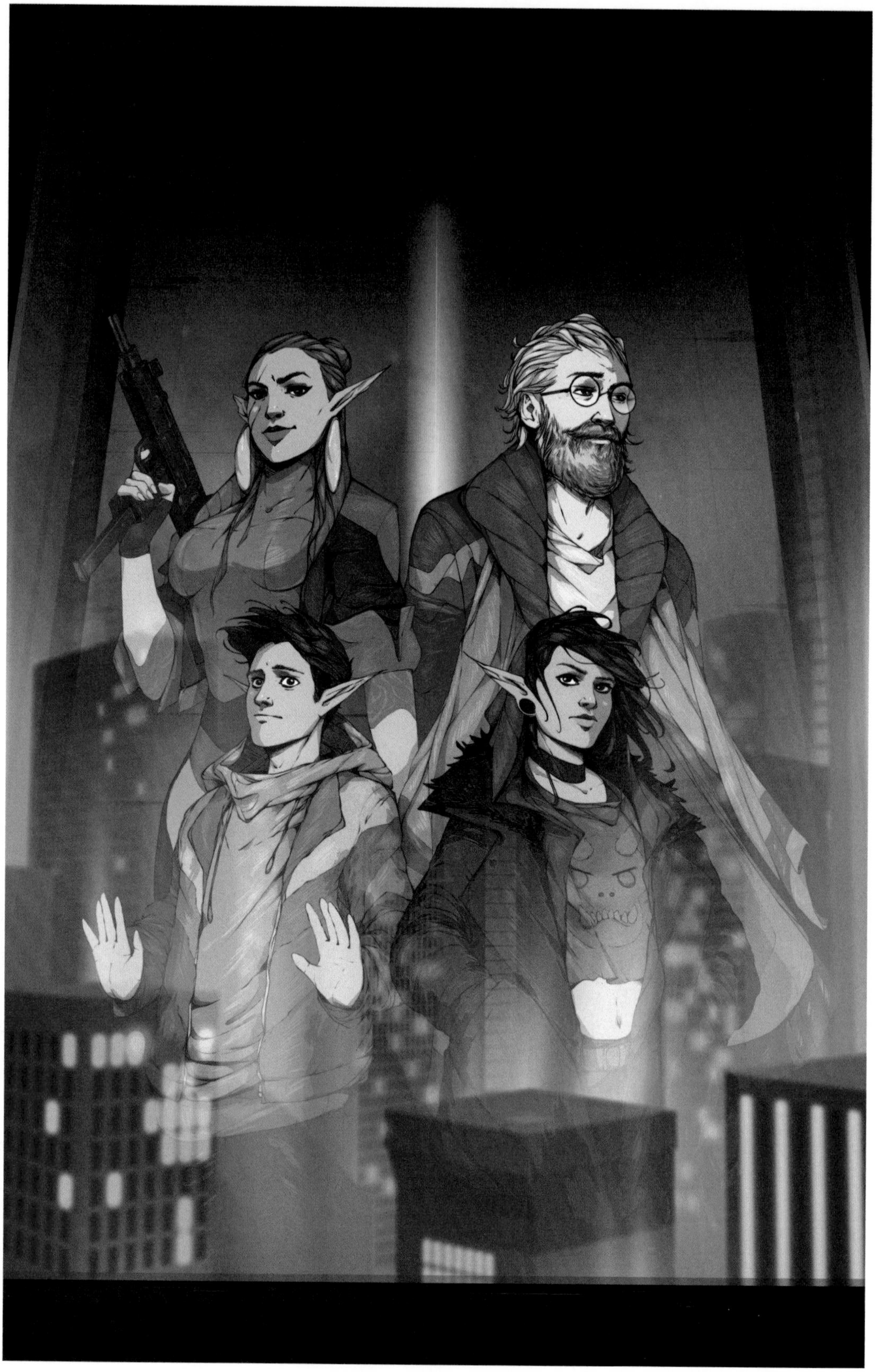

ISSUE #6 COVER • ARTWORK BY **TOMAS OLEKSAK**

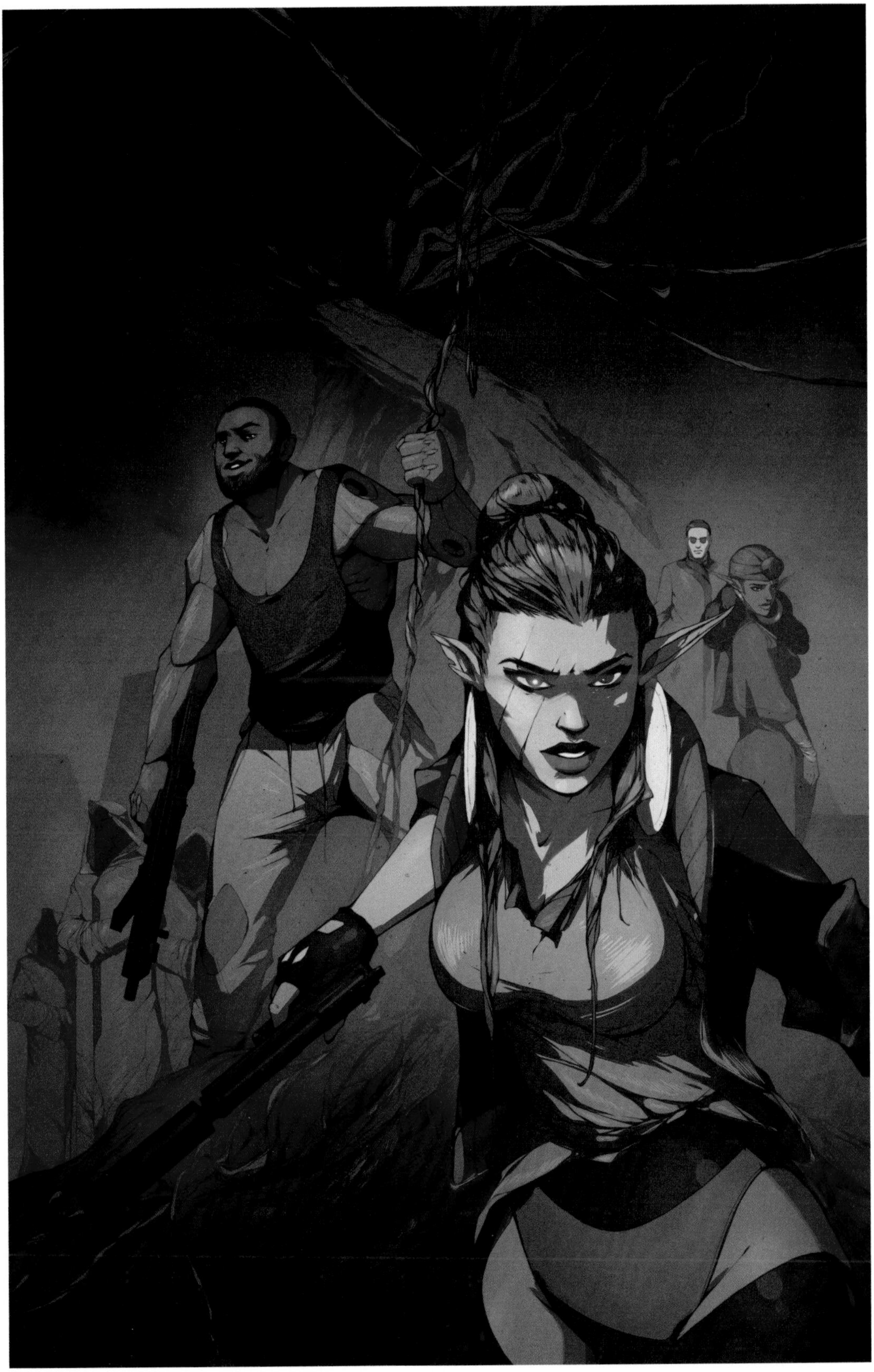

ISSUE #7 COVER • ARTWORK BY **TOMAS OLEKSAK**

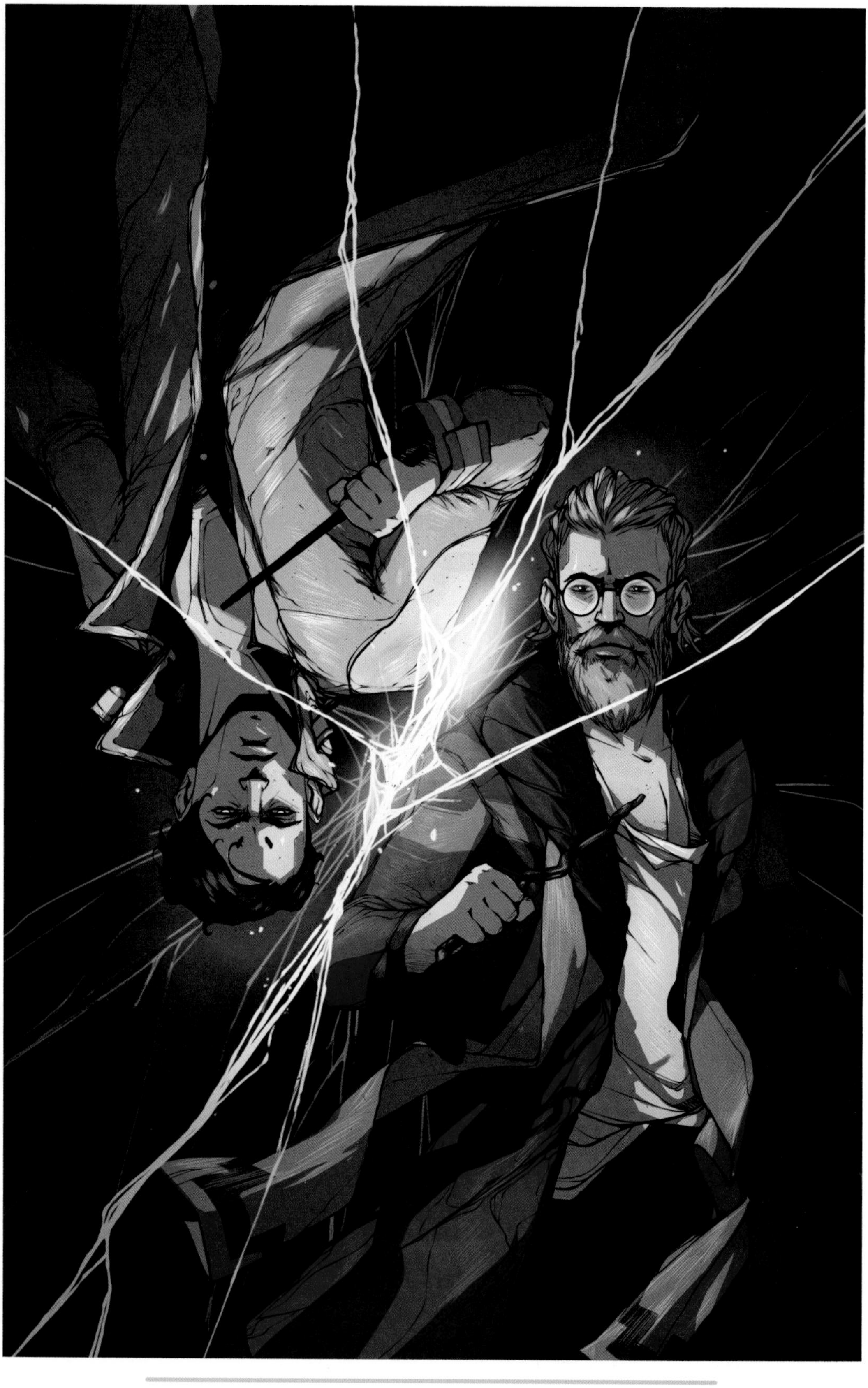

ISSUE #8 COVER • ARTWORK BY **TOMAS OLEKSAK**

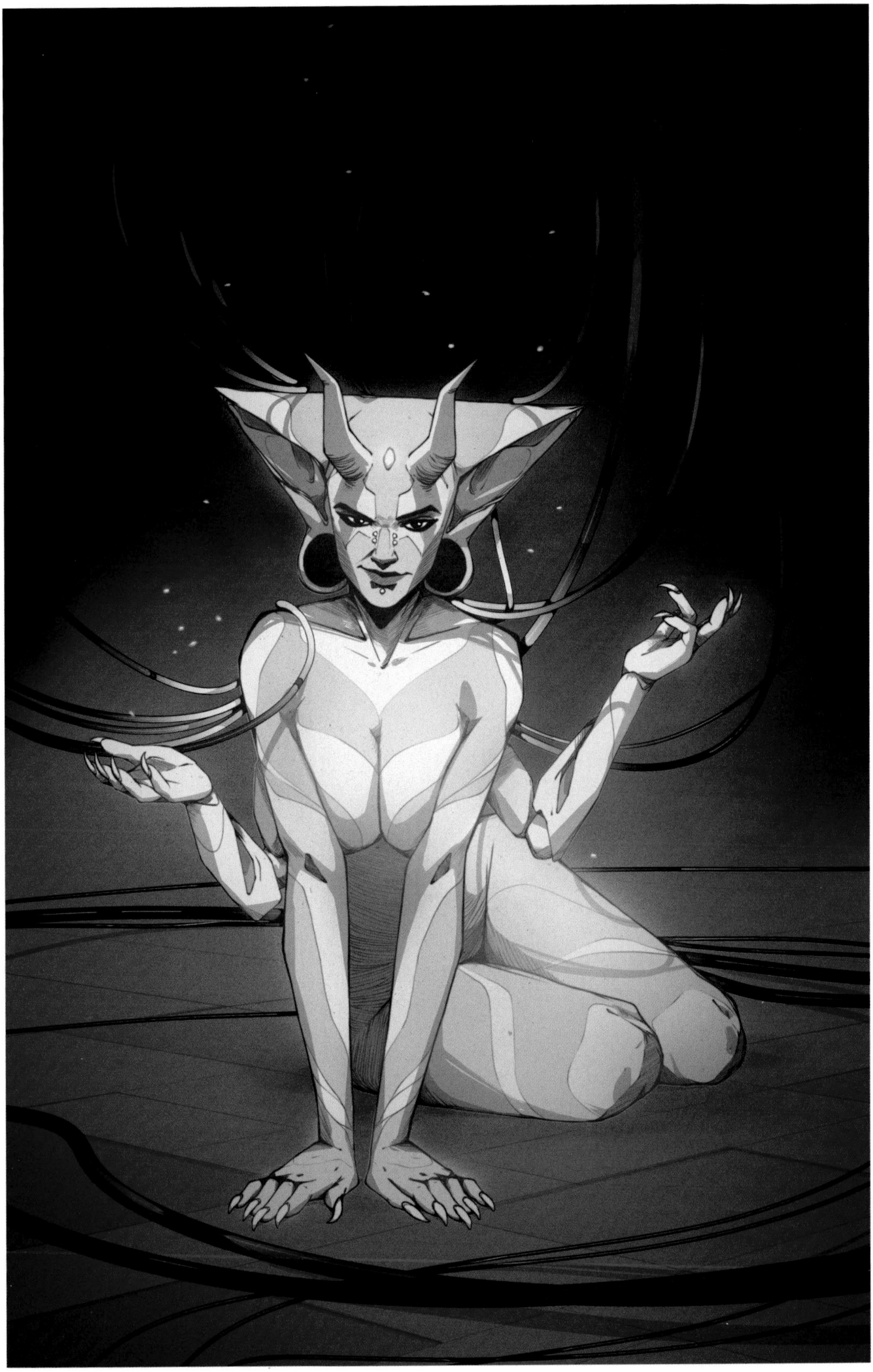

ISSUE #9 COVER • ARTWORK BY **TOMAS OLEKSAK**

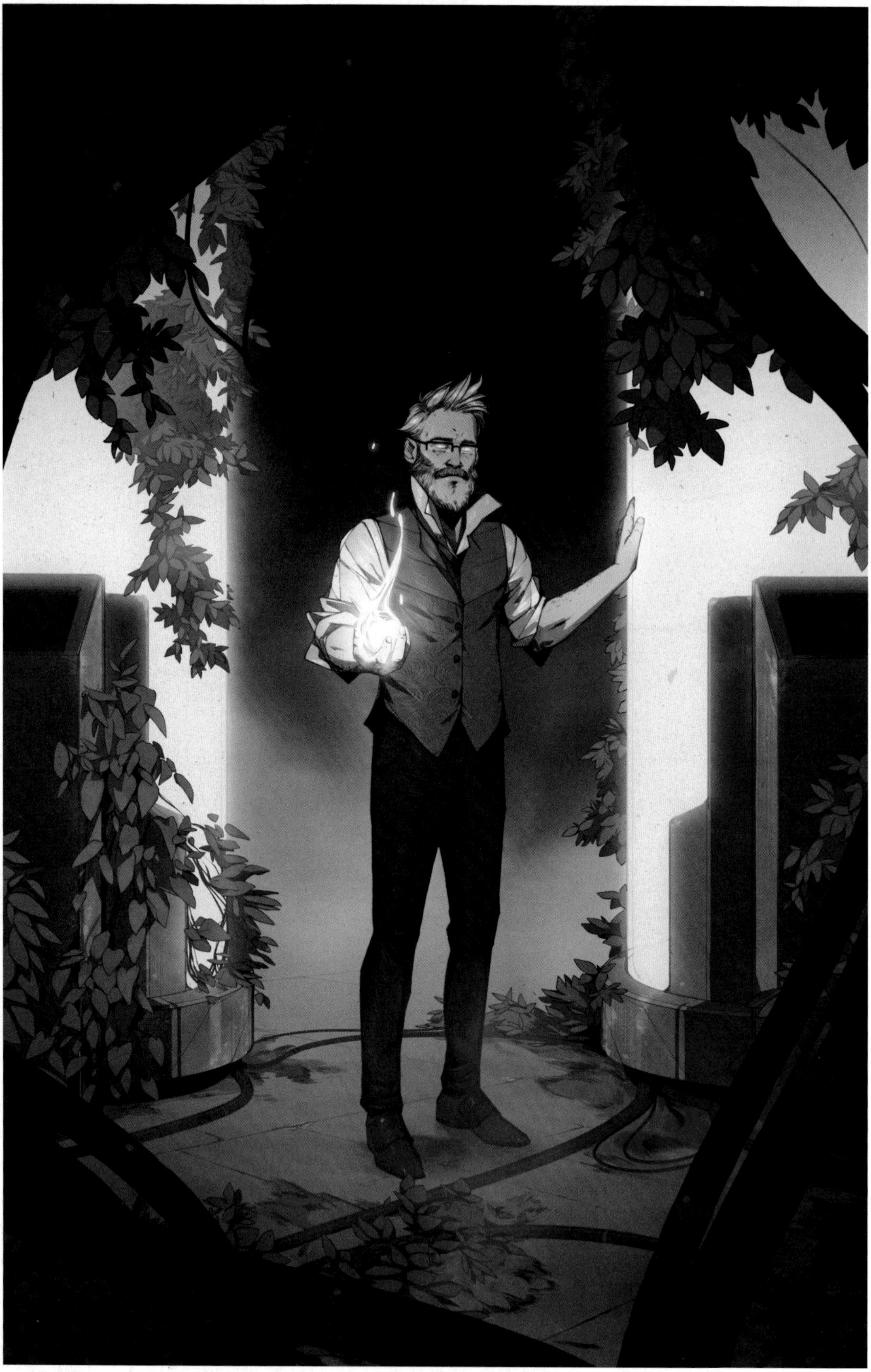

ISSUE #10 COVER • ARTWORK BY **TOMAS OLEKSAK**